A History of Modern Oman

An ideal introduction to the history of modern Oman from the eighteenth century to the present, this book combines the most recent scholarship on Omani history with insights drawn from a close analysis of the politics and international relations of contemporary Oman. Jeremy Jones and Nicholas Ridout offer a distinctive new approach to Omani history, building on postcolonial thought and integrating the study of politics and culture. The book addresses key topics, including Oman's historical cosmopolitanism, the distinctive role of Omani Islam in the country's social and political life, Oman's role in the global economy of the nineteenth century, insurrection and revolution in the twentieth century, the role of Sultan Qaboos in the era of oil and Oman's unique regional and diplomatic perspective on contemporary issues.

Jeremy Jones has an Oxford-based consulting business and has worked on Oman since the 1980s. His first book, *Negotiating Change: The New Politics of the Middle East* (2007), anticipated the Arab Spring. He is Senior Associate Member at the Oxford Centre for Islamic Studies.

Nicholas Ridout has worked with Jeremy Jones on research in Oman since 1989. Their first book together, *Oman, Culture and Diplomacy*, was published in 2012. He is also Professor of Theatre at Queen Mary University of London and has published extensively on theatre and performance.

A History of Modern Oman

JEREMY JONES

NICHOLAS RIDOUT

CAMBRIDGE
UNIVERSITY PRESS

CAMBRIDGE
UNIVERSITY PRESS

32 Avenue of the Americas, New York, NY 10013-2473, USA

Cambridge University Press is part of the University of Cambridge.

It furthers the University's mission by disseminating knowledge in the pursuit of education, learning and research at the highest international levels of excellence.

www.cambridge.org
Information on this title: www.cambridge.org/9781107402027

First published 2015

Printed in the United States of America

A catalog record for this publication is available from the British Library.

Library of Congress Cataloging in Publication Data
Jones, Jeremy, 1954–
A history of modern Oman / Jeremy Jones, Nicholas Ridout.
pages cm
Includes bibliographical references and index.
ISBN 978-1-107-00940-0 (hardback) – ISBN 978-1-107-40202-7 (pbk.)
1. Oman – History – 20th century. 2. Oman – History.
I. Ridout, Nicholas Peter. II. Title.
DS247.068J66 2015
953.53–dc23 2015016106

ISBN 978-1-107-00940-0 Hardback
ISBN 978-1-107-40202-7 Paperback

Contents

Figures

Maps

Acknowledgements

The authors wish to thank all the friends, citizens and officials in Oman who have generously given their time to conversations and discussions with the authors over the many years of their work in Oman. Thanks are also due to the Oxford Centre for Islamic Studies. They are grateful, also, to two anonymous readers for the Press, whose advice helped refine and develop the book. Special thanks, for assistance with the preparation of materials for the book, to Debbie Usher at the Middle East Centre Archive, St Anthony's College, Oxford, and to Orlagh Woods and Liz Heasman.

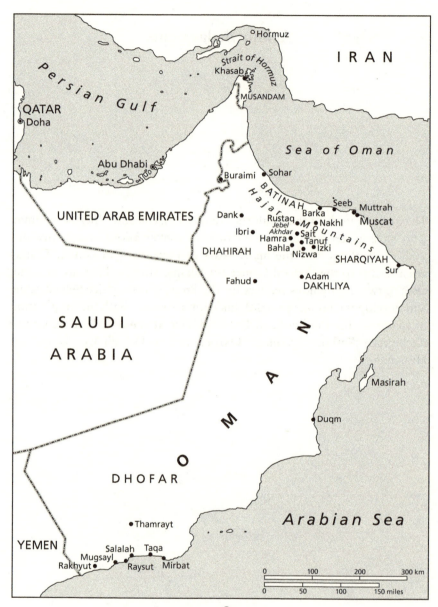

MAP 1. Oman.

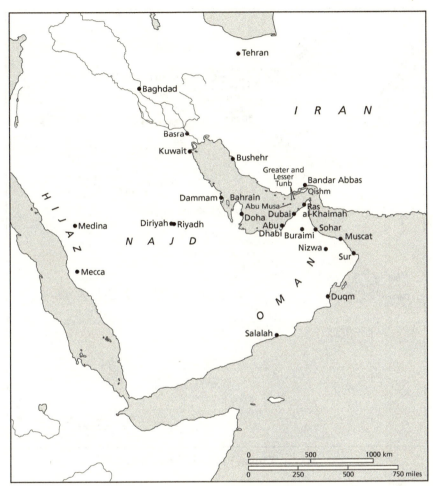

MAP 2. Oman in the Gulf.

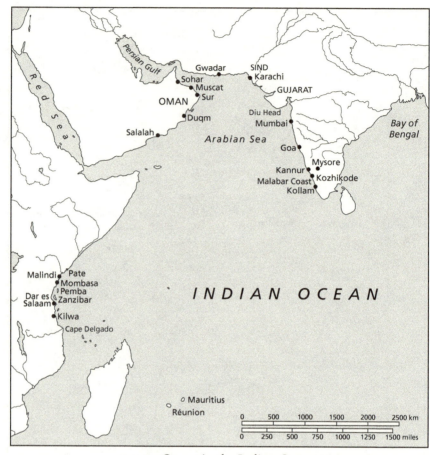

MAP 3. Oman in the Indian Ocean.

Introduction

What is modern Oman? Today, Oman looks and feels like most people's idea of a modern country. This is particularly true in the capital city, Muscat, with its busy freeways and malls full of the latest consumer goods, and its high levels of Internet penetration and smartphone use, which are evident to even the casual observer. But at the same time Oman today retains many features that might be considered typical of distinctly premodern or traditional society. It is ruled by a hereditary monarchy, everyday social life involves widespread religious observance, 'traditional' conceptions of the family are a powerful influence on the decisions made by individual Omanis, and even in the capital city, Omani men and women wear what most observers would instantly recognise as 'traditional' dress.

Most Omanis, too, probably think that it is the freeways and the technology, along with some of the more striking achievements of the contemporary state – the comprehensive welfare system and public education – that make their country modern. That is to say, they identify as modern those things in which Oman resembles countries whose economies and social systems are the result of a process of industrialisation that began, typically, in Europe and the United States in the nineteenth century. To call Oman modern in this sense, and to contrast its modern and traditional elements in this way, then, is to imply a process of linear development, to suggest a narrative of progress from a 'backward' or 'underdeveloped' state towards the achievement of a recognisable condition of modernity. This is a perspective shared by many Western accounts of Oman's history, and it is also the dominant commonsense Omani understanding of that history, often reinforced by the present government's own narrative of national 'renaissance' and economic development since 1970.

The reality is a little more complex. The achievement of the visible and commonsense modernity so evident in Oman today has indeed been quite remarkable. The familiar story of a country that was considered 'medieval' in its social arrangements and lack of infrastructure (paved roads, schools, hospitals and so on) in the mid-twentieth century, but which was transformed through the investment of oil revenues after 1970 into the self-evidently 'developed' nation of 2015, is, in many respects, entirely true. But it leaves out two complications. First, many underlying features of this contemporary Omani modernity can be traced to a much earlier period in the country's history, most particularly to its long participation in global trade networks. Second, several key aspects of what look like residues of Omani 'tradition' are in fact products of the very same earlier history. Above all, the hereditary monarchy of the Al Bu Said was itself an innovation, forged not in some 'medieval' past but, rather, in the late eighteenth century, at precisely the moment at which Oman decisively established itself as a significant participant in an increasingly global capitalist economy.

So it might make more sense to draw a distinction between two related senses of modern and modernisation in Oman. One is the familiar, everyday sense, referring to capitalist economic development, technological advances, centralised administration and the provision of public services. The other might refer to features of Omani society that look, in these terms, much less modern but which, in the context of a history of Oman such as this one, are in fact best understood as characteristics of a distinctively Omani modernity. These might include, therefore, the hereditary monarchy, the consolidation of a coherent 'traditional' national identity, as well as the country's participation in cosmopolitan networks of commerce and cultural exchange. At some points, these two senses of modernity converge, but not always.

Modernity, in the sense intended in this book, then, is a state of contradiction and tension among elements of a culture.

Modernity in Oman is not the resolution of this contradiction, but the experience of living with it: living with tensions between urban and rural patterns of life (and in the case of many Omanis, moving on a weekly basis between them) or negotiating the place of religious observance and practice in relation to a dominant global secularism. The example of Oman might also help us think about the nature of modernity

elsewhere in similar terms. To be modern is to live in the present a set
of tensions between a knowledge of the past and an imaginary future.
In other words, the condition of being modern involves the persistence
of the non-modern, a continual negotiation over what it is to be modern
and, in the case of Oman, what it is to be Oman or Omani.

POLITICAL GEOGRAPHY

The Sultanate of Oman, to give the modern nation its official title, is located
in the southeast of the Arabian Peninsula, with three land borders – with
the United Arab Emirates to the north and west, Saudi Arabia to the west
and Yemen to the south and west. To the east of Oman's long coastline is
the Indian Ocean. From the coastal capital of Oman, Muscat, to Karachi
on the other side of the Indian Ocean is a voyage of about 900 kilometres.
Rising up behind Muscat is a dramatic line of rugged dark mountains,
the Hajar range, which separates the two main axes of the traditional
Omani nation – the coast and the interior – from one another. Northwest
along the coast itself, between Muscat and another historical Omani
port, Sohar, is the narrow plain called the Batinah. This is the region
from which Omanis have traditionally ventured abroad, building multiple trade connections in the Gulf, across the Indian Ocean and even south
to the coast of eastern Africa. Crossing the Hajar mountains brings you
into the interior of the country, the Dakhliyah, where the people have
tended to focus more exclusively upon subsistence agriculture and where
Oman's traditional religious institutions are at their strongest, especially
in the old capital and oasis town, Nizwa. Rising in the heart of the interior is the plateau known as the Jebel Akhdar (Green Mountain), where
the altitude creates a cooler climate than in the desert below and where
fruit and flowers grow on mountainside terraces. North and west of the
Dakhliyah is the Dhahirah, beyond which lies the desert area of the Rub
al-Khali (Empty Quarter). Southeast and beyond Muscat in the opposite
direction from Sohar, the coast is rockier as it reaches down to another
famous port town, Sur. Inland from Sur is the desert region known as the
Sharqiyah. South of here, and for many centuries reached primarily by
sea, is the distinctive region of Dhofar, where another coastal plain sits at
the feet of mountains that separate the cultivable lowlands from the vast
expanses of the Arabian Desert. Dhofar is the only part of the Arabian
Peninsula with weather affected by the Indian Ocean monsoon, which
produces every July and August the season known as *khareef*, in which

mists and rains descend upon the hillsides of the Dhofari *jebel*, turning an otherwise largely barren landscape into a carpet of green decked with wild flowers. The relationship between coast and interior, the particular character of the Jebel Akhdar and the unique culture of Dhofar have all contributed significantly to the course of Oman's history, both ancient and modern, in ways we shall try to explain in the chapters that follow.

Perhaps the most significant determining factor in Oman's modern history has been its position at the Strait of Hormuz. The Strait of Hormuz is a narrow sea passage between the Persian Gulf and the Indian Ocean. One shore of the Strait is the tip of Oman's Musandam Peninsula, slightly less than 40 kilometres from the southern Iranian coast which forms its other shore. Once oil exports from the Gulf became crucial to the economies of the industrial world, from around the middle of the twentieth century, the Strait became one of the most important waterways in the world, with around 40 percent of all seaborne traded oil passing through it. Maintaining the secure passage of oil tankers from export terminals in major producing nations of the Gulf (Iraq, Iran, Saudi Arabia, Kuwait, United Arab Emirates) into the open ocean, and on to major consumers, has therefore long been a matter of the highest priority for producers and consumers alike. Since 1979, the unpredictable and sometimes confrontational policies of the Islamic Republic of Iran have given rise to fears among other producers and, especially, Western consumers that Iran might close the Strait, either through a deliberate blockade or by creating tensions and conflict that would deter ships from leaving or entering the Gulf. Between 1984 and 1988, in the second half of the war between Iran and Iraq, for example, Iraqi forces attacked shipping, including oil tankers, in an effort to provoke Iran into a closure of the Strait, thereby making the United States intervene to prevent the Iranians and thus enter the war on Iraq's side. In a more recent move that indicates how much regional producers would like to be free of such disruptions, in 2012 the UAE started to export oil via a new terminal in Fujairah, thereby avoiding the need to use the Strait of Hormuz. This is an advantage that Oman has always enjoyed – all its ports have direct access to the open ocean. Of the other Arab states of the Gulf only the UAE, via its short Sharjah and Fujairah littorals, and Saudi Arabia, via its Red Sea coastline, can avoid the use of the Strait for seaborne oil exports. Iraq, Kuwait, Bahrain and Qatar currently rely entirely upon the Strait of Hormuz. Not only does this mean that they each have a strategic interest in maintaining good relations with Oman, it also places upon Oman an obligation to its neighbours to maintain the good relations with Iran upon which their capacity jointly to guarantee the security of the Strait depends. Iran's own interest in the security of the Strait of Hormuz is considerable: according to a recent Iranian estimate, around 80 percent of Iran's foreign trade passes through it.[1]

Although Oman as a distinct geographical and political entity has a very long history, not all of the territory encompassed by the modern state has always been part of Oman. The regions of Batinah, Dakhliyah and Sharqiyah, with their key towns such as Muscat, Nizwa, Rustaq, Sohar and Sur, may be regarded as a more or less consistent core, even if, at times, there have been tensions and divisions between them and contests for political supremacy in Oman between leaders from within these various regions. Throughout most of Oman's history there has been a broad political, social and economic distinction between coast and interior, sometimes expressed in the name given to the country, Muscat and Oman. At times in Oman's history this distinction has widened to division between two different political entities. These have sometimes been conceptualised as a Sultanate, ruled by dynasties whose political power derives from control of the coast, and an Imamate, ruled by leaders in keeping with Oman's unique religious-political tradition of Ibadism (of which more shortly). The incorporation of Dhofar into this social and political system is of relatively recent origin, and its complete assimilation to the modern state was not achieved until after the name of the country was changed from Muscat and Oman to Sultanate of Oman in 1970 and the military conflict in the region was resolved in the mid-1970s. In addition to the consolidation of territory which led to the formation of the modern nation-state in its current form, changes have occurred because of other territories which have, at various times in Oman's history, formed part of Oman and contributed substantially to its economic, social and cultural development. Foremost among these is the East African archipelago of Zanzibar, which in the mid-nineteenth century formed part of a distributed network of Omani interests and possessions. Less well known is the province of Gwadar on the Makran coast of what is now Pakistan, which Oman eventually sold to the Pakistani government in 1958. So the process by which the modern nation came into being involved both acquiring and relinquishing land, until the nation was eventually consolidated in a single more or less contiguous territory.

---

[1] Asghar Jafari-Valdani, 'The Geopolitics of the Strait of Hormuz and the Iran–Oman Relations', *Iranian Review of Foreign Affairs*, 4.2 (2012), pp. 7–40 (13).

CULTURAL HISTORY

Oman is an Arab and a Muslim nation. That general characterisation disguises a great deal of cultural diversity, however. It is widely believed that some of the non-Arabic tribes in Dhofar are in fact the descendants of peoples who inhabited southern Arabia before the successive migrations of Arabs into the area. The historical record, both textual and archaeological, leaves room for doubt and contention over the dates of these migrations, normally referred to as the Azd migrations, and on the related question of the extent of Persian rule over and occupation of territory in what is now Oman.[2] There is some broad agreement that there were at least two major migrations, one of which involved tribes that moved from what is now Yemen, first into Dhofar and subsequently northwards. A second phase of Arab migration is generally understood to have followed and to have involved tribes entering what is now Oman through the territory from the north, around the Buraimi oasis (which marks the northern limit of the Omani region now known as the Dhahirah). Further migrations may also have brought new tribes into the mountains of central Oman. Omani tribal genealogies tend to trace descent from either the migration from the north or the migration from the south, and the principal division between Omani tribal confederations (the Hinawi and the Ghafiri) is held to express this distinction, even where, in practice, origins and affiliations are much more complex than this straightforward bipolarity would suggest.[3] These

---

[2] See, inter alia, J. C. Wilkinson, *Water and Tribal Settlement in South-East Arabia: A Study of the Aflaj of Oman* (Oxford: Clarendon Press, 1977); J. C. Wilkinson, 'Arab–Persian Land Relationships in Late Sasanid Oman', *Proceedings of the Seminar for Arabian Studies* 3 (1973), pp. 40–51; Brian Ulrich, *Constructing Al-Azd: Tribal Identity and Society in the Early Islamic Centuries* (PhD diss., University of Wisconsin-Madison, 2008); Brian Ulrich, 'The Azd Migrations Reconsidered: Narratives of Ab Muzayqiya and Malik b. Fahm in Historiographic Context', *Proceedings of the Seminar for Arabian Studies* 38 (2008), pp. 311–318; Derek Kennet, 'The Decline of Eastern Arabia in the Sasanian Period', *Arabian Archaeology and Epigraphy* 18 (2007), pp. 86–122; and D. Potts, *The Arabian Gulf in Antiquity*, vols. 1 and 2 (Oxford: Clarendon Press, 1990).

[3] The Hinawi–Ghafiri distinction seems to have entered Omani historiography in the early eighteenth century CE, when tribes which traced their origins to the southern migration (Yamanis) were led by a member of the Bani Hina in a political and military struggle for power with tribes which identified themselves with the migration from the north (Nizaris) under the leadership of a member of the Bani Ghafir. See Uzi Rabi, *The Emergence of States in a Tribal Society: Oman Under Said bin Taymur, 1932–1970* (Brighton: Sussex Academic Press, 2006), pp. 11–12. As Patricia Risso points out, the 'alleged fundamental tribal split among all Arabians', which this division reiterates, is 'oversimplified'. See Patricia Risso, *Oman and Muscat: An Early Modern History* (London: Croom Helm, 1986), p. 4. We will return to this issue in our discussion of the Ya'ariba civil war in Chapter 1.

Azd tribes came into contact, and eventually, it seems, conflict, with Persians who had settled in parts of what is now northern Oman, under both the Achaemenid (from the sixth century BCE) and Sasanid (from the third century BCE to the seventh century CE) Empires. During this period, following the Azd migrations and the rise of the Sasanid Empire, Rustaq and Sohar became the two most important Omani settlements, and the leaders of the Arab tribes, al-Julanda, exercised power from Rustaq on behalf of the Persians, whose headquarters were in Sohar.

Omani historiography offers the story of Malik bin Fahm as an origin narrative for Oman as an Arab nation. This story appears in the *Kashf al-ghumma*, an anonymous history, probably written in the first half of the eighteenth century and sometimes attributed to Sirhan bin Said bin Sirhan bin Mohammed. At the start of the story Malik bin Fahm lives in 'el-Sarat' in what is now Yemen. He decides to leave his homeland when one of his nephews kills a dog belonging to a neighbour who is under Malik's protection. Taking with him the people of his tribe who owe him allegiance, he travels towards Oman, learning on the way that the Persians are inhabiting Oman. He gathers a force of Arabs from the areas through which he passes and confronts the Persians, who send out an advance guard from their stronghold in Sohar. When the Persians refuse to reach an agreement with Malik bin Fahm which would allow him to settle in Oman, he prepares for confrontation on a plain near the town of Nizwa. The Persians attack, and after a battle of three days Malik bin Fahm kills the Persian commander in single combat and the Persian army flees the field. As a result of the ensuing treaty, the Persians are granted a year in which to evacuate Oman, and they withdraw to Sohar. During this period 'it is said' that the Persians destroyed many water channels (Sulayman bin Daoud having constructed ten thousand of them in Oman). The Persian ruler is incensed at news of Malik bin Fahm's victory, and instead of allowing the defeated Persians to return to their own country, he sends a troop of his most renowned warriors via Bahrain to Oman. Malik bin Fahm's smaller force defeats this second Persian attack and goes on to take control over the whole of Oman, 'governing wisely and well' for seventy years until his death at the age of 120. Book One of the *Kashf al-ghumma* ends as follows:

The Persians did not return to Oman after their expulsion by Malik until his reign terminated, and his children reigned in his place, and the kingdom of Oman came into the possession of el-Julanda-bin el-Mustatir el-Mawali, and Persia fell into the hands of the Benu Sasan. There was a peace between them and el-Julanda in Oman, and the Persians kept a force of 4000 warriors in Oman and a deputy with the kings of the el-Azd. The Persians abode on the sea coast, and the el-Azd ruled in the interior plains and hills and districts of Oman, the direction of affairs being entirely with them.[4]

This eighteenth-century history, quite probably written at a time when the Persians were once again exercising considerable influence in Oman, and just before their expulsion by the founder of the Al Bu Said dynasty, Ahmad bin Said, shows how the writing of ancient history – the story of Malik bin Fahm and his triumphs over the Persians – may have as much to say about the moment in which it is written as it does about the historical events it purports to relate. It affirms Omani autonomy and it does so specifically by contrasting it with the alternative, which is subjugation to Persian rule. By painting such a picture of the historical past it affirms a desire for a future in which the same autonomy is achieved. It is perhaps worth noting that three highly significant events, the arrival of the Arabs in Oman, Oman's embrace of Islam and the inauguration of the Al Bu Said dynasty, are all associated in Omani historiography with Omanis throwing off the Persian yoke.

There is in fact some considerable scholarly debate over the extent of Sasanid Persian rule in eastern Arabia generally, and Oman in particular, during this period. Some scholars have argued that the Persians in Oman ruled directly, exerted territorial control, owned land and contributed to a period of economic prosperity. Some recent work has challenged this view, suggesting more indirect control and disputing the evidence of a significant economic impact, other than from maritime trade.[5] It is, however, generally accepted that the Persians were responsible for developing viable agriculture in Oman through the construction of systems of irrigation channels known in Persian as *qanat* and in Omani Arabic as *aflaj* (sing. *falaj*). These are the channels attributed in the *Kashf al-ghumma* to the Persian Sulayman bin Daoud. The use of *aflaj* in Oman has been central to the maintenance of life there even into the twenty-first century, and Oman's *aflaj* are the most extensive outside Iran. The social interaction encouraged by the use of *aflaj*, which require the development of complex systems for the management of a scarce and essential collective resource,

---

[4] *Kashf al-Ghumma*, translated and annotated by E. C. Ross as 'Annals of Oman, from Early Times to the Year 1728 A.D. From an Arabic MS. by Sheykh Sirhan bin Said bin Sirhan bin Muhammad of the Benu Ali Tribe of Oman', in E. C. Ross, 'Political Agent at Muscat', *Journal of the Asiatic Society of Bengal*, pt. I, no. 2 (1874), pp. 111–196.

[5] For a summary of the competing scholarly accounts see Brian Ulrich, 'Oman and Bahrain in Late Antiquity: The Sasanians' Arabian Periphery', *Proceedings of the Seminar for Arabian Studies* 41 (2011), pp. 377–385.

has given Omani culture a strong material basis for cooperation, which, as we have suggested elsewhere, contributes to a more general cultural preference for non-confrontational and consensual decision-making.[6]

As the new religion founded by the Prophet Mohammed started to spread through the Arabian Peninsula, his ambassador Amr bin al-As brought news of Islam to the most prominent Omani Arab rulers, Jaifar and Abd al-Julanda. Following consultation with other tribal leaders and religious scholars, a decision was taken to embrace Islam. The alliance thus forged with the Muslims of Mecca and Medina strengthened al-Julanda political power to such an extent that the Omani rulers were able to force a Persian withdrawal from the Batinah. These Omani leaders also drew their coastal territory into the political ambit of the first Caliphate, and Omanis participated in its subsequent expansion, including the conversion of the Sasanid Persian Empire and a substantial portion of the eastern Roman Empire. It was in Basra, a city which soon became one of the main centres of Islamic political power, that the distinctive strand of Islamic thought and practice that would come to be associated most strongly with Oman – Ibadism – came into being. The origins of Ibadism – named after Abdullah bin Ibad, although its leading intellectual founder was Jabir bin Zaid, a scholar from Nizwa who had settled in Basra – lie in disputes over succession in the Caliphate, which began with the accession of Uthman, the third Caliph and the first not to have been a companion of the Prophet. Those who became the Ibadis were among those who opposed a dynastic succession in the Caliphate. Ibadism was brought to Oman in 747 CE, and a first attempt was made to establish an Imamate on the basis of Ibadi religious, political and legal principles, with an Arab tribal leader elected as the first Imam. Foremost among these principles were the equality of all Muslims and the opposition to tyrannical power, both of which were to be sustained through the leader of the Muslim community being chosen through a process of consultation (*shura*). The specific Ibadi emphasis on *shura* – which we will discuss, in terms of its modern application, in Chapter 7 – is one of the principal ways in which Ibadis are conventionally distinguished from Sunnis and Shias. There are a number of differences in religious doctrine and interpretation, too, as well as in everyday religious practice, by which

---

[6] See Jeremy Jones and Nicholas Ridout, *Oman, Culture and Diplomacy* (Edinburgh: Edinburgh University Press, 2012), pp. 54–57. On *aflaj*, see also Wilkinson, *Water and Tribal Settlement*, and Dale R. Lightfoot, 'The Origin and Diffusion of Qanats in Arabia: New Evidence from the Northern and Southern Peninsula', *Geographical Journal* 166.3 (2000), pp. 215–226.

Ibadis may be distinguished from other Muslims, but Ibadis themselves tend to avoid discussion of sectarian difference, sometimes referring to Ibadism as a *madhab* without a *madhab* (sect without a sect).[7] This is consistent with one of the distinctive positions adopted by the Ibadis at the time of their formation: unlike the Kharijites, who constituted another of the main groups opposed to dynastic succession in the early Caliphate, the Ibadis rejected the use of force as a way of settling such disputes.

Modern Oman has the largest proportion of Ibadis of any country in the world (there are significant communities of Ibadis in Libya, Tunisia and Algeria, as well as in Zanzibar, in the latter case as a direct result of the Omani presence). The Omani government does not include sectarian questions in its census, but the most reliable estimates suggest that Ibadis account for about 45 percent of the population, although many sources tend to reproduce claims that Ibadis constitute a majority and, in some cases, up to 75 percent of the population. Whatever the precise figure, what is important is the cultural and intellectual influence of Ibadism on Omani social and political life. The ruling Al Bu Said dynasty are Ibadis, and there are aspects of modern government, particularly under Sultan Qaboos, which, as we shall see, draw substantially on elements of Ibadi tradition. Nonetheless, the most long-standing political tension in the modern era can be characterised, at least in part, as that between the religious tradition of the 'elective' Imamate of the interior and the dynastic rulers of the coast, even though, as many historians have noted, the Imamate itself became a largely dynastic institution.[8] The Imamate's claim to political autonomy from the coast, or even, in some cases, to overall political leadership of Oman, rests upon its long and continuous role in the social and religious life of the country, and upon its adherence to its tradition of elective leadership. As we shall see, the consolidation of Al Bu Said rule in modern Oman has depended substantially on the dynasty's capacity to conduct the business of government with appropriate regard for Ibadi principles and sensibilities. The government risks opposition when its policies can be portrayed as out of touch with principles to which Imamate leaders, or

---

[7] Scholarly accounts in English of Ibadism include Ahmed Hamoud al-Maamiry, *Oman and Ibadism* (New Delhi: Lancers, 1980); Amr Khalifa al-Nami, *Studies in Ibadhism* (Open Mind, 2007); J. C. Wilkinson, *The Imamate Tradition of Oman* (Cambridge: Cambridge University Press, 1987); Khalid al-Azri, *Social and Gender Inequality in Oman: The Power of Religious and Political Tradition* (London: Routledge, 2012); and Valerie Hoffman, *The Essentials of Ibadism* (Syracuse, NY: Syracuse University Press, 2012).

[8] See, in particular, Wilkinson, *The Imamate Tradition*, pp. 9–17.

others seeking to reaffirm the centrality of Ibadism, might lay claim. The last major instance of such opposition came in the mid-1950s, and is the subject of Chapter 4. On this occasion the Imamate effectively became the flag under which various tribal leaders, backed by external powers, sought to challenge the decisive unification of the country as a modern nation. Subsequently, the Omani government has been largely successful in drawing on Ibadi cultural values while avoiding any major Islamist mobilisation based upon them. In this respect modern Oman seems to have found a much more comfortable accommodation between religious practice and institutions, on the one hand, and the modern and largely secular institutions of government, on the other, than have many other states in the region.

MARITIME TRADITION

As we have suggested, one of the ways in which the Muscat–Oman distinction has often been represented is as a difference between an inward-looking interior, where tribal affiliations and Ibadi-inflected social and religious conservatism tend to prevail, and an outward-looking, more 'liberal' and secular community along the coast and, especially in the modern period, in Muscat. This dichotomy does not fully account for either the complexity of relations between its two poles or the extent to which these relations have shifted from one historical moment to the next. However, it does contain a substantial element of truth. A distinction between the culture of the coast and the culture of the interior is visible and tangible today, and though all the terms of that difference would have taken different material forms at different moments in the past, it has been a consistent feature of Omani life and of the way in which Omanis understand their country. While the interior may at many moments in its history have exhibited many of the characteristics of a society closed in upon itself – small settlements in a desert or mountain landscape, an emphasis on continuity of place, people and customs – it may appear exceptionally inward-looking only because for much of Omani history the people of the coast have been so exceptionally outward-looking. One of the consequences of this cosmopolitanism is the cultural diversity of the population of modern Oman. Another is a sense of attachment to a network of commercial and cultural relations across the Indian Ocean, established by sailors, navigators and scientists who developed the ability to sail between Arabia and India, making use of the monsoon winds and their ability to navigate by the stars.

The Omani maritime tradition seems to have begun in the context of Sasanid Persian influence. Persians established themselves as intermediaries in the silk trade with China, which, in addition to the famous overland Silk Route, involved a seaborne trade by way of Ceylon (present-day Sri Lanka). In his celebrated account of Arab voyages in the Indian Ocean, George Hourani indicates that it is 'probable' that Persian ships were sailing as far as China before Islam took hold.[9] While Siraf on the southern Persian coast was the key Persian port, Sohar in Oman also became a vibrant centre for maritime trade. With the withdrawal of the Persians from the Arabian Peninsula, in the face of Arab Muslim expansion, Arabs, including Omanis, inherited the trade routes between the Gulf and Canton in China. For a period of several hundred years, between the rise of Islam during the seventh century and the collapse of the Tang dynasty in China at the end of the ninth century, this trade appears to have flourished, supported by the political continuity at each end of the route. Several texts indicate the presence of Omani and sometimes specifically 'Ibadi' merchants doing business in China. Raysut (near present-day Salalah in Dhofar) and Muscat both became important destinations along the voyages undertaken by Arab sailors across the Indian Ocean. Hourani's summary of a typical voyage during this period gives a vivid sense of the extent of this seafaring enterprise:

The China ships would sail down the Persian Gulf before it gets at all rough, in September or October. They would cross from Masqat to Malabar with the northeast monsoon, just as they do today. This was a month's voyage and we may put it in November–December, following al-Masudi [the celebrated Arab historian and geographer, whose texts, *The Meadows of Gold and Mines of Precious Gems* and the *Book of Admonition and Revision* are, in the words of the translators of *The Meadows of Gold*, 'notable attempts at "global" history].[10] The last two weeks of December could be spent trading in Kulam Mali [Kollam in present-day Kerala], for in any case no further progress could be made until the cyclones in the southern part of the Bay of Bengal came to an end, toward the close of December. A month of sailing to Kalah Bar [in present-day Kedah, Malaysia] would cover January. After a few weeks at Kalah, toward the end of the northeast monsoon, a ship might have a following wind through the Malacca Strait, and be in time to use the southern monsoon in the Sea of China. This is the summer monsoon, and in that sea it is gentler than the northeast of winter; in April and May it is light, and typhoons are of least frequency then. After a summer at Canton, one would

[9] George Hourani, *Arab Seafaring in the Indian Ocean in Ancient and Early Medieval Times*, revised and expanded by John Carswell (Princeton. NJ: Princeton University Press, 1995), p. 41.

[10] See Mas'udi, *From 'The Meadows of Gold'*, translated by Paul Lunde and Caroline Stone (London: Penguin Books, 2007).

return with the northeast monsoon to the Malacca Strait between October and December, and again cross the Bay of Bengal in January, from Kulam to Raysut in February or March, still with the northeast. But from Raysut one might well attain Masqat with the first gentle breeze of the southwest in April, and end the voyage once more in a smooth summer Gulf. Thus the round trip took a year and a half, leaving a summer at home before the next trip.[11]

A further sense of the commercial and political culture in which Omanis of this time participated may be obtained from a famous collection of stories compiled sometime after the middle of the tenth century by Burzurg ibn Shahriyar of Ramhormuz, called *Kitab Ajaib al-Hind* (*The Book of the Wonders of India*), which, Hourani notes, 'may be counted as a worthy forerunner of the Sindbad stories in the *Arabian Nights*'.[12] This includes the story of a Jewish merchant from Sohar, Ishaq bin Yahuda, who returns to Oman after an absence in the East of thirty years (in 300/912) bringing with him great accumulated wealth. He sets about dealing with the ruler of Oman, Ahmad bin Hilal, but his wealth excites jealousy, and 'an evil man' seeks to sully his reputation with the Vizier in Baghdad, who sends a eunuch to Oman to secure his arrest. Ahmad bin Hilal complies with the demand to surrender Ishaq to the Vizier's eunuch, but also promises Ishaq that he will contrive to assist him, too. Ahmad bin Hilal stirs up the merchants in the town, who, convinced that this sort of action against foreigners will be detrimental to their interests, close the markets, protesting that Baghdad is interfering with their freedom of trade. Ahmad bin Hilal writes to the Caliph in Baghdad to explain what has happened, and as a result, the Vizier's eunuch, rather than bringing Ishaq to the Vizier in Baghdad, takes 2,000 dinars from him and leaves. Ishaq is nonetheless outraged at this treatment, even though he has avoided arrest, and takes everything he owns onto his ship and sets sail again for China. On refusing to pay 20,000 dinars in transit dues at Sarira (Sumatra), he is assassinated. The story ends with the author recounting a story told him by a number of men who had seen Ishaq bin Yahuda in Oman that he had given Ahmad bin Hilal a vase full of golden fish, rubies and musk worth 50,000 dinars.[13]

The story of Ishaq bin Yahuda is of interest to historians of Oman for a number of reasons. It is one of a number of well-known stories

[11] Hourani, *Arab Seafaring*, pp. 74–75.
[12] Ibid., p. 68.
[13] Captain Buzurg ibn Shahriyar of Ramhormuz, *The Book of the Wonders of India, Mainland, Sea, and Islands*, edited and translated by G. S. P Freeman-Greville (London: East-West Publications, 1981), pp. 62–64.

which seem to have arisen from the role of Sohar in this Indian Ocean trade; legend has it that the famous Sindbad of the *Arabian Nights* was in fact from Sohar, even though evidence in the text has him as a merchant from Basra. It also gives a sense of the wealth and high stakes involved in the Indian Ocean trade at this time, although, as recent historians of the Indian Ocean have pointed out, such tales almost invariably emphasise the luxury goods market rather than the more substantial trade in everyday goods.[14] It is also noteworthy not only that its central figure is a Jewish merchant who is viewed sympathetically, but also that prejudice and machinations against him are reported as having been motivated by the jealousy of 'evil men'. Finally, the story of Ishaq seems to be one about free trade, in which the Jewish merchant, the Omanis and other merchants operating in Sohar (including, it seems, other foreigners) recognise that they share an interest in a trading environment in which there is little or no state interference. Oman is represented here as a thriving centre of maritime trade defending its rights against the attempts of the Caliphate in Baghdad to restrict or undermine them. What is important is not so much the empirical verifiability of the story itself as what it may tell us about the way in which Oman may have been imagined and conceptualised, both at the time of this early seafaring activity and in subsequent accounts. Just as the story of Malik bin Fahm in the *Kashf al-ghumma* tells us something about how Omanis in the eighteenth century viewed Omani identity in relation to their Persian neighbour, the story of Ishaq bin Yahuda and its reproduction in contemporary Omani texts, including recent tourist information presented by the Port of Sohar, may be taken as an index of the current value placed upon Oman's tradition of maritime trade, as, of course, are references to Sindbad, too.[15]

COSMOPOLITANISM

The Omani population today is distinctly cosmopolitan, a fact which is regarded both positively and negatively within the country, among citizens and government alike. It is seen as a positive consequence of Oman's maritime history, which government agencies appear keen to emphasise, especially where it is thought to communicate Oman's capacity to participate fully in globalised economic transactions. But it is also seen and experienced as problematic, to the extent that, since the 1970s, Oman

[14] See, e.g., Michael Pearson, *The Indian Ocean* (London: Routledge, 2003).
[15] http://www.portofsohar.com/tourist-information

has become increasingly dependent upon migrant labour, with serious consequences for its economic prospects and social development (these issues will be addressed more fully in Chapters 7 and 8). The origins of Oman's cosmopolitan population, however, as we have already suggested, lie much further back in the historical past than this most recent phase of economic migration. This cosmopolitanism is the consequence of hundreds of years of active Omani participation in trade and cultural exchange across and around the Indian Ocean and its littoral. Perhaps the least visible aspect of it is the wealth of family connections between Omanis and ancestors and contemporary relatives in nearby countries, including Yemen, Saudi Arabia and Iran, not to mention the numerous family and tribal connections to be found between Omanis and citizens of the United Arab Emirates. Through much of Oman's history, the borders between the territories upon which the modern states are now based were both fluid – they shifted, where they existed, over time – and porous – people moved readily across them, their interests and affiliations shaped by tribe, family and town rather than by national identity. However, there are also distinct and visible communities of varying origins whose presence in Oman is due to economic and cultural exchange far beyond the immediate region of Arabia and the Gulf. These are the communities whose origins lie in India, East Africa and Baluchistan.

Indians started to take up residence in Oman from the fifteenth century, although most accounts of Indian Ocean trade support the idea that there would have been considerable contact and interchange for several hundreds of years before any Indians actually started to live in Oman. In the sixteenth century, Indian merchants cooperated with the development of Portuguese maritime and commercial power in the Indian Ocean, which, as we shall see in Chapter 1, extended as far as the coast of Oman. But although the Portuguese presence in Oman would largely come to an end by the mid-seventeenth century, Indian merchants, from Sind and Gujarat, continued to build businesses and lives in Oman. Indeed, members of the Indian merchant community are widely held to have played a significant role in the expulsion of the Portuguese from the Omani coast in the mid-seventeenth century, for which they received in return privileges not normally accorded to non-Muslims, such as permission to build a Hindu temple.[16] Indian merchants have since been a consistent and powerful constituency, often working very closely with the Omani Arab

---

[16] See Calvin H. Allen, Jr., 'The Indian Merchant Community of Masqat', *Bulletin of the School of Oriental and African Studies* 44.1 (1981), pp. 39–53.

merchant elite. Sayyid Said took leading Indian merchants as partners in his development and expansion of Zanzibar in the first half of the nineteenth century, and some of present-day Oman's major businesses are Indian-owned and -managed. Another significant group of Omanis of Indian origin are Shia Muslims, known as Lawati, who are generally regarded as having had origins and routes to Oman very similar to those of their Hindu counterparts. Because they are Muslim they have integrated in a different way into Omani society, participating publicly, for example, in national politics in a way that Hindu Indians currently do not. Some Lawati now trace their genealogies to Arabs of the interior, and some use 'al-Lawati' as a kind of 'tribal' surname. The business community of Muttrah has a powerful Lawati element within it, and there is still a part of Muttrah, near the corniche, which is obviously a mainly Lawati area, even though it now includes non-Lawati residents.

Omanis of East African origin may be found throughout the country. Their integration into Omani society began with the extension of Omani economic and political power on the East African coast, and to some extent also the interior, as far as the Central Lakes, which began under the Ya'ariba in the seventeenth century (as the Omanis, having already driven the Portuguese from their own coast, began to supplant their positions in Africa). Some Omanis are of East African origin because they are descendants of Africans who came to Oman a long time ago, some of them as slaves. Others claim East African, and particularly Zanzibari, origin because their forebears were among the Omanis who migrated to Zanzibar, either to acquire land and develop business interests, as in the nineteenth century under Sayyid Said, or later, as economic migrants of a different kind, to search beyond Dakhliyah for work as labourers and shopkeepers. Descendants of these migrants returned to Oman (some, in fact, were not technically 'returning', having never seen Oman before) after the revolution of 1964 led to their expulsion from Zanzibar. Others returned or 'returned' in the 1970s, after spending time elsewhere in the Gulf. A significant number of these 'Zanzibaris' were literate and were able to contribute administrative expertise in the context of government-led economic and social development in the 1970s and 1980s.

The origins of Oman's significant Baluchi community lie in a territory which bears their name (Baluchistan), which currently straddles the border between Iran and Pakistan. The first Baluchis came to Oman during the Ya'ariba civil war, when Imam Sayf bin Sultan brought Baluchi soldiers from the region then known as Makran to support him in his conflict with Bilurub bin Himyar in the early eighteenth century. The connection between Oman and Makran (Baluchistan) was strengthened under the Al Bu Said, and Baluchi have continued to serve in large numbers in Oman's armed forces. In many cases Baluchi troops have been preferred because they are thought unlikely to harbour political affiliations which might make their loyalty questionable (this was a particular issue during the conflict between Sultan Said bin Taimur and the 'Imamate' in the 1950s). Like some Lawati, many Baluchi have taken 'al-Baluchi' as a form of tribal name, while others will continue to insist that they are not part of the tribal system of Oman.

In addition to these communities, there is a large and shifting population of expatriate workers in Oman today, many of whom are from India, Bangladesh and Pakistan. These workers started to arrive in significant numbers from the 1970s and contributed much of the manual labour necessary for the construction of the country's modern infrastructure. Today the expatriate workforce comprises about 800,000 people, many of whom are semi-skilled labourers and domestic employees. Unlike members of the long-standing communities discussed earlier, they are not Omani citizens, and although some are long-term residents, many are not. The Omani government has for several decades recognised that a continuing dependence upon expatriate labour will make it difficult to achieve full employment for Omani citizens. The question of how to manage this issue, which has both social and economic dimensions, is one of the most pressing facing the present government, as we shall see in Chapter 8.

THE SCOPE OF THIS BOOK

This book is about modern Oman. We will have occasion later in the volume to comment further on the concept of the 'modern' and related terms such as 'modernity' and 'modernisation'. For the time being, however, let us understand the term 'modern' as it relates to Oman as simply a way of marking a period. In the case of Oman, where the present ruling family, the Al Bu Said, came to power in the 1740s, it makes reasonable sense for the term 'modern' to refer to the period since then because there has been sufficient continuity (as well as a great deal of change) to make a coherent narrative possible and for that narrative to be useful in illuminating key features of the contemporary country. Our book begins, therefore, with the accession of Ahmad bin Said as Imam of Oman in 1749, but it also looks backward from that moment to offer an understanding of the political and economic situation which Ahmad bin Said inherited from the dynasty he supplanted – the Ya'ariba. This is important because, as we shall see, some of the key characteristics of the modern Omani state – and in particular the role of the merchant elite in underpinning state power – had already begun to emerge under Ya'ariba rule. Thus, although the accession of Ahmad bin Said is an important historical turning point, it did not immediately mark a radical change in the nature of Omani political and economic life. Modernity did not simply arrive in Oman: it took its shape from the dynamics of political and economic forces which had been present in Oman for some considerable time.

The first part of the book – 'Foundations' – covers the period between the accession of Imam Ahmad and that of Sultan Said bin Taimur in 1932. Its aim is to provide the background necessary for an understanding of the increasingly complex history of Oman in the twentieth century. The second part of the book – 'Modern History' – brings the story up to (more or less) the present day. Chapter 1, which charts the arise of the Al Bu Said, concludes with an account of the political struggles that followed the death of Imam Ahmad and which led eventually to the ascendancy of his son Sultan bin Ahmad. Chapter 2 charts the fortunes of the Omani state under Sultan bin Ahmad (1792–1804) and Said bin Sultan (1804–1856), under whose leadership Oman expanded its maritime power in the Gulf region and entered into increasingly complex political and economic relations with a new maritime power there: the British Empire. Said bin Sultan effectively moved his capital from Muscat to Zanzibar, extending and deepening Oman's engagement with flows of international trade. Chapter 3 begins after the death of Said bin Sultan in 1856 and charts the increasingly political involvement of the British in Oman affairs, which led eventually to the separation of Zanzibar from Oman. This began a period of economic decline for Oman, as the dominant position achieved by Western imperial powers in the Indian Ocean and beyond deprived Oman of its main source of economic growth and prosperity. During the second half of the nineteenth century and the first decades of the twentieth, this economic reversal contributed to further political instability and to renewed competition between the largely mercantile rulers of the coast and the mainly interior supporters of an Imamate revival. Chapter 3 concludes with an account of the confrontation between the Imamate revival and the Muscat leadership in the first two decades of the twentieth century and the temporary settlement between them which endured until the 1950s. Chapter 4 resumes the story of the political tensions between rival conceptions of the Omani state, focussing primarily on the efforts of Sultan Said bin Taimur (1932–1970) to unify the country as a modern nation-state in the face of economic hardship and substantial external challenges to his rule. Chapter 5 continues the story to include an account of the last major civil conflict in Omani history, in which a rebellion in the southern province of Dhofar, which began in the early 1960s, gained the support of the neighbouring socialist state of the People's Democratic Republic of Yemen and, through them, of both Communist China and the Soviet Union. It was only with the defeat of this major armed challenge in 1975 that Al Bu Said rule in Oman was once again secure. Chapters 6, 7 and 8 are concerned primarily with the economic and political development and the international relations of the Sultanate of Oman under its present ruler, Sultan Qaboos (b. 1940). The accession of Sultan Qaboos in a coup that overthrew his father in July 1970 has sometimes been represented as a decisive break in Omani history, ushering in a completely new phase in the nation's history. Just as in the case of Imam Ahmad, there is some truth in this interpretation, but it is also a story which, in its convenient periodisation, disguises important underlying continuities. For although Sultan Qaboos actively set in motion many processes of economic and social development, and is credited with the creation of the modern Sultanate of Oman (the name he chose to replace the earlier 'Muscat and Oman'), he did not do so by changing underlying principles but rather by effectively taking advantage of a vital underlying reality: the extraction and export of oil. Oman first exported oil in 1967, and although it is by no means as large an exporter as some of its neighbours, oil has dominated the economy ever since. One of the major issues confronting Oman today, alongside the question of employment alluded to earlier, will be how to maintain the standard of living achieved through oil in a future when there is no more oil. That time remains some decades away, but preparing for it is a major concern for the government and people of Oman, and some of the social tensions and political challenges described in the final chapter are likely to intensify as the end of the oil era approaches.

PART ONE

FOUNDATIONS

I

Oman and the Al Bu Said

Ahmad bin Said Al Bu Said, the first ruler of the Al Bu Said dynasty, was elected Imam in 1749. He rose to power in the context of a period of civil war among the Ya'ariba rulers who had preceded him. His historical significance today has a great deal to do with the fact that he founded the dynasty that has ruled Oman ever since, for a period of more than 250 years. This should not, however, be allowed to disguise the fact that his accession to power did not inaugurate a distinctive new era in Oman social, economic and political life. Instead it marked a resumption of patterns of government and economic organisation which had been established over the preceding century, under the rule of the Ya'ariba. What Ahmad's acquisition of power in the aftermath of the Ya'ariba civil war resumed, his successors, most notably Sayyid Said until his death in 1856, then developed and extended. Thus, although this history of modern Oman follows conventions of Omani historiography regarding the accession of Ahmad bin Said and the foundation of the Al Bu Said dynasty as a significant turning point in Omani history, we begin this chapter with a short account of the principal and significant events of the preceding century, in which Oman first established itself as a regional power whose economic and political reach extended far beyond the Arabian Peninsula and into East Africa. As we shall see, the foundation for this expansion was the ability of the Ya'ariba Imams to extend their political power from the interior of the country to its coast, where they successfully confronted and expelled the Portuguese, who had established and maintained naval dominance in the Indian Ocean, including the coast of Oman, since the beginning of the sixteenth century.

YA'ARIBA EXPANSION AND PORTUGUESE POWER

The Portuguese had first appeared in the region in the early sixteenth century. In 1498, Portuguese ships under the command of Vasco da Gama, which had earlier been the first European ships to sail past the Cape of Good Hope at the southern tip of Africa, successfully crossed the Indian Ocean, from Malindi to Kozhikode (Calicut) in India. There is an oft-repeated story that Vasco da Gama was assisted in making this crossing by an Arab pilot and navigator called Ibn Majid (Ahmad ibn Majid). Ibn Majid was indeed a navigator and a captain of merchant ships trading across the Indian Ocean. He was quite probably of Omani origin and was the author of two celebrated books in which he set out his knowledge and expertise. However, as several scholars have noted, the evidence linking Ibn Majid with the pilot who assisted Vasco da Gama is outweighed by plentiful other evidence that the pilot in question was a Gujarati.[1] Nonetheless, the perpetuation of the myth of Ibn Majid's involvement is testimony to the extent to which, at this time, it was Arab sailors and navigators who were believed to be the real experts in the Indian Ocean. The Portuguese entry into the lower Gulf followed soon after Vasco da Gama's arrival in India. Portugal was building an overseas empire, based around a new Estado da India (State of India) with its capital at Goa. As part of this project Portuguese state and merchant interests started to establish a string of coastal possessions which would function as a regional trade network under their exclusive control. One vital element in this network was the Kingdom of Hormuz, whose main centre was located on the island of Hormuz (after which the strait is named) and which lies just off the southern coast of Iran. For several hundred years Hormuz had been a wealthy trading centre, and by the time the Portuguese arrived, its rulers also held effective political control over most of the important towns on the Omani coast, including Muscat, Sohar and Qalhat (now largely in ruins after its destruction by the Portuguese). At this time the Nabhani Imams of Oman exercised real influence only in the interior. Portuguese forces, under the command of Afonso de Albuquerque, took control of Hormuz in 1515, having previously captured or destroyed Omani coastal towns. By this time the

---

[1] See, e.g., G. R. Tibbets, *Arab Navigation in the Indian Ocean Before the Coming of the Portuguese, Being a Translation of 'Kitab al-Fawaid fi usul al-bahr wal-qawaid'* (London: Royal Asiatic Society of Britain and Ireland, 1971), and Sanjay Subrahmanyam, *The Career and Legend of Vasco da Gama* (Cambridge: Cambridge University Press, 1999).

Portuguese had also established themselves in East Africa, starting with Kilwa in 1506, and subsequently in such places as Mombasa and Pate. The Portuguese constructed forts in their key locations, among them the two forts that still stand today in Muscat: Jalali and Mirani. So during the sixteenth century control of the Omani coast largely passed from the Kingdom of Hormuz to the Portuguese.

During the early seventeenth century Portugal started to face a range of challenges to the maritime military supremacy it had established in the Gulf. So, although ports like Muscat, Qalhat and Sur were still vital links in Portuguese trade routes, including those to Basra at the head of the Gulf and Gujarat and Goa on the western coast of India, Dutch, English and Ottoman forces were gaining ground and were gradually able to exert superior military and maritime power in the region. It was at this time that the first of Oman's Ya'ariba leaders, Nasir bin Murshid (1624–1649), acceded to the Imamate and began expanding the political influence of the Imamate beyond the interior, to which it had for some time limited itself. He took control of forts at both Nakhl and Rustaq for the Imamate and started to apply pressure on the Portuguese, even in their stronghold at Muscat. It fell, however, to his cousin and successor, Sultan bin Sayf (1649–1688), finally to take control over the key ports of Quriyat, Sur and Muscat, the last of which the Portuguese abandoned to Omani control in 1650. Possession of Muscat and other coastal towns then became the basis for a significant change in the basis of Imamate rule in Oman. Where previously the Imamate had concerned itself primarily with the maintenance of a just society on the basis of a familiar pattern of social relations associated with life in the interior, now, in the context of Ya'ariba expansion, the role of government became increasingly directed towards furthering the economic interests of merchants and traders, among whom Ya'ariba leaders themselves became prominent. Political succession within the Imamate started to take on strong dynastic characteristics; Imams were designated in advance, in some cases so that they acceded to power while still children. Those who wished to preserve the tradition of the Imamate as a religiously ordained community ruled by a leader elected from within the religious and social elite, viewed these developments with anxiety and alarm. The Imamate was in the process of transforming itself into something much more closely resembling the Sultanate that it was eventually to become under the Al Bu Said: a nation-state where political power would be underwritten by an increasingly close alliance between the traditional elite and an increasingly prosperous and internationally oriented merchant class. It was also in this later phase of Ya'ariba rule in Oman that Oman gradually wrested control of key possessions in East Africa from the retreating Portuguese and began to establish itself as a major maritime power: by the second half of the seventeenth century Omani shipbuilders were able to replicate the larger, gun-bearing ships of the kind the Portuguese had first used to secure their own maritime dominance in the region a hundred or so years earlier. Thus the alliance between the traditional elites and the new merchant elite also came to be backed by superior military force, creating the conjunction of forces that would facilitate the process of state forma-tion in the twentieth century (see Chapters 4–5). But this consolidation of power in the hands of an alliance between the Ya'ariba and other members of the merchant elite was not without its difficulties, and oppo-sition to their conduct of government began to express itself in explicit political moves.

On the death of the Ya'ariba Imam Sayf bin Sultan in 1711, his son Sultan bin Sayf's succession was resented by religious and tribal leaders in the interior. The Ya'ariba rulers of Oman not only had succeeded, as we have seen, in expelling from the Omani coast the Portuguese, who had been a persistent threat since the beginning of the sixteenth century, but had also built upon this success to establish an extensive range of external possessions and interests, most notably in East Africa, where Pemba, Zanzibar and Kilwa were all governed from a Ya'ariba regional stronghold on the coast at Mombasa. Their rule as Imams had been dynastic rather than elective in accordance with the Ibadi tradition of the Imamate, and while this appears to have been tolerated by the cus-todians of Ibadi tradition during times of external threat, such as when the Portuguese were on the coast, it appeared less justifiable in times of prosperity, such as that achieved by the time of the reign of Sultan bin Sayf. Therefore, when Sultan bin Sayf died in 1719, and his son, a sec-ond Sayf bin Sultan, was deemed too young to be a credible successor, the religious and tribal leaders succeeded in electing Muhanna bin Sultan as Imam instead. Upon Muhanna's death in 1721 the conflict between rival claims to the Imamate among the Ya'ariba escalated again as Omani tribes aligned themselves with one or the other of two opposing factions, one led by Khalaf bin Mubarak, chief of the Bani Hina, the other by Mohammed bin Nasir al-Ya'arubi, chief of the Bani Ghafiri.

This is the historical origin of the idea that Omani political life has been dominated by a division between Hinawi and Ghafiri tribal con-federations. In some accounts this division is also thought to coincide with a distinction between those whose origins lie with the Azd Arabs who migrated into Oman from the south, of Yemeni or Qahtani descent, conventionally claimed by Hinawis, and those who trace their descent to the Adnani or Nizari group who migrated into Oman from the north. According to Patricia Risso, this coincidence between Azdi genealogy and political affiliation emerged only during the nineteenth century, and in any case, affiliations tended to shift, with tribes changing sides, so that there have even been times when the Bani Ghafir tribe itself (after whom the Ghafiri group took its name) has been part of the Hinawi confederation.[2] At the time of the initial conflict around which the Hinawi–Ghafiri distinction arose, the Al Bu Said tribe adhered to the Hinawi faction. It was after the deaths of both the leaders of the two factions that the second Sayf bin Sultan was proclaimed Imam at Nizwa in 1728. A rival Imam, Bilurub bin Himyar, was elected five years later, and it was in the struggle between the second Sayf bin Sultan and Bilurub bin Himyar in the 1730s that Ahmad bin Said Al Bu Said entered Omani politics.

THE RISE OF AHMAD BIN SAID

As told by the nineteenth-century historian and loyal servant of the Al Bu Said, Ibn Ruzayq, the story of Ahmad bin Said's rise to power involves both his successful negotiation of the internecine struggles of the Ya'ariba and his success in eventually mobilising some measure of Omani national resistance to the intervention of Persian forces. The Persians, with the keen consent of an unusually powerful new leader, Nadir Shah, had been invited into Oman by Sayf bin Sultan to assist him in his struggle against Bilurub bin Himyar. Ahmad bin Said, who had been born in Adam and appears to have established himself as a relatively successful merchant, first became embroiled in the politics of the Ya'ariba civil war when an associate of Sayf bin Sultan recommended him to the Imam as 'the only man worthy of your confidence: he is discreet in judgement and very courageous'.[3] Shortly after this recommendation the Imam Sayf was on his way from Muscat to Rustaq when he encountered Ahmad bin Said, who was himself on a journey to Muttrah, presumably on mercantile business of some kind. The Imam instructed Ahmad bin Said to come and see him in Muscat as soon as he heard that the Iman had returned there from Rustaq. When he did so, the Imam took him into his service, first sending

---

[2] Risso, *Oman and Muscat*, pp. 42–43.
[3] Ibn Ruzayq, *History of the Imams and Seyyids of Oman*, translated by George Percy Badger (London: Hakluyt Society, 1871), p. 133.

him 'to transact some business for him' (134) and then promoting him through several positions before appointing him Wali of Sohar. Ahmad bin Said is also said to have married a daughter of the Imam Sayf bin Sultan, although this is not mentioned by Ibn Ruzayq, whose account of Ahmad bin Said's actions at this time tends to downplay any sense that Ahmad himself was actively seeking political power, even though one might choose to interpret his report of omens, such as a voice from nowhere that hails him as 'Imam of Oman', as a poetic figuration of a more prosaic political ambition.[4]

Ibn Ruzayq proceeds to recount how Imam Sayf grew jealous of Ahmad bin Said's success and popularity (this also suggests the political ambition that Ibn Ruzayq does not ascribe directly to Ahmad bin Said) and contrived to remove him from power and have him killed. But on his way to meet Imam Sayf (and fall into his trap) Ahmad bin Said encountered Ibn Ruzayq's own grandfather, who was an accountant and personal secretary to the Imam and privy to his ill intentions towards Ahmad bin Said. He informed Ahmad of the Imam's intentions, and Ahmad rose 'as swiftly as the wind' back to Sohar (135). Eventually Ahmad and the Iman were reconciled. It was at this point that the Persians appeared, responding to their invitation from Imam Sayf, who had earlier written to Nadir Shah to request his military assistance against Bilurub bin Himyar in the struggle for the Imamate. The arrival of Persian forces aroused the dismay of a group of Omani notables, who, in Ibn Ruzayq's account, sent the Imam an impassioned letter decrying his dependence upon the Persians, whom they suspected, not inaccurately, of ulterior motives, and urging the Imam to 'place your reliance rather on uprightness and piety' (140). The Persians proceeded to take advantage of their invitation by launching an invasion of the Dhahirah, where, Ibn Ruzayq reports, they slaughtered children and captured women to be sent back to Shiraz as slaves. They reached as far as Nizwa, from where Bilurub took flight, but when they were eventually unable to seize the fort they turned their attentions to the Batinah coast and took control of the city of Muscat (although its two forts continued to resist them). Bilurub was urged to lay aside his claim to the Imamate and joined forces with Sayf to force a Persian withdrawal as far as the region around Sohar, where another Persian force was besieging the city.

In 1741 Sultan bin Murshid was elected Imam, in preference to Bilurub, who had lost the support of the faction that had previously

---

[4] Ibid., pp. 157–158.

promoted him. This raised a further challenge to Sayf bin Sultan, who gathered a new military force at Barka, which was 'utterly routed' by the forces of the new rival Imam, Sultan bin Murshid. Sayf was pursued to Muscat, where he was forced to take refuge aboard a ship, which then, according to three accounts suggested by Ibn Ruzayq, was wrecked, seized by Ahmad bin Said or else permitted Sayf to make his way to the Persian forces, which he once again sought to enlist on his side in the contest with his new rival. In Ibn Ruzayq's narrative of this closing phase of the Ya'ariba civil war, which appears to cover the period from around 1744, even though Ibn Ruzayq himself has it ending with Ahmad becoming Imam in 1741, Ahmad bin Said's role appears quite simple: he is in Sohar, defending the city against the besieging Persians. Other accounts suggest a slightly more complex role, in which, once the Persians had succeeded in taking Sohar, Ahmad bin Said withdrew for a while to Barka, made common cause with Sultan bin Murshid in an attempt to retake Sohar from the Persians (an encounter in which Sultan bin Murshid was wounded and ultimately died), after which he succeeded in getting the Persians to appoint him as their own Wali at Sohar, rather than Sayf's. Sayf is said to have died a few days after Sultan bin Murshid, repenting bitterly his decision to invite the Persians into Oman. Ibn Ruzayq's narrative makes no mention of Ahmad bin Said's appointment as the Persians' Wali in Sohar, presumably because this would sit uneasily with an account of Ahmad bin Said's rise to power in which he otherwise appears to be an unwavering opponent of the Persians. Ibn Ruzayq also fails to mention that Bilurub bin Himyar was once again elected Imam following the death of Sultan bin Murshid. These two omissions allowed Ibn Ruzayq to move towards his famous set piece, in which Ahmad bin Sultan outwitted and eventually destroyed the Persians and acceded rapidly to the position of Imam.

First of all, his resistance to the Persians at Sohar (or, perhaps, if we think beyond Ibn Ruzayq's account, his tactical alliance with them) led the Persians, on learning of Sayf's death, to propose a deal with Ahmad, in which he would allow them to depart, taking with them their arms and ammunition. Ahmad agreed to this and also allowed the Persians to believe that the same deal would hold with their compatriots currently installed in Muscat. When the Persians left Sohar, Ahmad moved down the coast to Barka, where he had two sets of scales set up to enable goods imported from India to be weighed and thus landed and traded there. The effect, it is suggested, was to draw trade away from Muscat and Muttrah and towards Barka, simultaneously making Barka a key centre for commercial activity and depriving the Persians in Muscat and Muttrah of supplies. The compression of Ibn Ruzayq's narrative at this point makes it difficult to determine how long it took for this effect to take hold. The Persians, starting to 'despond' (151) at their predicament, sent a close relative of the late Sayf bin Sultan, one Majid bin Sultan, with a letter to the Shah requesting that they be permitted to return home. The Shah's affirmative response, sent with Majid bin Sultan, was intercepted by Ahmad bin Said at Sohar, who sent his own representative, Khamis bin Salim, to Muscat, accompanied by four hundred men, to deliver the letter to the Persians, who, believing Khamis to be acting on behalf of Majid, 'delivered up all the posts into his hands' (152). Khamis then installed the four hundred men he had brought with him from Sohar as a garrison.

With his own forces now in control of Muscat, Ahmad bin Said invited the Persians to Barka, where great quantities of meat were prepared for them, much to the fury of the local Omanis, who believed the Persians deserved death rather than hospitality. Once the Persian leaders were invited to eat, however, a proclamation was issued, informing the people that '[a]nyone who has a grudge against the Persians may now take his revenge' (153). The Persians were all killed, with the exception of two hundred who were taken to sea, on Ahmad bin Said's orders, ostensibly bound for Bandar Abbas. But the Barka sailors who were entrusted with this task set fire to the ships, swam back to shore, and left the Persians to drown. In Ibn Ruzayq's narrative this is the crowning event which effectively ends his Book One and after which Ahmad bin Said made a more or less ceremonial tour of key towns – Rustaq, Samail, Izki, Nizwa, Bahla – in all of which he was recognised as Imam.

As Patricia Risso notes, and as we have suggested in the foregoing account, Ibn Ruzayq's chronology for the period following 1728 is 'totally confused'.[5] Risso's own account, which we have drawn on here to indicate important ways in which Ibn Ruzayq's may be unreliable, draws on an untitled and anonymous manuscript which, Risso suggests, considering its consistency with other reliable accounts on veri-fiable matters and its 'non-polemical tone', is far more reliable for the period it covers (1728–1795) than Ibn Ruzayq's. Ibn Ruzayq, as Risso observes, was an historian 'patronized' by Sayyid Said bin Sultan, was therefore 'unsurprisingly' partisan in his account of Al Bu Said history and, as a prolific writer and copier, 'often failed to indicate his sources'.[6]

---

[5] Risso, *Oman and Muscat*, p. 226.
[6] Ibid., p. 226.

What Ibn Ruzayq's account leaves out is a final phase in the Ya'ariba civil war, in which the Persian ruler, Nadir Shah, facing pressure from Ottoman expansion in the Gulf, decided to withdraw his troops from Oman, thus helping Ahmad bin Said to consolidate further his position on the coast, as the Persians withdrew (one can see, incidentally, how Ibn Ruzayq's story is far from inconsistent with this, even if he offers a different account of Persian motivations). Meanwhile Bilurub was deposed, in 1748, and Ahmad bin Said, whose political position was strong enough for him to make a direct bid for power, sent Khalfan bin Mohammed Al Bu Said to lay siege to Nizwa. Nizwa accepted Khalfan as Ahmad's *wali*, and shortly thereafter Izki followed suit, giving Ahmad control of key locations in the interior as well as on the coast. In June 1749 Ahmad was elected Imam by a group of religious leaders which included the author of the letter that had deposed Bilurub the previous year.

So what can a contemporary historian of Oman conclude from a reading of Ibn Ruzayq's partisan and possibly myth-making history in relation to accounts drawing on different sources? Ibn Ruzayq's narrative emphasises a supernatural sense that Ahmad bin Said was destined to become Imam, and this, as we have already suggested, may take the place of calculation and ambition on Ahmad's part, which are largely absent from Ibn Ruzayq's account. All the same, he is presented as ruthless with opponents, capable of major feats of war, and prepared to exercise cunning and deceit in pursuit of larger objectives (as in the story of the massacre at Barka). Since other historical accounts suggest that the Persians were withdrawing their forces from Oman of their own accord rather than because of the pressure exerted upon them by Ahmad bin Said, we may reasonably imagine that Ibn Ruzayq's account of the massacre at Barka is designed to make a better historical narrative of the events, more befitting a man who was, at the time Ibn Ruzayq was writing, worthy of such praise as the founder of an Omani political dynasty that had held power for more than a century. The fact that this apotheosis shows Ahmad bin Said to be capable of political cunning and deception may also lead us to speculate that the story is a way of displaying those characteristics poetically, by a writer who has not otherwise presented his subject as engaged in the kind of political chicanery necessary to acquire power in the context of a civil war, including, for instance, his appointment as the Persian's *wali* at Sohar, which, Risso comments, was 'a feat which attests well to his diplomatic skill'.[7] In a sense, then, Ibn Ruzayq's

---

[7] Ibid., p. 41.

account may tell us more than a literal reading might initially suggest. The possibility that the author is writing metaphorically – allowing symbolic and fictional events to stand in for realities less easily rendered in literary form – is supported by his reference to the scales of Barka. This striking image – of scales being set up – and the brief reference to the effects this had on the direction of regional trade seem to point to the more general idea that Ahmad bin Said, like the successful Ya'ariba Imams before him, was building his political power on the basis of a dominant position in the country's coastal trade.

THE STRUGGLE FOR MUSCAT

Once established as Imam, Ahmad bin Said was able, as we suggested at the opening of this chapter, to resume the outward-looking and commercially oriented policies developed by the Ya'ariba which had fallen into decline during the civil war. Muscat would become the key location for the development of such policies, and control of the city would from now on be the prize in nearly all struggles for power among Omani leaders. After his accession, Ahmad bin Said continued to be troubled by residual aspects of the earlier conflict. These included domestic challenges from those who had not fully accepted his election in the first place and who wished to promote their own claims to the Imamate, and also the return, under a new leader, Karim Khan Zand, of the Persians as rivals for control of the waters of the southern Gulf. He successfully resisted both of these challenges, and by the end of the 1770s, Al Bu Saidi control of coastal Oman and of Muscat had been largely secured, and the basis for an expansion of power based on earlier Ya'ariba possessions beyond Oman itself had been laid.

However, there were also struggles for political power within the Al Bu Said themselves, as Imam Ahmad's sons competed for position both during and after his reign. Four sons in particular played prominent roles: Said, Qays, Sayf and Sultan. On his accession, Imam Ahmad had appointed Said as Wali of Rustaq and Qays as Wali of Sohar. Sayf and Sultan were sons of the same mother, and in 1781 they joined forces in an attempt to seize power in Muscat. Their action does not seem to have been an attempt to secure the Imamate itself for either of them, but may rather have been designed to support their own commercial interests. As Sultan bin Ahmad's subsequent career shows (see Chapter 2), control of Muscat would accomplish this. In December Sayf and Sultan took their brother Said hostage and held in him Muscat's Jalali Fort. Ahmad responded by laying siege to the fort from both land and sea, forcing Sayf and Sultan to flee Oman altogether, for Makran. Here the local ruler granted them possession of the coastal town of Gwadar, a port which would later become an important point in Oman's nineteenth-century maritime trade network and would remain an Omani possession until its sale to Pakistan by Sultan Said bin Taimur in 1958.[8] As we shall see, Sultan bin Ahmad would eventually emerge as the undisputed political ruler of Oman after a struggle of some years following the death of his father, Imam Ahmad.

By the end of Imam Ahmad's reign, then, Muscat was establishing itself as the leading port of trade between the Gulf and India and, with the coffee trade, the lower reaches of the Red Sea, too.[9] In East Africa, where the Ya'ariba had earlier begun to establish Omani political and economic power, the period of Omani civil war had allowed local leaders to regain considerable autonomy and had even permitted the Portuguese briefly to regain control of Mombasa. It would not be until after the death of Imam Ahmad that his successors would begin to reassert Omani political and economic power in East Africa, beyond the stronghold of Zanzibar. A resurgence in the African–Indian Ocean slave trade, generated by French plantation developments in Réunion and Mauritius, more or less simultaneous with a shift in the ivory trade route north from the area of Portuguese dominance in Mozambique, would be crucial to the revival of Omani interests there (see Chapter 2).

Imam Ahmad died in December 1783. He had designated his son Said as the next Imam, and Said bin Ahmad was duly elected. However, this dynastic succession was contested by advocates of a return to a more traditional Imamate, and attempts were apparently made to set up a rival Imamate under Ahmad's son Qays, the Wali of Rustaq, in 1785. These proved unsuccessful, however. On Imam Ahmad's death, both Sayf and Sultan had returned to Muscat with the aim of contesting Said's rule, but their military advance into northern Omani towns, supported by troops from Ras al-Khaimah, was checked by Said's forces, and both brothers

---

[8] For further discussion of how the offer of Gwadar to Sultan and Sayf came about, see Beatrice Nicolini, 'Historical and Political Links between Gwadar and Muscat from Nineteenth Century Testimonies', *Proceedings of the Seminar for Arabian Studies* 32 (2001), pp. 281–286. For more on Makran and its role in Oman's nineteenth-century trade network, see Beatrice Nicolini, *Makran, Oman and Zanzibar: Three-Terminal Cultural Corridor in the Western Indian Ocean (1799–1856)* (Leiden: Brill, 2004).

[9] See Wilkinson, *Imamate Tradition of Oman*, pp. 50–51; Calvin H. Allen, Jr., 'The Indian Merchant Community of Masquat', *Bulletin of the School of Oriental and African Studies* 44.1 (1981), p. 41; and Risso, *Oman and Muscat*, p. 61.

withdrew from direct challenges. Said also faced a persistent challenge to his political authority from his own son, Hamad, to whom he ceded control over Muscat in 1789. Said's concession of Muscat to his son may in fact have served to Said's own advantage, as Hamad's control of the key port city may have been preferable to him to further advances by his brother Sultan. In any case, and despite these domestic difficulties, during the period in which Said was Imam and Hamad controlled Muscat, Omanis were successful in building upon the resumption of Oman's maritime trade made possible during Imam Ahmad's reign, in extending Omani influence in East Africa once again, with the slave trade becoming increasingly lucrative, and in opening new commercial relations with the powerful Muslim state of Mysore.

Hamad bin Said died of smallpox in 1792, and the following year a decisive accommodation between the three leading members of the Al Bu Said family was reached. Said remained Imam and retired, with a pension, to Rustaq, a title and a location which might suggest, according to earlier practice, that he held the pre-eminent position. However, his power did not extend much beyond Rustaq, and it was generally recognised that the title of Imam no longer carried with it the assumption of full political control. Said's position was in any case further weakened by the fact that many of the religious elite were known to favour Qays, who remained in control of Sohar. The key position, however, fell to Sultan bin Ahmad, who had successfully built up his own naval power, partly based in Gwadar, and who now, crucially, held uncontested control of Muscat, which was becoming both the political and commercial centre of Oman. Such was the advantage gained from possession of Muscat that Sultan bin Ahmad appears to have seen no need to lay claim to the Imamate. Although Sultan bin Ahmad and his successors did claim political authority over the whole of Oman at this time, local powers of various kinds continued to enjoy various degrees of autonomy, and political conflict between those who looked to the sea and to commerce, on the one hand, and those who sought a restoration of the traditional Imamate, on the other, would return, particularly at times when the prosperity of the commercially driven nation was threatened (see, especially, Chapter 3). But for the next half century, it was the mercantile Oman that prevailed, first under Sultan bin Ahmad and then under his son, Said bin Sultan. It is to the history of this period that we turn in the chapter that follows.

2

Oman, Zanzibar and Empire

Between Sultan bin Ahmad's rise to power in Muscat in 1792 and the death of his son and successor, Sayyid Said bin Sultan, en route to his home in Zanzibar in 1856, Oman established itself as a major commercial and maritime power in the Indian Ocean. The collection of ports, islands and associated territories assembled through the exertion of Muscat's maritime power has sometimes been referred to as an 'empire', and more recently as a 'thalassocracy'.[1] The term 'empire' suggests the coordinated exercise of political power from an all-powerful centre (Rome, Istanbul, London) and does not really capture the reality of the Omani network, while 'thalassocracy' has the advantage of indicating that political rule is exercised over a network by means of maritime power and connection rather than through the operations of a centralising state. Although it is perhaps an awkward and unfamiliar term, it does more effectively name the nature of Oman political and commercial power in the first half of the nineteenth century. In addition to building their network of trade relationships across the region, Omani merchants and traders also started to become part of a larger and incipiently global commercial system. The long-standing Indian Ocean network in which they had operated for centuries became increasingly integrated with the long-range trade of European and American industrial capitalism. This means that Oman was at this time a significant participant in an historical transformation which many historians have seen as establishing the essential foundations

[1] See Marcus P. M. Vink, 'Indian Ocean Studies and the "New Thalassology"', *Journal of Global History* 2.1 (2007), pp. 41–62.

of the present 'world-system' of globalised capitalism.[2] The sequence of events set out in this chapter must therefore be understood in relation to complex and long-range interactions with multiple national and commercial actors. Space does not permit us to trace all of these interactions or to provide for each event involving the key Omani protagonists a detailed account of how their actions affected and were affected by those of the many other participants in the expanding network of relations. Instead we shall briefly summarise some of the key features of Oman's immediate regional environment and aspects of its increasing integration into the globalising system of economic and political relationships being generated by the colonial expansion of European capitalism in the early nineteenth century.

EUROPEAN CAPITALISM COMES TO THE GULF

The most significant novel feature of the regional environment was, of course, the very fact of European colonial expansion itself. While the Portuguese, as we have already seen, were the first Europeans to establish a significant colonial presence in the region – with particularly direct consequences for Oman – it would be the Dutch, the French and, above all, the British whose activities would have the most far-reaching consequences for the Omanis. But even before Britain emerged as the key foreign power with whom an Omani leader would have to reckon, the entire Indian Ocean network of political and economic relations, in which Oman had participated for centuries, had already been transformed, as Dutch, French and British East India companies (all founded in the first two decades of the seventeenth century) vied with one another to establish control of trade in commodities and raw materials across the region. By 1750 the intervention of these companies, with the backing of their respective governments, had wrought a transformation in the trade of the region. It is this transformation that Immanuel Wallerstein has described as having entailed 'a restructuring of production processes and the creation of a political entity (or entities) operating within the rules of the interstate system'.[3] K. N. Chaudhuri has suggested that this intervention brought to an end a period in which the main markets of the

---

[2] See, in particular, Immanuel Wallerstein, *The Modern World-System II: Mercantilism and the Consolidation of the European World-Economy* (Berkeley: University of California Press, 2011).

[3] Immanuel Wallerstein, 'Incorporation of Indian Subcontinent into Capitalist World-Economy', *Economic and Political Weekly*, 21.4 (1986), pp. PE 28–PE 39.

region were, in effect, politically neutral.[4] The rulers of the states of the Indian Ocean littoral before 1750 generally participated in a tacit agreement in which the traders of the region, wherever they came from, were permitted to do their business anywhere around the regional network. The mid-eighteenth-century transformation involved the reorganisation of much regional production towards meeting the needs of European consumers, accompanied by aggressive efforts on the part of the companies, often backed by force of arms, to secure exclusive positions in key commercial locations. In short, regional trade after 1750 became highly politicised because of its integration into a system that would be dominated by a capitalist system of production. The dominant merchant groups before this transformation were not driven by the need to maximise the extraction of surplus value. The new capitalist enterprises which came to dominate the region's trade during the eighteenth century, however, were driven by this imperative and, backed by the military power of European nation-states, generated amongst themselves a fierce competition for control of resources and access to resources.

Britain would eventually emerge as the most successful of the European powers, establishing an extensive empire based substantially upon its colonisation of the Indian subcontinent. Through the nineteenth century, as we shall see, Britain also developed a system of economic, political and military administration in the Gulf, coordinated on behalf of the British government in India by a Residency, initially established by the East India Company in Bushehr in 1763. Under British administration most of the Arab Emirates and Shaikhdoms of the Gulf entered into treaties or became British Protectorates, so that their foreign policies were effectively directed by the British, and British agents (many of whom were recruited from the local population) worked closely with local rulers and merchants to ensure that British interests were protected and advanced.[5] This system, initially established as an extension of the British administration of India, would eventually be dismantled in 1971, nearly twenty-five years after Indian independence, once the British government in London had concluded that it could no longer afford the military deployment that underpinned its political role in the Gulf. Oman never became a British Protectorate (although in 1890 Zanzibar did), but its political and

---

[4] K. N. Chaudhuri, *Trade and Civilisation in the Indian Ocean: An Economic History from the Rise of Islam to 1750* (Cambridge: Cambridge University Press, 1985).

[5] See James Onley, *The Arabian Frontier of the British Raj: Merchants, Rulers, and the British in the Nineteenth-Century Gulf* (Oxford: Oxford University Press, 2007), and also Chapter 3, this volume.

economic relationship with Britain would prove to be of enormous significance for Oman, largely shaping the terms of its engagement with the capitalist world-system from the late eighteenth century onwards.

The first significant contacts between Omanis and the British East India Company took place much earlier, around 1624, when Omani merchants active on the western coast of India started doing business with Company merchants. The British sought to develop these commercial relationships with a view to participating in the already long-established trade between Oman's ports (Muscat, Seeb, Sohar) and Gujarat, and in 1645 Imam Nasir bin Murshid responded to this interest by inviting the East India Company to do business in Oman. Imam Nasir's initiative was economic and political: as we have seen in Chapter 1, the Portuguese still held the key ports of Muscat, Quriyat and Sur at this time, and the Imam, who already had the support of Indian merchants in his efforts to expel them, almost certainly saw a relationship with the British as advantageous to this campaign. An agreement between the Imam and a representative of the East India Company was signed in 1646, granting the Company trading privileges in Sohar, and discussions were also held around this time over the possible establishment of a Company factory at Muscat, leading at one point to formal negotiations, which were, however, inconclusive. Subsequent efforts by the East India Company to secure agreement with Omani rulers (both Ya'ariba and Al Bu Said) to set up a factory were unsuccessful.[6] When Sultan bin Ahmad came to power in Muscat in 1792, the British – having consolidated their position in India through the subjugation of Indian rulers and the establishment of military superiority over their principal European rivals, the French – now exercised such control over the conduct of Indian Ocean trade that Omani commercial interests were much more directly threatened than ever before. Of particular significance for Muscat was the British military victory over Tipu Sultan of Mysore at the Battle of Srirangapatna (Seringapatam) in 1792. Muscat–Mysore trade and political cooperation had established excellent conditions for the further development of Oman's Indian Ocean trade network. Tipu Sultan's defeat not only was a setback for this relationship but also resulted in the British gaining new territorial possessions on the Malabar coast (including the ports of Kozhikode and Kannur), from which British policy threatened to exclude Omani traders. The British, who had initially been regarded in Oman as

---

[6] M. Reda Bhacker, *Trade and Empire in Muscat and Zanzibar: The Roots of British Domination* (London: Routledge, 1994), pp. 31–32.

valuable new business partners, were now emerging as a substantial challenge to Omani interests.

REGIONAL RIVALRIES

While the expansion of British power in India and the Gulf was the dominant feature of the external environment facing Sultan bin Ahmad, the activities of a range of other actors were also significant. Foremost among these regional actors, and so close at hand as to require constant attention from Sultan bin Ahmad, were the coastal tribe of the Qawasim and the Islamic revivalist movement of the Wahhabis. The Qawasim controlled both Ras al-Khaimah and Sharjah and, since the mid-eighteenth century, had established themselves as a significant maritime power in the lower Gulf – a position which would lead them into a persistent rivalry with Oman. The present-day rulers of Ras al-Khaimah and Sharjah in the United Arab Emirates are Qawasim. Wahhabism was a religious movement named after its founder, Mohammed ibn Abd al-Wahhab, who preached an austere return to the religious practices and values of Mohammed's time, insisting upon the authority of the Quran and Hadith, in opposition to the claims of later legal and religious scholarship. In 1740 al-Wahhab entered into an alliance with Mohammed ibn Saud to establish an Emirate in the Najd, the central highlands of the Arabian Peninsula, which became the first Saudi state.[7] Their alliance was hugely successful and led to campaigns to extend the power of the Emirate, which started to threaten Oman from 1800 onwards. Wahhabism's emphasis on the Arab origins of Islam, as well as its accusation that contemporary rulers had betrayed Islam's basic values, would become the ideological basis of political and military campaigns against both the Ottomans and Persians, and also against fellow Arabs whose religious beliefs supposedly made them 'infidels'. Oman's Ibadi rulers were therefore among the targets of Wahhabi hostility. The formation of an alliance between the Qawasim and the Wahhabis constituted a substantial challenge to Sultan bin Ahmad's control of Omani territory. At the same time, this alliance came to be perceived by the British as a significant threat to their own interests, as it threatened their capacity to exercise influence on the Gulf littoral. These, then, as we shall see, were the circumstances in which Oman and Britain entered into a political and military alliance that was to have far-reaching consequences for the political order in the lower

---

[7] See Pascal Menoret, *The Saudi Enigma: A History* (London: Zed Books, 2005), pp. 43–52.

Gulf region and for Oman's position in the wider global political and economic system taking shape in the context of colonialism.

Complex interactions between Oman's interests and these two regional rivals, further and massively complicated by increasing British political involvement, would shape Omani policy during the reign of Sultan bin Ahmad (1792–1804) and through the first phase of his son Sayyid Said's reign (from 1804 to about 1828). Oman's successful negotiation of these relationships was one of the key factors in the establishment of the Omani thalassocracy and created the conditions that enabled Oman's expansion in East Africa, with the development of Zanzibar as Sayyid Said's political and commercial capital in the second phase of his reign. This chapter therefore proceeds in three sections: the first tells the story of Sultan bin Ahmad's reign; the second and third concern the two phases of Sayyid Said's.

SAYYID SULTAN BIN AHMAD, 1792–1804: THE FOUNDATIONS OF OMANI POWER

As we have already seen (Chapter 1) Sultan bin Ahmad's rise to power began on the death of his father, Ahmad bin Said, in 1783. For about five years after Imam Ahmad's death, Muscat was under the control of his brother Said bin Ahmad, who had been elected Imam on his father's death. Sultan and his brother Sayf had initially returned from Gwadar and had launched a military campaign, in an alliance with Saqr bin Rashid of Ras al-Khaimah, with the aim of having Sayf replace Said. Checked by Said's troops, the two brothers withdrew, with Sayf effectively ending his involvement in domestic political struggle, while Sultan took up residence in the Sharqiyah, marrying into a local tribe, al-Wahiba. He appears to have continued to represent a threat, first to Said and then, after Said ceded control of Muscat to his son, Hamad, in 1789, to Hamad also, against whom he appears to have made occasional incursions, including at least one attempt to take control of Muttrah.

It is clear that Muscat itself was a significant aspect of this prolonged struggle for political pre-eminence among the successors of Ahmad bin Said. Under Said and Hamad, Muscat had grown in economic importance, and control over this now dominant commercial capital would be essential for anyone with ambitions to rule Oman as a whole. By 1790, half of all commerce between India and the Gulf passed through Muscat. At the same time Muscat's share of the trade in Yemeni coffee increased substantially. Hamad regularised import tariffs, introducing a flat rate for foreign traders of all denominations, replacing a previous system in which Christians had paid only 5 percent, Muslims 6 percent and Hindus and Jews 9 percent.[8] This policy was presumably aimed at encouraging trade, especially from India, where Hamad made a particular effort to increase the scale of commercial relations with Sind. Muscat would from now on thrive as a merchant city in periods when the country's rulers could use it to consolidate Oman's network of external relations. Conversely, it would fall into decline when Oman's external networks were under threat. Muscat would also be the key location for the development of Oman's relationship with the British: the more successful Muscat's merchants and traders became, the higher it appeared in the list of British regional priorities.

When Hamad died in 1792, Sultan, with the crucial political support of the Muscat merchant class trumping the political power of the religious leaders of Rustaq, who expressed their allegiance to Imam Said, succeeded in gaining control of Muscat. He immediately resumed the expansion of Oman's maritime and commercial interests, which had endured a brief hiatus following Hamad's death. Among his crucial early initiatives was the seizure of Hormuz and Qishm from the Bani Ma'in. Because the Shaikh of the Bani Ma'in also held the lease to the Persian port of Bandar Abbas, this also passed to Sultan bin Ahmad. Within a year of taking power in Muscat, then, Sultan bin Ahmad had strengthened Oman's position at the crucial Strait of Hormuz, exerting considerable control over both the Arab and Persian coasts. This would be the basis for subsequent Omani efforts to secure a dominant position in the region. It was also the position the Qawasim would seek to challenge, and it was also the grounds for the intensification of both British and French interest in securing an alliance with Muscat. Britain would eventually succeed in securing an Omani alliance, initially formalised in a treaty in 1798.

The British and the French had long been engaged in a struggle for political control in India, which had continued even at times when the two countries were officially at peace with one another in the European sphere. While Britain had decisively gained the upper hand by the mid-eighteenth century – taking control of Bengal by defeating an alliance between the French and the Bengali ruler at the Battle of Palashi (Plassey) in 1757 – France maintained significant possessions mainly in the south and east of the subcontinent, as well as two important Indian Ocean

[8] Bhacker, *Trade and Empire*, p. 26.

islands, Île de France (Mauritius) and Île Bourbon (Réunion), where its naval power was concentrated and where substantial slave plantations had been established, producing sugar and coffee for European consumption. As we shall see, these plantation economies would later be emulated by the Omani rulers of Zanzibar. As Sultan bin Ahmad came to power in Muscat, Britain and France were on the brink of a period of intensified military confrontation across several fronts, occasioned primarily by British participation in a coalition of European monarchies united in their aim to defeat the republican government established in France in 1792, as a result of the revolution which had begun in 1789. Under republican rule tensions arose between the French colonial rulers of Île de France and Bourbon over slavery – fundamental to the island economies but vigorously opposed by powerful elements within the new revolutionary regime. In 1794 the French Convention (republican France's first elected legislative assembly) voted to abolish slavery in France and all its colonies. French colonists, already politically divided over the revolution itself and fearful of the kind of slave rebellion that had already broken out in Saint Domingue (present-day Haiti, at that time the most important French colony in the Caribbean), resisted the efforts of the government in Paris to enforce abolition, and Île de France effectively operated as an independent state from 1796 until its reincorporation under Napoléon Bonaparte following his coup d'état in Paris in 1803. The combination of intense French–British competition and the complications and divisions on the French side in the throes of revolution goes some way to explaining how the British achieved their objective of a treaty with Muscat at the expense of the French.

Britain's immediate and longer-term interests in securing an alliance with Muscat were fairly clear. A long-term interest in expanding the volume and profitability of the commercial activities of the British East India Company was sharpened by the pursuit of competition (and outright conflict) with France, whose challenge to British interests was most forcefully underlined in July 1798 when French forces under the command of Napoléon embarked on an invasion of Egypt. British commercial interests in the Gulf depended on the continued security of Basra, where the East India Company had established its first 'factory' (or trading post) in the region in 1620. It was from Basra that the Company conducted its trade with Persia, and it was through the Gulf and Basra that an overland route to European markets for Indian textiles had been forged. For much of the eighteenth century, Britain's interests in the region were limited to the protection of its commercial assets through the security of Bombay–Basra shipping, the maintenance of local trade between Muscat, Persia and Basra and the protection of British subjects doing business in the region. But at the end of the century the resurgence of the French, signalled so vividly by Napoléon's invasion of Egypt, along with continued regional instability, led the East India Company to call for the intervention of the Royal Navy in the Gulf to protect its shipping from the threats posed by both regional and international competition. These threats included the maritime operations of both the Omanis and the Qawasim, which the British routinely understood and reported as 'piracy', especially after a Qawasim attack on an East India Company ship in 1797. As local commerce dwindled in significance when compared with the traffic between Britain and British India, the strategic importance of the Gulf led to the direct politicisation of the British presence in the region.

The question of 'piracy' in the Gulf during this period has been a subject of much scholarly debate. The British documentary record tends to reflect the interests of its authors – the agents of the British government and the East India Company – who defined threats and challenges to their own commercial interests as 'piracy' as part of a process of affirming the principles of property and sovereignty that underpinned the emergent capitalist and colonialist world-system. For those whose perspectives were not shaped by this set of values, the 'pirates' of the British archive might be viewed as having acted in legitimate pursuit of their own commercial interests. Sultan bin Muhammad al-Qasimi, the present Qawasim ruler of Sharjah, in a book that seeks to absolve his historical predecessors from the charge of piracy, argues, for example, that attacks on shipping were an accepted aspect of city-state rivalries. He also claims that many of the actions attributed by the British to Qawasim piracy may in fact have been carried out by Omanis. This suggests that the British accusation of 'piracy' may have been politically expedient (either consciously or unconsciously) and that it was levelled primarily at those against whom the British wished to take action rather than against those with whom they wanted to make an alliance.[9]

---

[9] Some key texts in the scholarly discussion of this issue include Mohammed al-Qasimi, *The Myth of Arab Piracy* (London: Routledge, 1988); Charles E. Davies, *The Blood-Red Arab Flag: An Investigation into Qasimi Piracy, 1797–1820* (Exeter: University of Exeter Press, 1997); Patricia Risso, 'Cross-Cultural Perceptions of Piracy: Maritime Violence in the Western Indian Ocean During a Long Eighteenth Century,' *Journal of World History* 12.2 (2001), pp. 293–319; and Khaldoun Nasser al-Naqeeb, *Society and State in the Gulf and Arab Peninsula: A Different Perspective* (London: Routledge, 2012).

The entry of the Royal Navy into the Gulf therefore marked the beginning of a much more interventionist and politically motivated British presence in the region, of which the treaty with Muscat would be an early indication. For the British, even if their long-term aims were yet to become clear, the treaty with Muscat set the stage for a century-long effort to secure the Gulf as 'a British lake', as the last nineteenth-century British Viceroy of India, Lord Curzon, was to call it. It is perhaps curious, and certainly requires some explanation, that the system of Protectorates established by treaties between Gulf rulers and the British did not, in the end, include Oman. This will be addressed in Chapter 3.

The immediate question for historians of Oman, however, is what led Oman to enter into formal treaty relations with the British at this time, after nearly 150 years in which British requests had been persistently denied. In the most general terms Oman's action is best understood as a move to take a position within the 'globalising' world-system by extending and enhancing its participation in existing Indian Ocean networks. Not even the most far-sighted leader could have foreseen what this step would eventually entail. Instead it is reasonable to assume that Sultan bin Ahmad's decision to sign a treaty with the British was a response to a set of more immediate and pragmatic considerations, many of them commercial. It is when these considerations are examined as a whole, in retrospect, and with their consequences in mind that the treaty can be seen as a crucial stage in the process by which Oman came to be part of the global capitalist system. The more immediate commercial considerations would have been underpinned by a perception that the British were a much more powerful political and economic force than the French. This perception would have been sharpened by recent British threats to Omani commercial privileges, including free access to Indian ports. It may also have been accompanied by a reasonable expectation on the part of Sultan bin Ahmad and his merchant associates (many of whom were Indian) that new commercial opportunities in India might flow from such a political alliance with the British.

The treaty was signed on October 12, 1798. Among its seven articles, three specified commitments on the part of Sayyid Sultan bin Ahmad to limit his relations with the French. The first was not to grant either the French or the Dutch a factory at Muscat, Gombroon (Bandar Abbas) or any other port within his jurisdiction. The second was an undertaking to dismiss a French doctor (doctors were often, it seems, spies) from his service. The third affirmed that French ships seeking water in Muscat should not be permitted to enter the port if English ships were present and that, in the event of any hostilities arising from this, Muscat should take the English side (but would not participate in any naval conflict between the English and the French on 'the high seas').[10] In addition, Sayyid Sultan agreed, in Article Seven, that the British might establish and fortify a factory at Bandar Abbas. It was Article Two, however, that probably had the most lasting consequences, affirming that the 'friendship' between Muscat and the British involved treating one another's friends as friends and one another's enemies as one's own. Sayyid Sultan's successor, Sayyid Said, would soon find that the British were less willing than he might have expected to take positive action against Muscat's enemies. This would be a source of some tension in the emerging Omani–British relationship, whose first major test was already taking shape in the form of a de facto alliance between the Qawasim of Ras al-Khaimah and a newly expansionist Saudi/Wahhabi state, which had designs on the conquest, subjugation and conversion of Oman to its religious and political revival.

The Wahhabi challenge to Oman began in earnest in 1800. The Saudi Amir, Abd al-Aziz, had already reportedly sent to Omani leaders an exposition of Wahhabi doctrine (in the form of a treatise, *Kashf al-Shubhat*, by the movement's founder, Mohammed ibn Abd al-Wahab) accompanied by an invitation to convert to the new religious movement. In response to the predictable Omani rejection of this offer, Abd al-Aziz dispatched a military force under the command of a Nubian slave general, Salim al-Hariq, to attempt the capture of the Omani town of Sohar. Between them, Qays and Sultan successfully prevented the Wahhabi advance and Salim al-Hariq withdrew his force to the oasis of Buraimi, where he established a Saudi/Wahhabi base, recruited Dhahirah tribal leaders as allies and started to raise *zakat*, an Islamic tax collected to support the poor, from the local population. Buraimi would be the political and military base for Wahhabi actions against Oman for the next two decades, and the legacy of the Saudi occupation of the oasis would assume new significance in the 1950s, when the rulers of the third Saudi state would use it as the basis for a provocative territorial claim, as we shall see in Chapter 4. At this stage the Wahhabis had already secured the submission and conversion of the Qawasim after several years of attacks, ending in the successful siege of Ras al-Khaimah in 1799. This meant that the Wahhabis could now rely on the Qawasim as military and political

---

[10] See Risso, *Oman and Muscat*, pp. 218–219.

allies in their subsequent efforts to bring Oman under their sway. The Qawasim had already been challenging Oman both on land and at sea. The combination of these two previously antagonistic forces substantially increased the pressure on the Omani position and started to limit Sultan bin Ahmad in his attempt to expand Omani military and commercial power in the Gulf.

Sultan bin Ahmad had been seeking to use his maritime strength to gain even greater control over the flow of trade through the Gulf. But Wahhabi expansion would frustrate his efforts, first frustrating him in attempts to seize control of Bahrain and then making a direct assault on Sultan's own power based in Muscat. The Wahhabi move on Muscat exploited divisions within Sultan bin Ahmad's own family when, following an unsuccessful attempt to seize power in Muscat, Sultan's nephew, Badr bin Sayf, took up residence in Diriyah, where he converted to Wahhabism and where he started participating, alongside the Wahhabi General Salim al-Hariq, in actions on the Batinah, with the apparent objective of seizing Sohar. This action seems to have been designed by the Saudi/Wahhabi leadership to complement action against Muscat by sea. However, the Saudi/Wahhabi action was abruptly halted when Amir Abd al-Aziz was assassinated in Diriyah, and Salim al-Hariq withdrew once again to Buraimi. The direct Wahhabi threat appeared to be diminishing, and Sultan bin Ahmad entertained hopes that now the Ottoman leadership might lend some support to his efforts to repel them. But on his return, in November 1804, from a disappointing visit to Basra, where he found little evidence to support hopes of decisive Ottoman intervention, Sultan bin Ahmad was killed while going ashore at Qishm. The identity of his killers is unclear, and even if they were, as seems probable, Qawasim, there is nothing to suggest that Sultan's death was a deliberate political assassination rather than the result of a typical act of opportunist violence. His death left Oman with several rivals competing for power with one another: his nephew Badr bin Sayf (now allied to the Wahhabis), his brother Qays bin Ahmad (Wali of Sohar) and two of his sons, Salim and Said. Although it was Badr bin Sayf who would initially gain the upper hand in Muscat, it was Said, only sixteen years old at the time, who would eventually emerge the victor in this political struggle.[11]

---

[11] See Ibid. and J. B. Kelly, *Britain and the Persian Gulf, 1795–1880* (Oxford: Clarendon Press, 1968). See also Jones and Ridout, *Oman, Culture and Diplomacy*, for a more detailed account of these events.

SAYYID SAID IN MUSCAT, 1804–1828:
WAHHABIS, QAWASIM AND BRITISH

Sayyid Said would eventually build on Sultan bin Ahmad's establishment of Muscat as the basis for the expansion of Omani maritime and commercial power. This was not achieved without political and military struggles in which the existence of Oman as an emerging nation-state was repeatedly under threat from three directions: from the rise of Wahhabi power in Saudi Arabia, from the rivalrous ambitions of the Qawasim rulers of neighbouring Gulf cities and from the expansion and intensification of British imperial power in the region. As we shall see, Muscat's emergence out of these struggles to become a pre-eminent and increasingly cosmopolitan port city in the first decades of the nineteenth century led the British to regard Muscat and its ruler as key players in their own efforts to establish commercial and political power in the Gulf, with the result that an alliance with the British would become an enduring aspect of Omani political continuity.

Before these external struggles took place, however, there was an internal Omani competition for political supremacy. In the initial contest for power after the death of Sultan bin Ahmad, it was Sayyid Said's brother Qays, Wali of Sohar, who made the first move. With the support of the Imam Said, still effectively in political retirement in Rustaq, he led a force through the Batinah in an attempt to take control of Muscat. He was halted in his advance by the intervention of his sister Sayyida Moza, who engineered the return of her nephew Badr bin Sayf and his appointment as regent. Her intention was that Badr should step aside after two years, by which time the young Said bin Sultan (also her nephew) would come of age and assume power. But Badr, who, it will be recalled, had already made an unsuccessful attempt to take Muscat on his own behalf only a year earlier, clearly saw this as a new opportunity to assert his primacy at Muscat on a permanent basis. He sent for Wahhabi military assistance to repel Qays's advance and to force him into agreeing to Badr's position in Muscat. Qays's compliance was short-lived, however, and Badr was obliged to call once more on Wahhabi forces, by both land and sea, when Qays made a renewed assault on Muscat while Badr himself, with British assistance, was seeking to recover Qishm and Bandar Abbas from the Bani Ma'in (allies, it will be recalled, of the Qawasim). Qays was eventually forced to retreat and to give up key possessions, including the forts of Nizwa and Bahla. Without the backing of Imam Said, and facing a range of tribal opposition, as well as the Wahhabi troops

acting on Badr's behalf, he withdrew to Sohar and definitively conceded
Muscat to Badr. Badr's own position was hardly secure even now, however. His intention to take power for himself was in clear contradiction
of Sayyida Moza's purposes in having him recalled to Muscat, and even
with Qays's challenge effectively overcome, he lacked significant political
support, both within his own family and in influential sectors of Muscat
and wider Omani society. Both the merchants and the religious traditionalists viewed his dependence upon Wahhabi power with grave concern.
Not only did Badr's relationship with the Wahhabis represent a form
of political subjugation to an external power – unwelcome enough in
itself – but it led to an increasingly active presence in Muscat of Wahhabi
preachers, who both sought converts and intervened to limit the rights of
religious minorities, including those of the significant number of Hindus
who played an integral role in Muscat's commercial life. They also forced
an intolerant interpretation of Muslim religious observance on Muslim
residents and traders. These actions were inimical to the well-established
working relationship between the religious and the commercial elements
in Omani society, where Ibadi traditions of tolerance had for many years
afforded an excellent climate for the cosmopolitan economy upon which
Muscat was establishing its political pre-eminence. In July 1806, recognising that Badr had no intention of relinquishing power, Sayyida Moza
made her move, urging Said, who was now the Wali of Barka, to move
decisively against Badr. Sayyid Said invited his cousin to Barka, where
he had him assassinated.[12] Sayyid Said then made his way immediately
to Muscat, where his appointment as ruler was announced, for which
he readily secured the support of Qays in Sohar. At sixteen years of age,
Sayyid Said faced a very unstable political situation. The Saudi/Wahhabi
state was posing a major challenge to the economic base and the territorial and cultural integrity of the Muscat-based Omani state in which
he had just taken power. The Qawasim, politically emboldened after the
death of Sultan bin Ahmad, were threatening to secure for themselves the
political and military control over the lower Gulf that Imam Ahmad had
previously achieved. In this perilous context it was particularly worrying
that Sayyid Said's supposed allies, the British, whom he understood to be
bound to support him against his enemies under the terms of the 1798
treaty, now refused even to recognise his authority.

[12] The most well-known and roughly contemporaneous account of this action is to be
found in Vincenzo Maurizi, *History of Seyd Said* (Cambridge: Oleander Press, 1984),
pp. xxviii–xxx. Maurizi, also known as Shaikh Mansur, served as Sayyid Said's doctor
and may well have been a French spy.

Like his father before him, Sayyid Said seems to have hoped that if one of the European powers in the region would not support him, the other might, and turned accordingly to the French, with whom he concluded a treaty in 1807. Shortly thereafter the French also signed a treaty with the Persians, and the British received intelligence suggesting that they were also seeking to secure agreements with both the Wahhabis and the Ottomans. This seems to have been enough for the British to engage for the first time with Sayyid Said (suddenly and pragmatically putting to one side previous reservations about the circumstances of the young ruler's accession to power). Wahhabi influence in Muscat was growing, and Sayyid Said was under strong pressure to join forces with the Wahhabis and their Qawasim allies in operations in the Gulf against the British. In 1809 a British envoy to Muscat was able to win Sayyid Said's participation, instead, in a British military operation against the Qawasim at Ras al-Khaimah. Sayyid Said seems to have anticipated that success would lead to the recovery of Omani possessions such as Shinas (recently seized by the Qawasim of Ras al-Khaimah), but his hopes were dashed when the British effectively withdrew from the confrontation upon the appearance of a Wahhabi military force. While Sayyid Said was forced to sue for peace with the Wahhabis, the British reached an agreement with them not to interfere in any of their conflicts with other Muslims in the region, in return for a Wahhabi promise not to attack British shipping in the Gulf. As a result of this agreement the British declined to offer Sayyid Said any support against renewed Wahhabi incursions in 1810, instead advising him to accede to whatever peace terms he could obtain. Turning again to the French for support, presumably on the basis of the 1807 treaty, Sayyid Said was again rebuffed, with the French recommending not only that he make peace with the Wahhabis but that he also agree to demands that the Omanis convert to Wahhabism. At this point neither colonial power, it seemed, could be a dependable ally for Oman, and Sayyid Said's position must have seemed very precarious indeed. He had come to power partly because he was able to mobilise political support against Badr bin Sayf's embrace of Wahhabism, but now he seemed to lack the military or political capacity to resist continued threats to the Omani political and religious autonomy he had initially sought to defend.

Omani fortunes were soon to recover from this low point, however, initially because of developments elsewhere in the Arabian Peninsula. After the short-lived French occupation of 1798, a new Egyptian regime, led by an Albanian, Mohammed Ali, had asserted itself and had by this time become sufficiently powerful to confront the Wahhabis. Acting on behalf of the Ottoman Sultan, in whose name he ruled Egypt, Mohammed Ali launched an invasion of the Hijaz, which resulted in the capture of both Mecca and Medina in 1811. The first Wahhabi/Saudi state was eventually and decisively defeated and overthrown by Egyptian forces led by Mohammed Ali's son, Ibrahim Pasha, in 1818. Diriyah was sacked and, as a result, Wahhabi control of Buraimi (which, it will be recalled, was the key staging post for Wahhabi incursions into Oman) lapsed. The collapse of the first Wahhabi/Saudi state created conditions under which it now became possible for the British to move against the Qawasim (since they no longer enjoyed the political and military support of their erstwhile Wahhabi allies), and in 1819, again with Omani participation, the British launched a military campaign to take Ras al-Khaimah. The success of this operation formed the basis for the establishment of a formal system of British political and military pre-eminence in the Gulf. This first took the form of a General Treaty of Peace in 1820 in which the Qawasim and other *shaikhs* and rulers of the lower Gulf (Abu Dhabi, Sharjah, Dubai, Ajman and Umm al-Quwain) agreed to cooperate with the British in eliminating the maritime conflicts and opportunism the British defined in the English translation of the Treaty as 'plunder and piracy'.[13] The Treaty also bound its signatories to desist from participation in the slave trade, the restriction and eventual abolition of which, as will shortly be seen, had started to become a priority for British policy in the region.

Sayyid Said was not among the signatories. For some of the local rulers, then, it seems that the General Treaty may have been seen, at least in part, as an alliance in which the British might protect them against the Omanis. This certainly appears to have been the view of the rulers of Bahrain, who appealed for British protection against threats of attack and demands for tribute from Sayyid Said in 1820, 1823, 1828 and 1829.[14] More broadly, it appears that the Arab signatories generally understood the Treaty in terms of existing practices of protection, in which weaker powers could apply to stronger ones for protection against either third party threats or, indeed, threats from the very power to which they were appealing for protection. In this sense, as James Onley argues, the subsequent development of a system of British Protectorates in the Gulf arose

---

[13] See Aitchison, Sir C. U., *A collection of treaties, engagements, and Sunnuds relating to India and Neighbouring Countries*, vol. VII: *Containing the treaties etc. relating to Sind, Baloochistan, Persia and Herat; Turkish Arabia and the Persian Gulf; and the Arabian and African Coasts* (Calcutta: O. T. Cutter, Military Orphan Press, 1865), p. 249.

[14] See James Onley, 'The Politics of Protection in the Gulf: The Arab Rulers and the British Resident in the Nineteenth Century', *New Arabian Studies* 6 (2004), pp. 30–92.

not simply as a top-down imposition on the part of the colonial power, but as a reciprocal, if, by definition, unequal arrangement between the local rulers and the British.[15] Oman's position outside the 1820 General Peace Treaty would be echoed in Oman's preservation of both de jure and de facto independence, even at the end of the nineteenth century, and eventually in the very separate path of nation-state formation taken by Oman when compared with those taken by Bahrain, Qatar and the seven members of the United Arab Emirates in the second half of the twentieth century. While it might in retrospect appear to be an exclusion which would enable Oman's very separate and, in many respects, rather successful political and economic course, at the time it may also have had some more negative immediate consequences, limiting the scope of Oman's political and commercial activities in the Gulf and securing a pre-eminent position for a colonial power with which Oman's relations were, at this stage, at best ambivalent.

SAYYID SAID IN ZANZIBAR, 1828–1856: CAPITALISM, PLANTATION SLAVERY AND THE BRITISH

In the two decades after the 1820 Treaty, the political and economic centre of Omani power shifted decisively from Muscat to Zanzibar. Zanzibar is more than 2,000 miles away from Muscat, in the Indian Ocean just off the coast of East Africa. Today it forms part of the Republic of Tanzania. In the nineteenth century it fell decisively under Omani political control. Omani business interests and political and cultural influence persisted long after direct political authority came to an end, only to be decisively and violently repudiated in the revolutionary movement of 1964, in which most of the remaining ruling class of Omani origin fled into exile. The history of Zanzibar is therefore an important part of Oman's history, and Zanzibar, its people and its culture played an important role in the shaping of modern Oman, as this and the subsequent chapter seek to show.

If the assertion of British power in the Gulf in the early nineteenth century served as a spur for Sayyid Said to develop both political and commercial assets elsewhere, then long-standing Omani interests in the East

---

[15] See James Onley, *Britain and the Gulf Shaikhdoms, 1820–1971: The Politics of Protection* (Doha: Georgetown University School of Foreign Service in Qatar, Center for International and Regional Studies, 2009).

African coast offered encouragement to the development of Zanzibar and
its hinterland as the location of new activities or, rather, at least initially, the
resumption of old ones. This move was to have far-reaching consequences,
leading as it did to the development of an entirely novel commercial and
political network under Omani rule, which played a central role in the
incorporation of both Oman and East Africa into the wider global networks of modern capitalism. The circumstances of this shift involved the
interaction of complex factors, including, as we suggested at the start of
the chapter, the capitalist globalisation of the nineteenth century, but also
involving significant transformations in economic relations in the Indian
Ocean and East Africa. Sayyid Said was not in total command of these
processes – no one was – and it would therefore be misleading to suggest
that he was the sole architect of this new Omani network. It would be
more accurate to propose that he rode the currents of a period of turbu-
lent change to great advantage.[16] However, as we shall see in Chapter 3,
much of what was achieved – at least politically – during his reign was to
be undone and undermined in the second half of the nineteenth century by
the very processes of capitalist globalisation and British colonial expansion that Sayyid Said had exploited so effectively in the first half.

Omanis had started to play a significant political and economic role
along the East African coast two hundred years earlier, during the period
in which the Ya'ariba first developed the merchant politics that the Al Bu
Said would revive and extend. They did so initially in competition with
the Portuguese, first presenting themselves as alternative allies for the
local Swahili ruling class against European domination and gradually
asserting their own pre-eminence, both politically and economically. By
1699 the key port city of Mombasa was under Omani control, and a new
ruling elite (of Omani-Arab origin), the Mazrui, were appointed to govern there on behalf of the Omanis. It was also at this time that wealthy
Omanis, including the ruling elite, started to invest some of the profits
they had secured from their trading activities in the cultivation of dates
for export (principally to India through Bombay) and employed slaves on
plantations in order to do so. East Africa was the primary source of this
new slave workforce. Sayf bin Sultan (1692–1711) was reported to have
owned thirty thousand date palms and to have employed seventeen hundred slaves on his plantations in Oman.[17] But as the Ya'ariba civil war

---

[16] We have discussed the competing accounts of Sayyid Said's role and motivations in Jones
and Ridout, *Oman, Culture and Diplomacy*, pp. 111–113.
[17] Adbul Sheriff, *Slaves, Spices & Ivory in Zanzibar* (London: James Currey, 1987), p. 19.

in Oman (see Chapter 1) started to consume both material resources and political attention, active Omani involvement in East African affairs went into abeyance. Once it was resumed, at the beginning of the Al Bu Said period, the Mazrui rulers of Mombasa were sufficiently well integrated with the local Swahili elite to resist further Omani attempts to assert control. Because Mombasa, still the most obvious place from which to exercise political and economic influence in the region, was out of reach at this time, the Omanis established their new regional headquarters on the island of Unguja – more generally known as Zanzibar – in 1744.[18] An Omani Governor was appointed, but the indigenous people of the islands continued to be governed by their own local ruler, the Mwinyi Mkuu. From Zanzibar, Omani forces persisted, sporadically, in their attempts to wrest Mombasa from the Mazrui. This struggle was resumed under Sayyid Said in the 1820s, resulting in the Omani capture, first of Pemba (upon which Mombasa relied for much of its food) in 1823 and then of some crucial coastal ports near Mombasa in 1825. At this point the Mazrui, feeling their position to be genuinely under threat, sought British protection against the Omani challenge. The British naval commander in the region initially offered this protection, but it was later withdrawn, as the British government in India decided instead to support the Omanis, and the Mazrui were compelled to accept the resumption of Omani supervision and to pay tribute. Thus the Omani position in Zanzibar, and with it the capacity to control an entire network of prosperous small city-states in the region, was secured in the context of the very same British ascendancy that the move towards East Africa might have been an attempt to circumvent. Perhaps more precisely, Omani commercial and political action – increasingly inseparable at this time – operated flexibly in relation to circumstances in which the British presence loomed large. As we shall see in both this and the subsequent chapter, divergent Omani and British interests would from time to time bring the two countries and their representatives into direct conflict, especially in Zanzibar and over the direction of both its economy and politics.

Sayyid Said first visited Zanzibar in 1802, when he was just eleven years old, and for the first time as an adult in 1828, during the course of Omani attempts to take control of Mombasa. By 1832 he had moved there, eventually establishing it as his capital. On the occasion of his 1828

---

[18] The island commonly known as Zanzibar is in fact called Unguja, and Zanzibar is more properly the name for the archipelago of which it is the principal island. The other main inhabited island is Pemba.

visit he seems to have set in train preparations for a move, ordering new building at Bait al-Mtoni, a house and estate just to the north of the main town on Zanzibar, where he would come to reside and develop his administration. In doing so he was following an established pattern of Omani migration to Zanzibar, which had gathered pace in the early years of the nineteenth century, with a significant number of merchants, notably but not exclusively from the Hirth, leaving Oman for Zanzibar via Sur (then a thriving commercial port). At this time, in addition to undertaking the campaign to take Mombasa from the Mazrui, Sayyid Said was seeking to press a claim to Bahrain (which was repulsed in 1829) as well as taking temporary control of Dhofar (also in 1829). By the time he had established himself in Zanzibar, he had effectively relinquished control of Dhofar, suggesting that he may have been testing the feasibility of various alternatives to continued rule from Muscat. In December 1829 he sailed again for Zanzibar and began to spend ever more extended periods of time there, becoming more or less permanently resident there once the Mazrui at Mombasa had finally capitulated to complete Omani control in 1837. Sayyid Said was also persuaded that his political position would benefit from the commercial opportunities that Zanzibar would now provide. His Indian business associate, Shivji Topan, who had been developing a profitable trade at Zanzibar and whose son Ibji had been given control of Zanzibar's customs by Sayyid Said in 1818, seems to have been closely involved in the move to Zanzibar and may even have suggested the idea.[19] Another son of Shivji Topan, Jairam Shivji, would take over the customs farm at Zanzibar, which would remain in the family into the 1880s (along with the customs farm at Muscat, too, which had earlier been held by the Gopal Bhimani family). Indian merchants like Jairam Shivji had been operating in Zanzibar since at least the beginning of the nineteenth century, in a trade that saw ivory from the African mainland exported via Zanzibar to Bombay and Indian cloth imported to Zanzibar. Over time the terms of this trade with the homeland deteriorated and Indian merchants sought to establish for themselves a position in which they were independent of commercial networks back in India.

---

[19] For the idea that Sayyid Said travelled on a ship belonging to Shivji Topan, see Bhacker, *Trade and Empire.* p. 71. For the idea that he did so at Shivji Topan's suggestion, see Gijsbert Oonk, 'Gujarati Business Communities in East Africa: Success and Failure Stories', *Economic and Political Weekly*, 40.20 (May 14–20, 2005), p. 2081n. For the additional suggestion that the Gopal Bhimani family – also Bhattias from Kutch – were 'instrumental in encouraging Said b. Sultan to extend Albusaidi control over East Africa', see Bhacker, *Trade and Empire*, p. 72.

An alliance with Omani merchants and their merchant ruler, Sayyid Said, which afforded them religious tolerance and preferential tariffs, helped them achieve this. It was this alliance, headed by Sayyid Said, that would lay the foundations for Zanzibar's remarkable commercial and cultural pre-eminence in the region over the next fifty years.

That pre-eminence was also built on the labour of slaves. It is important to recognise the extent to which this represented a social and economic innovation, achieved in the interests of modern capitalist development and not, as has sometimes been imagined, the continuation of some age-old, 'Oriental' or 'Islamic' system of slavery. Two distinctions have to be made. The first is between two different practices of slavery, one of which, as we shall shortly see, was part of a social distribution of roles and relations in the Indian Ocean before the colonial period, while the other, the more recent, was a system of labour created in colonial plantations, first in the Caribbean and later in the Indian Ocean, to contribute directly to the capitalist production of commodities for sale in a globalising economy (its typical products were for mass luxury consumption: sugar, coffee, tobacco, and the like). The second distinction pertains specifically to Zanzibar and involves a shift from an economy in which income was obtained through the trade in slaves to an economy in which profit was obtained through the exploitation of their labour, on plantations, which, on Zanzibar, were dedicated mainly to the production of cloves (another product for mass luxury consumption). We shall return shortly to an account of this transformation of the Zanzibar economy and its use of slaves, but first we must explain in more detail the first of these two distinctions: between slavery in the Indian Ocean generally, and in Oman in particular, in the precolonial period and the plantation slavery that succeeded it under colonial regimes.

Slavery was a long-standing institution in Oman, regulated, as elsewhere in the Muslim world, by specific guidance drawn from both the Quran and the Hadith and subsequently elaborated by legal scholars. Omani merchants participated in the Indian Ocean slave trade. Omani-governed ports, especially Zanzibar, became major centres for the sale of slaves. As we shall see, the economy of Zanzibar, and by extension the expanding Omani state, owed a substantial part of its wealth and prosperity to this traffic, particularly in the early stages of its development in the first half of the nineteenth century. Yet, until the eighteenth century, with the introduction of plantation slavery to the Mascarenes (the islands of Mauritius and Réunion, recently colonised, as we have seen, by France), slavery in the Indian Ocean region as a whole, including

Oman, had been very different in character from the slavery associated with the circum-Atlantic traffic in which European traders acquired slaves in West Africa for sale and transportation to the Caribbean and other destinations in the Americas, where they would be put to work on plantations.

Gwyn Campbell offers an overview of how slavery functioned across the diverse cultures and societies of what he calls the IOW (Indian Ocean World): 'The meaning of slavery in the IOW becomes clearer if Western notions of a division of society into free and slave, and of slaves as property, are replaced by a vision of society as a hierarchy of dependency in which 'slaves' constituted one of a number of unfree groups from which menial labour was drawn to provide services both productive and nominally unproductive.'[20] Slaves in the Indian Ocean world, including Oman, did not form a unique category of persons, unlike slaves in the circum-Atlantic world, who were generally understood to be and almost universally treated as less than human, and were therefore excluded altogether from the life worlds of the non-slave population. Campbell also notes a number of further key differences: a large proportion (if not the majority) of slaves in the Indian Ocean world were female, while nearly all of those taken in the circum-Atlantic trade were male;[21] slaves were regularly employed in a far wider range of roles in the Indian Ocean world than the manual labour in which slaves were used in the colonial Americas, and some of them eventually rose to positions of power and responsibility; violence and coercion, while used in some cases, were hardly exclusive to slave populations, as slaves were just one kind of unfree labour; social barriers between slave and non-slave populations were generally far more porous in the Indian Ocean world than in the so-called 'New World' of the colonised Americas.

In Oman, slavery shared many of these general Indian Ocean characteristics, but also some particularities derived both from pre-Islamic Arabian societies and from Islam (although it is important to note that the idea that there is a specific form of 'Islamic slavery' is largely a product of the Orientalist imagination). Islamic law prohibited the enslavement of

---

[20] Gywn Campbell, 'Introduction', in *The Structure of Slavery in Indian Ocean Africa and Asia* (London: Frank Cass, 2004), p. xxii.

[21] In Zanzibar's plantation slavery there were probably more men than women, although the male majority never approached the levels seen in Caribbean plantations. See Abdul Sheriff, 'Localisation and Social Composition of the East African Slave Trade, 1858–1873', in W. G. Clarence-Smith (ed.), *The Economics of the Indian Ocean Slave Trade in the Nineteenth Century* (London: Frank Cass, 1989), pp. 131–145.

Muslims: slaves were accordingly acquired in the context of conquest or conflict with non-Muslim peoples. At the same time, however, slaves were quite readily assimilated into the societies in which they were enslaved: it was the responsibility, for example, of slave owners to ensure that slaves were converted to Islam. This assimilation was also often effected practically through concubinage and sometimes through marriage. The children of such unions were considered free, and their mothers, upon the deaths of the fathers/owners, would be freed. The general tendency, at least within early Islamic societies, to view all people as equal, at least in spiritual terms, even if not within a hierarchical social organisation, facilitated assimilation. This tendency may have been more marked in Oman than elsewhere, because of the retention of this egalitarian emphasis in Ibadi thought: it was technically possible, according to Ibadi legal theory, for a slave to become an Imam (although there is no evidence that any slave ever approached the kind of status that would make this a reality).

In Oman at the end of the eighteenth century, slaves fulfilled a number of social and economic functions. Most were probably domestic servants, either in small households or in the often large retinues of major *shaikhs* and merchants. Some slaves, as elsewhere in the Indian Ocean world, could rise, as slaves, to positions of power and responsibility. This was particularly the case among those slaves employed as soldiers, sailors and guards. Because the only social bond between a slave and the rest of the community was the one with her or his owner, a slave was often regarded as more likely to be loyal than a fellow Omani, who would also typically owe allegiances to family and tribe or, in the context of tribal conflict, might be induced to switch allegiance in a way a slave would not. One example of this was Sulayman bin Suwaylim, who rose to become Sultan Faisal bin Turki's *wazir* (chief minister) in Muscat in the late nineteenth century. In general, and with the exception of those slaves who worked on the date plantations in the Batinah (such as those employed, as we have seen, by Sayf bin Sultan), slaves were not seen as primarily a source of manual labour. Indeed, as Frederick Cooper suggests, they were, at least until the situation started to change in the nineteenth century, 'as much an item of consumption – as domestics or living displays of wealth – as of production'.[22]

The second distinction, then, involves a historical transition between this system of slavery, which existed in multiple variations across a range

<hr>

[22] Frederick Cooper, *Plantation Slavery on the East Coast of Africa* (New Haven, CT: Yale University Press, 1977), p. 37.

of Indian Ocean cultures, including Oman's, in the precolonial period, and a new system which resembled that developed by the European colonisers of the Americas and which started to take hold in the Indian Ocean from the mid-eighteenth century. The main impetus for this was the development of plantations on the French-occupied islands of Mauritius and Réunion from around 1735.[23] These plantations depended exclusively upon the labour of slaves, now required in much larger numbers than before. Slaves captured in East Africa and then sold in commercial centres like Zanzibar met much of this new demand. This expanded trade became a rich source of income for merchants who participated in this traffic and also, by way of customs revenue, for rulers in locations where slaves were bought and sold, which included Muscat, Sur and, increasingly, Zanzibar.

It was this trade, whose new economic significance was a direct result of colonial penetration of the region, that British abolitionist initiatives would seek to restrict and eventually eliminate. This involvement followed the passage of the first British anti-slavery legislation, entitled An Act for the Abolition of the Slave Trade, which ruled that from May 1, 1807, 'the *African* Slave Trade, and all manner of dealing and trading in the Purchase, Sale, Barter, or Transfer of Slaves, or of Persons intended to be sold, transferred, used, or dealt with as Slaves, practiced or carried on, in, at, to or from any Part of the Coast or Countries of *Africa*, shall be, and the same is hereby utterly abolished, prohibited, and declared to be unlawful'.[24] As a British law, the Act applied only to British subjects or to trade taking place within the British Empire. However, in the second decade of the nineteenth century, representatives of the British government sought to extend its application throughout the Indian Ocean region. Their efforts were facilitated by Britain's naval superiority and political control in the western Indian Ocean.

The first significant encounter between Sayyid Said and this new British activism on the subject of slavery took place in 1821. Fairfax Moresby, a senior British naval officer based in Mauritius (which the British had taken from France in 1810), started seizing ships suspected of carrying

---

[23] See Edward A. Alpers, 'The East African Slave Trade', in Z. A. Konczacki and J. M. Konczacki, eds., *An Economic History of Tropical Africa*, vol. 1: *The Pre-Colonial Period* (London: Frank Cass, 1977), pp. 206–215, for an overview of this development in general, and Sheriff, *Slaves, Spices*, and Cooper, *Plantation Slavery*, for details of its consequences for Zanzibar in particular.

[24] An Act for the Abolition of the Slave Trade, March 25, 1807, http://www.pdavis.nl/Legis_06.htm (accessed August 1, 2014), emphasis in original.

slaves to and from Zanzibar. He also wrote to Sayyid Said asking for his support in bringing the trade to an end. He initially received no response, but travelled again to Zanzibar in 1822 with a treaty which he presented to Sayyid Said for signature. Sayyid Said signed what would thereafter be known as the Moresby Treaty.[25] The Moresby Treaty stipulated that the Omani government seize and punish captain and crew – as pirates – aboard vessels found to be carrying slaves to 'any port outside His Highness's dominions'. Applied to all movements east of a line drawn from Cape Delgado to Diu Head on the western coast of India, the Treaty thus exempted trade from Zanzibar into the Gulf itself, suggesting that it was designed mainly to block the traffic south into the Indian Ocean to locations such as Mauritius, where, it will be recalled, Moresby was based at the time. It also prohibited any sale of slaves to Christians. Sayyid Said complained that the loss of income (in customs revenue) arising from signing the Treaty came to MT$50,000 a year, a sum which he may well have exaggerated (although Maurizi, interestingly, claims that in Muscat, at the time of his visit there in 1809, Sayyid Said derived 'an annual revenue of 75,000 dollars' from the slave trade).[26] Sayyid Said would increase his estimate of these losses in subsequent years in the hope of gaining maximum compensation from the British in return for his acquiescence.[27] Additional articles would be added to the Treaty in 1839, specifying a 'general right of search for British warships with respect to Arab vessels'; in 1845, reaffirming the British right to search and extending the scope of the restrictions to the northward trade, too; and again in 1850, providing British access to Omani territory to destroy slave-trading facilities. By 1850, the British Consul in Zanzibar, Atkins Hamerton, was able to claim that the foreign slave trade (in which slaves were exported from East Africa to destinations beyond) had been reduced by 80 percent.[28]

It was in response to the restrictions introduced by the Moresby Treaty that the Omani merchant class in Zanzibar started to seek alternatives to the foreign slave trade, and with consequences for the local trade and the Zanzibar economy as a whole that the British abolitionists almost certainly had not anticipated: the transformation of an economy that profited from the slave trade to one almost entirely dependent upon slave labour. In 1828, Sayyid Said revealed in a letter to his agent in Bombay,

[25] Norman Robert Bennett, *A History of the Arab State of Zanzibar* (London: Methuen, 1978), pp. 19–20.
[26] Maurizi, *History of Seyd Said*, p. 29.
[27] Sheriff, *Slaves, Spices*, p. 47.
[28] Ibid., p. 223.

that '[i]n consequence of the abolition of the slave trade the collections of Zanzibar have been diminished; it has therefore been deemed necessary to make plantations of sugar cane in the islands.'[29] In the same year, Edmund Roberts, an American merchant who would soon come to play a major role in the development of Omani and Zanzibari relations with the United States (as discussed later), wrote to a business associate that the Omanis on Zanzibar 'for some time past have turned their attention to the cultivation of spices, the sugar cane, coffee, etc., all of which ... will soon be articles of export'.[30] Despite experiments with sugar and indigo, the commodity that would succeed was cloves. It appears that cloves had already been introduced to Zanzibar from plantations in the Mascarenes before Sayyid Said arrived in 1828. But it was under Sayyid Said that they really took off. Sayyid Said himself had large plantations developed, as did his *wazir*, Sulayman bin Hamed, and the influential Shaikh of the Hirth, Abdallah bin Salim al-Harthi. Some Swahili landowners and even some Indian merchants also invested. At the height of the 'clove mania' that ensued, at the start of the 1850s, the slave population on Zanzibar appears to have increased about six- or sevenfold since the first British attempt to suppress the slave trade in the early 1820s.[31]

Thus in Zanzibar the transition from a precolonial to a colonial regime of slavery was not limited to its effects upon the trade in slaves. Indeed, precisely because of British efforts to restrict the trade, with which Sayyid Said had cooperated, the economy in Zanzibar underwent a major transformation. Instead of selling slaves to labour on plantations elsewhere and profiting from the slave trade, Omanis in Zanzibar acquired slaves in order to profit instead from their labour. Initially this created a massive economic boom in Zanzibar, which more or less cornered the global market in cloves. This boom financed the consolidation of Omani power in the region and was the basis for its mid-nineteenth-century predominance. Eventually, however, like many mono-cultures, the clove-dependent economy of Zanzibar proved vulnerable. Omani merchants who had moved out of trade into plantation ownership started to lose money as overproduction of cloves led to a sharp decline in price. Many were forced either to sell or to mortgage their plantations to Indian merchants whose commitment to trade rather

---

[29] Sayyid Said to Shoostree, n.d., Consultation, July 9, 1828, Maharashtra State Archives, August 1828, cited in ibid., p. 48.

[30] Roberts to Woodbury, December 19, 1828, Library of Congress, Roberts Papers VI, cited in ibid., p. 50.

[31] See Cooper, *Plantation Slavery*, p. 56, and Sheriff, *Slaves, Spices*, p. 60.

than plantation ownership (in the main) had secured them more sustainable revenues, primarily through their position in the ivory trade, which experienced exponential growth in the same period. By the end of the period of the 'clove economy', economic power in Zanzibar lay primarily in the hands of the Indian merchants. This power was not only economic: their financial dealings, primarily as providers of loans to the plantation owners and other members of the Omani ruling elite, gave them substantial political influence. Furthermore, because they were eventually incorporated into the British Empire as British subjects, the Indian merchants became a means by which the British government would come to exercise ever greater political influence over Zanzibar, especially in the period after the death of Sayyid Said (see Chapter 3).

As already indicated, the success of the Indian merchants on Zanzibar in the mid-nineteenth century owed much to their participation in the ivory trade, which turned out to be a more enduring business than cloves. Although clove production continued well into the later nineteenth century, the profits it generated dwindled, while ivory's did not. Furthermore, because the Indian merchants stuck to trade, rather than redirecting their business activities and resources into plantation ownership and deriving profit from production, they continued to reap the benefits of a prolonged period in which the terms of trade were exceptionally advantageous for Zanzibar. This is because the major exports either from Zanzibar itself or traded through it from the African mainland – such as cloves and, especially, ivory – were rare enough for long enough to command high prices in the West, while the manufactured goods imported into Zanzibar from the West, and contributing to the emergence of a modern consumer culture there, tended to fall in price over the same period as a result of technological innovations in mass production. It was such innovations that also led to the massive increase in demand for ivory that would underpin Zanzibar's continuing economic and consumer boom. The development, at the very end of the eighteenth century, of a technology that mechanised the manufacture of combs from ivory was followed by the development of machinery for the mass production of other ivory items, such as piano keys and billiard balls. As mass middle-class leisure consumption grew in the nineteenth century, the demand for ivory for these products grew with it. The key site for much of this production was the United States, and it was in the context of the ivory trade that the first significant contacts between Omanis and Americans took place.

The American trader Edmund Roberts met Sayyid Said in Zanzibar in 1828, apparently seeking to remove obstacles to trade there in which he was already engaged. Sayyid Said's response was to suggest that these might be removed by the establishment of a commercial treaty between Oman and the United States. Roberts obtained from the U.S. government the commission to negotiate such a treaty, which was eventually signed in Muscat in 1833. It provided American traders with favourable terms, comparable to those enjoyed by the British in areas of Omani jurisdiction, including, of course, Zanzibar. These initial commercial contacts led shortly to more extensive diplomatic relations between Oman and the United States, including the appointment of an American Consul to Zanzibar in 1837 and the first voyage by an Omani ship to the United States in 1840. The American Consul in Zanzibar, Richard Waters, achieved a dominant position among foreign merchants there, developed and sustained by a business relationship with the customs master, Jairam Shivji. His position was resented, above all, by British merchants, for whom the increasing pluralisation of Western participation in Zanzibari commerce, led by the arrival of the Americans and actively encouraged by Sayyid Said and Zanzibari merchants, was experienced as a challenge to their pre-eminence. The assertion of British political control in Zanzibar in the later part of the nineteenth century – discussed in Chapter 3 – may be understood in this context as well as that of the reconfiguration of British rule in India after 1857: indeed, the two processes may be seen as complementary, with political demands for greater systematisation and control leading to an intensification of power that might be expected to carry economic benefits (economic expansion was, after all, the prime mover of imperial design).

The voyage in 1840 of Sayyid Said's ship, the *Sultanah*, to New York, carrying his envoy to the U.S. government, Ahmad bin Na'aman, along with gifts for the American President, Martin van Buren, is generally seen as the symbolic inauguration of a relationship that would have far-reaching consequences for Oman in the latter half of the twentieth century, even though the extent of U.S. global political hegemony could not have been anticipated by either party at the time. At the time, at least as far as the Omanis were concerned, the relationship with the United States was important primarily because it involved Omanis' and Zanzibar's deepening participation in the commodity capitalism of the nineteenth century and their integration into networks of economic, cultural and social exchange. The voyage of the *Sultanah* to New York was followed in subsequent years by a series of other voyages to major European ports on trade missions whose long-term consequence was increasingly to bring the mass-produced luxuries now enjoyed by the middle classes of the West into the homes and lives of Omanis on Zanzibar.[32]

Sayyid Said died in 1856, returning to Zanzibar from Bandar Abbas. His death introduced a new phase of instability into Omani government and brought to an end the political union between Oman and Zanzibar, even though economic, cultural and political relations between these two distant places would continue to be important. Zanzibar's rise as a cosmopolitan commercial centre continued after his death, but it did so under increasing political influence from the British government, whose role in Oman itself, as we shall see, also became more and more assertive and determining. Opposition and active resistance to British power, and to the policies followed by Omani rulers who increasingly had to accommodate it, would become significant features of the political landscape in both polities in the decades after Sayyid Said's death. In the process important seeds of some of the most significant events of the twentieth century, and of the direction of modern Oman, would be sown. This is the story of Chapter 3.

[32] See Jeremy Prestholdt, *Domesticating the World: African Consumerism and the Genealogies of Globalisation* (Berkeley: University of California Press, 2008), especially chs. 3 and 4.

3

Oman in the Age of British Ascendancy
and the Arab *Nahda*

In the period between the death of Sayyid Said in 1856 and the accession of his namesake, Sultan Said bin Taimur, in 1932, Oman experienced a complex process of change, often described in terms of decline and marginalisation. As British imperial consolidation in the second half of the nineteenth century played a major role in the development of a global economy dominated by the industrialised nations of the North, and driven by their colonial appropriations, both Oman and Zanzibar, which had been very much part of this process in the first half of the century, found themselves increasingly excluded from it. The separation of the two main parts of Sayyid Said's 'thalassocracy' – Oman and Zanzibar – from one another was a major factor in this process of decline. The marginalisation of Oman itself involved the decline of local and regional trade in the Gulf, as a result of the development of steamer traffic in the Indian Ocean and the gradual replacement of a regional economy dominated by Indian manufactures and trade networks by a system dominated by the British. This had substantial political consequences for an Omani elite whose power had been built on its participation in the earlier interregional trading networks. In effect, Oman was simply left out of the action, as trade no longer passed through its formerly thriving port cities. In Zanzibar, a slightly different process ensued, in which trade continued apace, but the commercial and political alliance between the Omani ruling elite and the Indian merchant class gave way to increasing British domination. In Zanzibar, the action was seized by the British from the Omanis. However, although these changes did significantly limit Omani participation in the emerging networks of the globalising economy, there were related developments that served to incorporate Oman and Omanis into new transnational networks, including, most significantly, those that involved intellectual and political opposition to the emergent colonial world order. In this chapter we show how these new movements, shaped by a renewal of Muslim religious and political thought – the Arab *nahda* – interacted with long-standing aspects of Omani religious and political culture to offer an alternative to Al Bu Said rule, identified by many during this period as excessively dependent upon British power.

THE PARTITION OF OMAN AND ZANZIBAR

In 1844 Sayyid Said, in a letter to Lord Aberdeen (the British Foreign Secretary), had indicated, in pursuance of the 1840 treaty with Queen Victoria he had signed in Muscat, that after his death his 'African possessions' should be assigned to his son Khalid and his 'possessions in Oman in Arabia, in the Persian Gulf and on the coast of Persia' to his son Thuwaini.[1] Whether or not Sayyid Said had intended this to institute the partition of his possessions after his death, it clearly established a formal basis upon which the British government could subsequently claim some role in determining the succession, and it is not surprising, given this opportunity, first by this letter and then by the course of events, that the British should have intervened to effect partition. Ten years later, in 1854, Sayyid Said was in Persia negotiating the renewal of his lease on Bandar Abbas. It was during the course of this absence that his son Khalid bin Said, who had been ruling Zanzibar on Sayyid Said's behalf, died. On Khalid's death his brother Majid bin Said assumed control of government in Zanzibar, but not without opposition from long-standing opponents of Sayyid Said's rule, the Barawina. Apparently in order to shore up his position in Zanzibar, Sayyid Said cut short his negotiations with the Persians, agreeing to much less favourable terms than before, and set sail for Zanzibar. He never reached the island, however, dying at sea on October 19, 1856. A week later his ship reached Zanzibar and his nineteen-year-old son, Barghash bin Said, who had travelled with him to Persia, made a failed attempt to seize power in Zanzibar from his older brother, Majid. Majid was backed by the British and on November 2, 1856, was proclaimed ruler of Zanzibar. The question of overall political control remained unresolved, however, as Majid's accession in Zanzibar simply placed him on equal footing with his brother Thuwaini, who ruled

---

[1] See Appendix 2: Said B Sultan's 1844 Letter to Aberdeen, cited in Bhacker, *Trade and Empire*, p. 200.

in Muscat: neither man could make an uncontested claim to the position previously occupied by their father. Indeed, at first, neither of them attempted to do so, each seeming to prefer to secure his own position rather than aspire to take precedence over the other.

A delegation sent by Thuwaini to Zanzibar proposed that the two brothers seek a mutually agreeable solution, and Majid responded by offering an annual subsidy of MT$40,000 in return for recognition of his sovereignty in Zanzibar. At the same time Majid sought to protect his own position by offering an annual payment to Abdallah bin Salim al-Barwani, a leading member of the opposition in his father's day. In the event Majid found himself unable to meet these financial commitments, and in 1857 Abdallah bin Salim started to organise with Barghash with a view to having Barghash replace Majid in power. At this time the British in India were facing an acute political crisis, in the form of the First War of Indian Independence (often referred to in British histories as 'the Indian Mutiny'). There was no British political agent in Zanzibar at this time, and it was widely rumoured that, if the Indian War of Independence were successful, the British might never return. This almost certainly encouraged Barghash to imagine that Majid's position – dependent as it had been upon British support – might be irretrievably weakened. Possibly in anticipation of just this eventuality, Thuwaini in Muscat took this opportunity to assemble a naval force to make his own move against Majid, perhaps, for the first time, believing that he could achieve control of the entirety of his late father's dominions. But by this time the British had dispatched a new Consul, Christopher Rigby, to Zanzibar, and he acted to defend Majid against both threats. A British warship intercepted Thuwaini's fleet in February 1859, and Thuwaini was compelled to agree that any claims he might have to sovereignty in Zanzibar should be submitted to British arbitration. Thus, through force of arms and as a result of dissension among the Omani elite, the local British authorities began to secure for themselves a decisive political role in the affairs of Zanzibar that they had not enjoyed before. A second attempt by Barghash to seize power later the same year was swiftly repelled by British use of force, and Barghash himself was exiled to Bombay.

As a result of these events it is clear that the British came to see Majid as incapable of governing Zanzibar without their support, let alone controlling both Oman and Zanzibar. At the same time, by siding with Majid against Thuwaini, they had effectively ruled Thuwaini out as a potential ruler of a unified state. Furthermore, the British conception of a state as a unified territory with a central sovereign authority did not readily correspond to the way in which the Oman–Zanzibar polity had come into being, nor with how it had been governed. To British eyes it made much more sense to see Oman and Zanzibar as two separate states. Zanzibar's promising commercial performance would certainly have been an added incentive for the British to encourage partition. British prospects of deriving substantial profits from Zanzibari commerce would be best enhanced without the complications arising from its continued participation in an expanded Omani state. A commission established by the British Governor General of India, Earl Canning, which included as one of its members William Coghlan, British Political Resident in Aden, who recommended separation, accordingly ratified the existing situation, awarding Zanzibar to Majid and Muscat to Thuwaini and requiring Majid to provide Thuwaini with an annual subsidy, in line with the agreement they had earlier reached, of MT$40,000. More than just ratifying the status quo, however, the Canning Award made it clear, at least as far as the British were concerned, that Majid and Thuwaini now ruled two separate states. Both were to be addressed from now on as 'Sultan', a term used by the British to indicate the unchallenged ruler of a single state. While this term may have rhetorically elevated each Omani ruler to a status equivalent to that of the Ottoman Sultan, in practice the Canning Award made both men dependent upon British patronage and support in ways that no Ottoman Sultan would have contemplated.

The Canning Award was consistent with a wider reformulation of British policy in the region at this time, much of which was undertaken, at least partly, in response to the First War of Indian Independence of 1857. The Government of India Act of 1858 closed down the British East India Company and transferred its powers to the British government. A Secretary of State for India, who took charge of a new government department called the India Office, was appointed to the cabinet in Westminster, and the Governor General of India acquired the additional title of Viceroy and established a Foreign Department of his own government that would eventually assume full responsibility for the conduct of relations with external powers in the western Indian Ocean, including Oman. These political arrangements reflected a move towards a greater centralisation of British colonial power, assisted by the extension of modern communications and transport into the Indian Ocean and the Gulf and accompanied by an increasingly activist political, social and cultural mission on the part of colonial agents and officials, throughout the British Raj and among its various dependencies, protectorates and allied territories. The status, identity, social lives and religious behaviour of colonial subjects started to become issues on which British officials would come to believe they should take views, and over which they should exercise authority, and whose lives they should organise according to emergent categories for systematic and rational classification and organisation. In Oman and Zanzibar this had a number of significant consequences, including the categorisation of subject peoples according to new and spurious pseudo-scientific race theories in which white Europeans were understood to possess natural superiority; an increasing incomprehension of and hostility towards manifestations of non-Christian religious practices; and a growing tendency to view all opposition, however motivated, to those local rulers whose compliance had won them British support as the activity of 'terrorists' or 'fanatics'[2] or, to use terms still employed in the 1960s by some authors, 'extremists' and 'zealots'.[3]

These changes in Britain's conduct of its colonial and imperial policy were part and parcel of a process of economic and technological transformation. One way of describing this process is that the administration of political, social and cultural activities in the Empire was increasingly organised according to a 'rational' calculus that prioritised productivity and the maximisation of surplus value for the owners of industrial and commercial enterprises. The enhanced bureaucratisation of British rule, with its systems of racial classification, for example, produced forms of knowledge that permitted increasingly efficient uses of human labour for production and profit. The inculcation of supposedly 'Christian' or 'British' values among colonial subjects was not merely a moral project; it served also to promote modes of discipline and attitudes to time and work supposed by colonial administrators to be more conducive to productivity than the perceived 'indolence' widely identified as a characteristic of 'Oriental' peoples.

Two letters written by the British Consul, Christopher Rigby, shortly after his arrival in Zanzibar reflect very well the perspective of many colonial administrators on the subjects upon whom this moral and disciplinary transformation was to be wrought. In May 1860 he wrote expressing his surprise at the prosperity of Zanzibari commerce, apparently astonished that so much could have been achieved despite the fallibility of Arab leadership: 'The trade is certainly surprising, when it is

---

[2] See Robert Geran Landen, *Oman Since 1856* (Princeton, NJ: Princeton University Press, 1967), p. 204.
[3] See, e.g., J. B. Kelly, 'Sultanate and Imamate in Oman', *Royal Institute of International Affairs*, December 1959, p. 6.

considered that it has been developed under the primitive rule of an Arab chief.'[4] In a letter of July 1861, he shared his impressions of the Omanis in Zanzibar, finding them 'all wasting their substance in drunkenness and debauchery, the degraded victims of the system of slavery, by which they regard any kind of honest industry as beneath an Arab, and only befitting negro slaves'.[5] Rigby's views are consistent with the broader changes in British policy and its execution. Numerous scholars have noted a significant change, from the mid-nineteenth century, of the uses to which the bureaucratic apparatus of colonial administration were put (maps, surveys, censuses, etc.), in which the simple gathering of information about colonial subjects (often for the purposes of taxation) gave way to the imposition of discipline upon them.[6] Arjun Appadurai has summarised the outcomes of the intensified and systematic counting and classification of colonial subjects in India – where this process reached furthest and deepest into everyday life – as follows: 'It is enumeration, in association with new forms of categorization, that creates the link between the orientalizing thrust of the British state, which saw India as a museum or zoo of difference and of differences, and the project of reform, which involved cleaning up the sleazy, flabby, frail, feminine, obsequious bodies of natives into clean, virile, muscular, moral and loyal bodies that could be moved into the subjectivities proper to colonialism.'[7]

In other words, the 'reforms' that colonial administrators like Rigby and others who interacted with Omani leaders and citizens in the second half of the nineteenth century would seek to implement aimed, at least in part, at the production of a disciplined workforce which, unlike the slaves of the plantations, would actively desire to work in the interests of imperial capitalism. By the same token, these reforms justified, as their political corollary, British interventions to eliminate, or exclude from power and influence, religious or political movements or leaders who offered alternative values or views of the purpose of life. In Zanzibar and the East African coast more generally, as Randall Pouwels has observed, 'the British managed to affect gravely the relationship of the Sultans to their

4 Bhacker, *Trade and Empire*, p. 173.

5 Ibid., p. 171.

6 See Arjun Appadurai, 'Number in the Colonial Imagination', in Carol A. Breckenridge and Peter van der Veer (eds.), *Orientalism and the Postcolonial Predicament* (Philadelphia: University of Pennsylvania Press, 1993), pp. 314–339 who refers to work on this topic by Bernard Cohn, Nicholas B. Dirks, David Ludden, David Arnold, Ranajit Guha and Dipesh Chakrabarty.

7 Ibid., p. 335.

subjects; to re-create the form and function of the old Sultanate to resemble something more like the European notion of a proper governing institution; and, finally, to alter the essential socio-economic underpinnings of life within the coastal towns.'[8] In Oman itself, where the direct economic rewards of implementing this new disciplinary regime were less immediate for the British, the political priorities called for a focus on the dangers posed by 'rebellious' tribes and 'fanatical' religious traditionalists, who, often in combination, threatened the positions of rulers more inclined to embrace at least some of the British conceptions of 'modern' and 'rational' government. Thus, towards the end of the period under consideration in this chapter, we shall see how the adoption of 'reformed' government structures by the Sultan in Muscat became an objective of British policy in Oman.

A less direct but no less serious consequence, for Oman, of the changing nature of the British involvement in the Gulf was the onset of severe economic decline. This began in Oman in the 1860s and, despite periodic upturns, continued more or less consistently through the remainder of the nineteenth century. It occurred as part of a wider stagnation in the Gulf as a whole, from which the region began to emerge fully only with the commercial exploitation of oil in the 1930s and from which Oman itself, where oil was discovered in commercial quantities only in 1964, took even longer to recover than many of its neighbours. Particularly serious for Oman, and for the viability of the political and economic system developed over the preceding century by the Al Bu Said, was the sharp decline in the 'secondary distributive system' or 'carrying trade' within the Gulf, in which Omani merchants and their Indian partners had played a major role and for which Muscat had established itself as one of the major centres.[9] This decline was caused by the establishment of direct shipping routes between Britain and India, facilitated by the introduction of steamers to the route from 1862 and by the opening of the Suez Canal in 1869. Maritime traffic between Oman and Zanzibar dropped off suddenly as a result of the post-Said political tensions. There was also substantial migration from Oman to Zanzibar and other places as the lack of economic opportunities became apparent. Further migrations, particularly from the Indian business community, occurred from 1868, when the

---

[8] Randall L. Pouwels, *Horn and Crescent: Cultural Change and Traditional Islam on the East African Coast, 800–1900* (Cambridge: Cambridge University Press, 1987), p. 163.
[9] Landen's analysis of this decline remains authoritative in this regard. See Landen, *Oman Since 1856.*

Imamate of Azzan bin Qays brought in a range of economic, social and cultural restrictions that limited the scope of business practices and religious observances by Hindus (as discussed later).[10] Although the volume of trade in the Gulf in the ten years since 1862 had increased, a rapidly declining percentage of this trade was handled by Arabs or Omanis, and profits from it accrued disproportionately to British companies and their Indian agents. Oman's own shipping industry collapsed. Furthermore, not only were all Omani ships left in Zanzibar in 1861, but by 1863 the last remaining ships at Muscat had been sold off, presumably as part of the attempt to fill state coffers depleted by debt. The chronic indebtedness of successive Omani rulers, up to and including Sultan Said bin Taimur (1932–1970), would be a significant factor in limiting the scope and independence of Omani political action for the next century, and its damaging consequences, in terms of both poverty and dependency, clearly had a formative influence on the thinking of Sultan Said bin Taimur (as we shall see in Chapter 4).

In this first phase of the post-Said era, then, British actions consolidated the foundations of British 'domination' or 'indirect rule'.[11] For many Omanis in both Zanzibar and Oman (but for slightly different reasons) this process resulted in their exclusion from many of the benefits of nineteenth-century globalisation, although they were by no means insulated from many of its more damaging consequences: the processes that Landen calls 'disruptive modernization'.[12] While Zanzibar did not experience the same kind of collapse suffered by Oman, its economy fell ever more substantially into foreign hands. Our account of the next period of Omani history will reveal how Omani opposition to British domination mobilised traditional religious and political resources as well as involved Omanis in subaltern transnational networks that developed alongside and in opposition to those established by European colonial capitalism. The decline of those commercial activities (manufacture, shipping, trade, including slave trade) which had been the foundations of Al Bu Said rule created conditions in which opposition could grow.

---

[10] Calvin H. Allen has contested the extent of this economic decline. See Calvin H. Allen, 'The Indian Merchant Community of Masquat', *Bulletin of the School of Oriental and African Studies* 44.1 (1981), pp. 39–53.

[11] These are the terms used by Bhacker, *Trade and Empire*, and Landen, *Oman Since 1856*, respectively.

[12] See Landen, *Oman Since 1856*, pp. 109–159.

OMAN AND THE *NAHDA*, 1861–1871

Over the next few decades the British, having established themselves as the arbiters of power in both Oman and Zanzibar as part of the implementation of a newly prescriptive approach to the management of dependent or subject polities, found themselves facing, as did the Omani rulers whom they backed, a series of opposition movements that came increasingly to identify themselves with other Arab and Muslim groups in a transnational context. Omani opposition to the ruling compromise between the Al Bu Said and the British over the period between 1861 and at least 1920 is therefore best understood not simply as an expression of local feeling through the revival of old Omani ideas about religion and political legitimacy, but also as part of a wider articulation of anti-colonial, 'pan-Arabist' and 'modernist' Muslim politics, to which participants at the time and some scholars subsequently gave the name *nahda* (awakening), while others have written of it as an Islamic 'modernism'. The extent of Omani participation (the Omani *nahda*) in this set of new political ideas and modes of organisation is clearest in relation to the movement for the restoration of the Imamate that took hold in Oman from around 1913. However, intimations of the emergence of anti-colonial ideas and practices organised through the revival of religious politics in an Omani context can also be detected in the establishment of a short-lived Imamate (1868–1871) under the rule of Azzan bin Qays, who was brought to power by a religious and political movement inspired by the activist Ibadi scholarship of Said bin Khalfan al-Khalili. In this section we therefore give an account of political developments in Oman, rather than in Zanzibar, in the period from 1861 (the Canning Award) to 1871, when Azzan bin Qays was killed in the defence of Muttrah and Turki bin Said took back control of Muscat from the Imamate forces. In a subsequent section on Oman during the reigns of Sultan Turki and his son Faisal, and the resurgence of Imamate politics in the early twentieth century, we will explore the continued significance of Zanzibar and its intellectual milieu for the development of ideas and the course of events in Oman. Before turning to these two moments of the Omani *nahda*, however, we must briefly outline the emergence of the new Arab and Muslim political consciousness of which the Omani experience formed part.[13]

---

[13] It is worth recalling that one of the most influential Omani historical accounts of the Imamate movement is Mohammed bin Abdallah al-Salimi's *Nahdat al-A'yan bi'Hurriyat 'Uman*. The author, who was the son of the prominent Omani religious scholar Abdallah al-Salimi, chose the term *nahda* to name the process whose history he presents. The adoption of the same term to name the transformation of the Sultanate under Sultan

This *nahda*, involving the emergence of a 'modernist' Islam intertwined with the growth of a pan-Arab consciousness, was a complex and far-reaching phenomenon. Oman, it might be said, sat, geographically at least, between its two poles – Egypt and India – and although it is widely believed to have been largely unaffected by these wider developments, there is in fact good reason to suppose that neither the ruling elite nor the religious establishment nor the more general population, especially in such cosmopolitan locations as Muscat, were entirely isolated from such trends.

In India the Mutiny (or First War of Indian Independence) of 1857 had highlighted the extent to which British rule posed not simply a political challenge but also a religious, cultural or even existential threat to the multiple cultures of the subcontinent, including its Muslim population; in this first major uprising against British rule, British hostility to both Hindu and Muslim culture and religious practices was a major source of popular fury, and this widespread sentiment and the brutality of the British suppression of the uprising demanded a response from Indian intellectuals. Indian Muslim intellectuals sought to respond by seeking to bring the scientific rationalism associated with the European Enlightenment (and those of its practical manifestations that had contributed to the success of British conquest) into a productive and pluralist dialogue with religious doctrine and tradition.[14] In Egypt, similar ideas started to take shape around the idea of reform among writers and intellectuals who were, as the historian Albert Hourani has written, 'committed ... in some way to the movement of reform, but also in another sense upholders of Islamic tradition and wishing to show that modern reform was not only a legitimate but a necessary implication of the teaching of Islam'.[15] In the second half of the nineteenth century, Mohammed Abduh and his student and collaborator, Rashid Rida, emerged as leading figures in an intellectual movement that not only responded to the challenges of modernity, but sought to do so by insisting upon its own embrace of consciously modern values. They called for a rigorous renovation of a religion, which, they claimed, had fallen into a decline characterised by intellectual weakness, subservience to conservative political regimes and religious institutions

---

Qaboos after 1970 suggests that it continues to have valuable and inclusive historical and ideological resonance for Omanis.

[14] See Mansoor Moaddel, *Islamic Modernism, Nationalism, and Fundamentalism: Episode and Discourse* (Chicago, University of Chicago Press, 2005), pp. 60–74.

[15] Albert Hourani, *Arabic Thought in the Liberal Age, 1798–1939* (Cambridge: Cambridge University Press, 1983), pp. 67–68.

and the persistence of superstition. Their project was to preserve and to reform, and in the process strengthen, both religion itself and Muslim society as well, the better to contend with the demands of modernity and to overthrow the political domination of the 'modern' European colonial powers.

In Zanzibar, such ideas began to permeate an increasingly cosmopolitan and literate intelligentsia fairly early on, from the middle of the nineteenth century, to such an extent that Zanzibar became not simply a place of refuge for Omani political leaders avoiding retribution back in Oman, but also a source of spiritual and ideological inspiration for some of those seeking to organise opposition to the rulers in Muscat. As Amal Ghazal has argued in a work that focusses on the development of such ideas among Ibadi scholars and intellectuals, what took shape in Zanzibar, in a highly literate and cosmopolitan context, was a kind of 'Salafist' Ibadism, in which a literary renaissance, sustained, as we shall see, by the active support of Sultan Barghash, who established Zanzibar's first printing press in 1870, grew into a vigorous new religious and political movement. Ibadi concepts of legitimate political authority, the continued validity of *ijtihad* (scholarly interpretation of sacred texts) and the idea of the Imamate as an ideal religious and political state coincided productively with the simultaneous movement in Sunni circles towards the revival of religious thought as a way of countering the corruptions of both colonial rule and the institutionalised Islam of the contemporary Arab world. This is the movement which became known as 'Salafism' and which is not to be confused with the twenty-first century movement often known by the same name, which rejects scientific rationalism and *ijtihad* altogether in the name of a fundamentalist approach to the sacred texts and an exclusivist and often violent approach to religious politics.[16] As Ghazal notes, 'The Omani elite in Zanzibar stood at the centre of these changes, taking place simultaneously among Ibadi communities in Zanzibar, Oman and Mzab [the region of Algeria in which Ibadism is concentrated]. Not only did Omanis in Zanzibar sponsor the scholars spearheading this Ibadi revival, political developments within Zanzibar itself had a transformative effect on the Ibadi *nahda*. This was especially evident in Oman where the *nahda* became a militarized movement aiming at overthrowing al-Busaidi rule in Muscat and establishing the Imamate.'[17] In Zanzibar

---

[16] See Amal Ghazal, *Islamic Reform and Arab Nationalism: Expanding the Crescent from the Mediterranean to the Indian Ocean (1880s–1930s)* (London: Routledge, 2010), p. 20.
[17] Ibid., p. 21.

and Oman, as elsewhere, both the religious and the pan-Arabist dimensions of this movement were occasioned by and articulated resistance to colonial domination and therefore, most particularly in our case, opposition to the fact and the consequences of British involvement in Omani and Zanzibari political affairs.

Most accounts of the brief re-establishment of the Imamate in Oman under Azzan bin Qays tend to describe its leaders and adherents as 'conservative'[18] or even, more pejoratively, as 'intolerant'[19] or 'medieval-style'[20] and conceive of it simply as an attempt to turn the clock back or to turn decisively away from the realities of modern life. This ignores the fact that in its determined opposition to British rule, in its movement away from an already well-established pattern of political rule by the Al Bu Said and by its very nature as a self-conscious 'renewal' of Ibadi Islam (indeed, John C. Wilkinson calls it 'neo-Ibadism') it was quintessentially 'modern' in character. Wilkinson makes the connection between the movement and its wider modern context, noting that, by the mid-nineteenth century, 'the Ibadis' experience of the imperial powers was putting them on a common footing with the rest of the Islamic world and leading to some effort to find common ground with them.'[21] And, as Ghazal's research in Zanzibar shows, the *nahda* in Oman enjoyed substantial ideological support in Zanzibar, including that of the intellectually engaged population. A simple dichotomy in which the colonial power and its merchant allies are understood to represent progress and modernity and their opponents reaction and the medieval simply does not hold in this case. This tendency to see the Omani experience as somehow isolated (and therefore only retrograde and 'conservative') rather than connected with wider modern developments to which it is clearly related is also a consequence of a historiography that follows colonial decision-making: few chronicles of developments in Oman after 1861 sufficiently account for the continued significance of the Oman–Zanzibar relationship, as though the Canning Award had suddenly consigned the two places to entirely different historical narratives. Again, Ghazal's research is an important counterpoint here: 'In order better to assess the impact of the split in the Omani dynasty on the Ibadi *ulama*, the relationship between Oman and Zanzibar should be analyzed in terms of historical continuity and even interdependency. As the following events

[18] This is the term used by Landen, for example. See his *Oman Since 1856*.
[19] J. B. Kelly, *Eastern Arabian Frontiers* (Westport, CT: Praeger, 1964), p. 86.
[20] Landen, *Oman Since 1856*, p. 295.
[21] Wilkinson, *Imamate Tradition of Oman*, p. 243.

demonstrate, the spiritual and political bonds between the two Omani communities persisted long after the split and stimulated the two *coups d'états* in Oman, launched in 1868 and 1913 respectively.'[22]

We have already seen how external economic circumstances had made it increasingly difficult for Thuwaini bin Said to maintain the basis for Al Bu Said rule in Muscat (to which his political control in the early 1860s had been largely confined). In the absence of the economic resources arising from commercial activities upon which successive Al Bu Said rulers had come to rely, Thuwaini faced internal opposition to his rule from multiple sources. His younger brother, Turki bin Said, Wali of Sohar, resisted his pre-eminence and sought to establish an independent power based in Sohar and the Batinah. The tribes of the Sharqiyah, most of whose leaders owed allegiance to the traditionally dominant Hirth, were an ever-present potential political threat. At the same time Oman faced a renewed challenge from the Saudi/Wahhabi Emirate of the Nejd, which, as before, would present itself as a powerful military and political ally for rival Omani leaders seeking to challenge whoever currently held sway in Muscat (it seems that at this time Thuwaini's son Salim may have been soliciting Wahhabi support for his own political ambitions). In addition, within the Al Bu Said family itself, the Qays branch (descendants of Imam Ahmad bin Said's second son, Qays) had from time to time challenged the claims of the Sultan branch (from which Thuwaini and his father, Sayyid Said, were descended), and as a result Thuwaini was unable to count on the loyalty of the senior member of this branch, Azzan bin Qays. The Qays branch of the family had traditionally enjoyed good relations with powerful elements of the Ibadi religious leadership. For most of the period of Al Bu Said rule, the religious leadership had been broadly supportive and had not turned questions about the legitimacy of the Al Bu Said into active political opposition. But as the tangible benefits of the Al Bu Said leadership began to disappear, religious and political questions that had lain dormant for perhaps a century were revived. Popular discontent was rising, sharpened by economic hardship and often articulated as hostility to the system of customs farming dominated by Indian merchants, many of whom were now British subjects and who therefore received British political support. Opposition to Al Bu Said rule also grew in proportion to the conviction among adherents of the Ibadi religious leadership that their rulers were insufficiently robust in their observance and preservation of religious practices and principles. The foundations

[22] Ghazal, *Islamic Reform*, p. 24.

of an opposition movement articulated through appeals to both Omani (Arab) and religious tradition were taking shape.

During the first half of the 1860s there were sporadic clashes between forces loyal to Azzan bin Qays and those mobilised by Thuwaini. In 1864 Azzan bin Qays sought to strengthen his position by an alliance with the Wahhabis. This development and a related uprising in Sur and its environs, sparked by the Bani Bu Ali, an Omani tribe which had converted to Wahhabism, provoked British intervention, ostensibly in support of Thuwaini (as the British had for decades regarded Wahhabi expansion as a threat to their dominance of the Gulf coast). The British bombarded the Saudi coastal towns of Dammam and Qatif, provided Thuwaini with additional arms and ammunition and successfully pressured Majid in Zanzibar to pay arrears on the annual subsidy to assist Thuwaini in his increasingly difficult financial circumstances. Thus strengthened, Thuwaini assembled a military expedition to confront the Wahhabis at Buraimi. This confrontation over Buraimi never materialised, however, as Thuwaini was assassinated in Sohar by his son Salim, apparently with a Wahhabi accomplice and possibly incited by Wahhabi political interests with whom Salim had apparently been developing relations. J. B. Kelly speculates that this assassination may have been planned in advance by Abdallah bin Faisal, son of the Wahhabi Imam.[23] But already the Wahhabi threat was subsiding: the powerful Imam, Faisal ibn Turki, had died in 1865 and a power struggle among his sons consumed the energies that had previously been directed to expansionism in the Gulf and operations in Oman. His son and immediate successor, Abdallah ibn Faisal, signed an agreement with the British in which he promised not to attack any of Britain's Arab allies, including and 'especially' the rulers of Muscat. Thus, whatever the nature of Salim bin Thuwaini's relationship with the Wahhabi Emirate, his rule from 1866 neither benefited from its support nor had to deal with the threat it might pose. However, Salim's grip on power was never properly secured, and under his brief rule the debt crisis appears to have deepened, weakening an already precarious position considerably. His uncle Turki bin Said, whom he had initially imprisoned on the grounds that he presented a clear threat to his leadership, was released, at British urging, and was soon mobilising against him,

---

[23] J. B. Kelly, 'A Prevalence of Furies: Tribes, Politics and Religion in Oman and Trucial Oman', in Derek Hopwood (ed.), *The Arabian Peninsula* (London: George Allen & Unwin, 1972), pp. 107–141 (113).

gathering support from among the Hirth in the Sharqiyah. After Salim had wrongly imprisoned the Hirth leader, Salih bin Ali (who had been expelled from Zanzibar in 1859 for his part in Barghash's rebellion against Majid, as described earlier), on suspicion of conspiring with Turki against him, Salih bin Ali started to develop a new opposition coalition against Salim. It was this three-part alliance – between Salih bin Ali, the religious scholar and *qadi* Said bin Khalfan al-Khalili and Azzan bin Qays – that was then able to move decisively against Salim. Although the British had recognised Salim's succession, they offered him no practical support, withdrawing to their boats in the harbour as the opposition coalition was poised to capture Muscat. The city was taken, Salim fled and in October 1868 an election in Muscat led to the proclamation of Azzan bin Qays as Imam. According to long-standing Ibadi tradition, since Azzan bin Qays was not himself a religious scholar of pre-eminent standing, he was confirmed (by public acclamation, following his nomination by the tribal and religious leaders) as a *da'if* (weak) Imam, whose decisions were subject to the approval of the appropriate religious authorities. This meant that Said bin Khalfan al-Khalili became the crucial ideological and political decision-maker for the short period of Azzan's Imamate.

The new Imamate enjoyed some early political success. Because it already had broad support among many of the tribes of the interior, it was able to assert its authority far more widely there than had previous rulers based in Muscat, and those tribes who did not immediately pledge their allegiance to the new Imamate were the objects of concerted military operations that eventually secured their submission over the course of 1869. One significant absentee from the tribal leaders who accepted the rule of Imam Azzan bin Qays was Sayf bin Sulayman al-Nabhani of the Bani Riyam, who, two years later, would join forces with Salim bin Thuwaini to overthrow the Imamate. His son and successor, Himyar bin Sayf, would later emerge as a leading figure in the pro-Imamate coalition of 1895–1913, and his grandson, Sulayman bin Himyar, would become a leading figure in the Imamate movement that took up arms against Sultan Said bin Taimur in the 1950s (see Chapter 4). Secure in its hold over the interior, and taking advantage of the dissension among the Saudi/ Wahhabi leadership after the death of Imam Faisal ibn Turki, the forces of Azzan's Imamate were also able to forge an alliance with the Na'im *shaikhs* of the Dhahirah and the ruler of Abu Dhabi to take back Buraimi from the Saudis, expelling their garrison by force and reaffirming Omani political supremacy over the oasis and its people. The Saudis did not take back control of Buraimi until 1954, when, as we shall see in Chapter 4, their actions triggered a political crisis with both local and international dimensions.

However, the Imamate also faced considerable difficulties. Foremost among these, at least to begin with, were financial problems exacerbated by the hostile attitudes towards the Imamate on the part of Sultan Majid of Zanzibar and representatives of the British government of India. Sultan Majid refused to pay the annual subsidy of MT$40,000 (and the British, supposedly responsible under the terms of the Canning Award for ensuring its payment, abstained from applying any pressure on Sultan Majid to do so, presumably on the basis that they refused to recognise Azzan bin Qays as the legitimate ruler of Oman). The senior British official in the region, Colonel Lewis Pelly, essentially failed to distinguish between the religious and political character of the Imamate and the radically different Wahhabis, whom the British had traditionally opposed. Furthermore, the economic and social policies implemented at the urging of Said bin Khalfan al-Khalili, which included the abolition of the lucrative practice of customs farming, restrictions on the sale of alcohol and tobacco and prohibitions against the playing of music, discouraged the Indian merchant community and gave their British patrons and partners the sense that the Imamate was hostile to the kind of free-trade regime to which they were committed. British officials, and as a result many subsequent commentators, have equated these policies with xenophobia and a hostility to trade as such. This is misleading. On the economic front, Said bin Khalfan al-Khalili first appointed a customs director, who began by reducing customs duties at Muscat – just as successful Al Bu Said rulers had done in the past – in order to stimulate trade and, when this policy proved unsuccessful (because in a period of declining commercial activity its main effect was to depress revenues), sought to have an Indian company take over the administration of Muscat's customs. It was the British who intervened to stop him from doing so. From this evidence one might conclude that far from being opposed to either trade or foreigners as such, the Imamate's economic policies were pro-trade and involved a continued willingness to work with foreigners. The Imamate may have differed from its immediate predecessors only by seeking to place commercial activities at Muscat more firmly under its own control, implementing policies that in the twentieth century might have been called nationalisation (British hostility to such practices in the region during the twentieth century would be evident in its actions over the Suez Canal in 1956). Because this attempt to 'nationalise' economic activity in the interests of Arab Omanis (the government's principal political constituency) was accompanied by the enforcement of cultural prohibitions shaped by religious doctrine, it is easy to see how these two aspects of policy might be understood, by the British whose interests they threatened, as part and parcel of a consistent xenophobia. It may be more productive, however, for historians to think of the policies implemented under the Imamate of Azzan bin Qays as responses to the political complexities of the colonial encounter, which were almost inevitably contradictory and largely reactive, coming as they did at a time before the consolidation of a cohesive anti-colonial nationalist movement. Recognising the incipient anti-colonialism in the Imamate movement at this juncture helps account for the political support enjoyed by the Imamate movement in the 1950s from the postcolonial Arab League.

The political hostility towards the Imamate had serious and tangible consequences. As a result of the decline in customs revenues and the non-payment of the Zanzibar subsidies, the government found itself obliged to seek revenue from unusual sources and also to cut its own expenditure. Among its revenue-generation schemes were the confiscation of assets from people associated with the previous regime and attempts to raise emergency loans. Both of these measures contributed to the growth of political opposition at home. At the same time the government was often unable to sustain the levels of subsidy for key allies, even including Salih bin Ali, or for former opponents, such as the Wahhabis, from whom such payments traditionally purchased neutrality if not active support.[24] Weakened by the economic consequences of its political isolation, the Imamate faced a direct and existential challenge when Sultan Majid of Zanzibar, simultaneously seeking to assert his own claim to paramountcy in Oman itself and to forestall any resurgence of a similar uprising by Imamate sympathisers in Zanzibar, initiated and financed a campaign by Turki bin Said, returning from exile in India, which was to drive Azzan bin Qays from power. Sultan Majid's financial support allowed Turki to secure the backing of Omani tribal leaders who had until now supported the Imamate, and with substantial tribal forces at his disposal, along with leaders of the Emirates of Dubai, Ajman and Ras al-Khaimah, he launched a military operation that Azzan was unable to resist. Azzan's main forces were ambushed near Dank in September 1870, and by January 1871 Turki's soldiers took Muscat. Azzan bin Qays died defending Muttrah. Said bin Khalfan al-Khalili surrendered under conditions negotiated with

[24] See Landen, *Oman Since 1856*, pp. 310–312.

Turki by Colonel Pelly, according to which Said bin Khalfan himself was to be protected and key aspects of Imamate policies, including the confiscations, were not to be reversed. These conditions were not adhered to; confiscated properties were returned and Said bin Khalfan al-Khalili died two days later while under arrest. Muhammad al-Salimi, the strongly pro-Imamate historian of this period, states that Said bin Khalfan and his son were buried alive.[25]

TWO DIMENSIONS OF 'MODERNISATION': OMAN AND ZANZIBAR, 1871–1920

Sultan Majid of Zanzibar did not live to see the success of his campaign to overthrow the Imamate. On his death, on October 7, 1870, he was succeeded by his brother and erstwhile rival, Barghash, who had returned to Zanzibar some years earlier from exile in Bombay. Barghash ruled Zanzibar until his death in March 1888, during which time he oversaw a further phase in the economic, social and political development of the new Sultanate. The most visible and tangible achievements of the period were those that transformed the material culture of the island through the creation of a distinctive modern city in Zanzibar's Stone Town and, with it, a cosmopolitan culture of consumption. At the same time, however, Barghash fostered a climate of intellectual and religious tolerance in which Ibadi scholars and religious leaders played a significant role. These developments were significant in places far beyond Zanzibar itself, including Oman, where the tradition of Imamate opposition to Al Bu Said rule was nurtured through practical and intellectual connections between Muscat and Zanzibar. Therefore, although many histories of Oman treat developments in Zanzibar and Oman separately after the Canning Award of 1861 divided the two parts of Sayyid Said's state, here we choose to continue to treat the two together, up until the death of Barghash in 1888 and the eventual declaration of Zanzibar as a British Protectorate in 1890. We do so because maintaining this dual focus enables us to see how events in both Oman and Zanzibar involved divergent but related processes of 'modernisation', in both of which religion appeared not, as it is sometimes represented, as a purely regressive and anti-modern element, but as a vital part of the process of modernisation itself. In neither case was this 'modernisation' the simple unilinear

---

[25] Muhammad al-Salimi, *Nahdat*, p. 332, cited in Wilkinson, *Imamate Tradition of Oman*, p. 237.

process in which, for example, a 'traditional' and religious way of life is superseded by a supposedly progressive, secular and technologically advanced one. Instead, both were experiences of complex interactions between alternative visions of political power, religion and economics.

When Barghash took power in 1870, Azzan bin Qays was still in power in Muscat, as we have seen. There was substantial support for his Imamate among the Zanzibaris, especially on Pemba, and the idea that the two Sultanates might be reunited under Imamate rule was still entertained among intellectuals and religious leaders committed to the Ibadi revival, also more generally known as *mutawiah*. At the start of his reign, Barghash decided to build a political alliance with the *mutawiah* (some of them had been among his supporters in 1859) and responded to their articulation of popular anxieties on a number of related issues: the role of non-Ibadi people in all quarters of public and commercial life; the lax application of religious law; the ruler's acquiescence with British pressure to end the slave trade. Barghash reformed the courts and appointed *qadis* who would apply religious law more thoroughly, and he placed some restrictions on the scope of Indian business activities. This turn in policy clearly worried the British, who feared that it could lead to both Muscat and Oman falling under the control of forces actively hostile to their political and economic interests.[26] Barghash, however, succeeded in managing the apparent contradictions between, on the one hand, his relations with the British (which improved considerably after initial tensions) and, on the other, his alliance with the *mutawiah*. His position was complicated by the fact that, whatever his sympathies with the *mutawiah* and his pragmatic interest in maintaining their political support, he may not have welcomed the idea of a reunification of Oman and Zanzibar under an Imamate (unless, of course, he could aspire to lead it himself): he is said to have celebrated the fall of Azzan's Imamate with a 101-gun salute.[27]

His support for Ibadi intellectual life endured well beyond the period in which it was of immediate political value to him, however. He also sponsored the publication of numerous works of Ibadi religious scholarship and set up a printing press – the first in either Zanzibar or Oman – as part of a project for the wider dissemination of Ibadi thought. In 1871–1872 he travelled to Egypt, Syria and Palestine; during the journey he also performed the *hajj* and encountered, presumably in Cairo, some of the literary, religious and political ideas associated with the

---

[26] See Bennett, *A History of the Arab State of Zanzibar*, pp. 91–92.
[27] Attributed to Abdallah al-Salimi, cited in Ghazal, *Islamic Reform*, p. 26.

FIGURE 1. Sultan Barghash, a *carte de visite*, 1865.
Source: SSPL/Getty Images

wider Arab *nahda*.[28] Barghash's activities thus laid the foundations for
the development of a sophisticated and cosmopolitan intellectual culture.
Ibadi scholars were welcomed and encouraged in their work throughout
Barghash's reign, and the culture they fostered continued to thrive after
his death. They forged strong connections with fellow intellectuals in
the Arab world, subscribed to journals such as *Al-Manar* (established in
Cairo by Mohammed Abduh and edited after his death by Rashid Rida)
and published their own journal, *Al-Najah* (established in 1910), as the
organ of a new political party, Hizb al-Islah (Reform Party).[29]

  One of the leading figures in this intellectual culture was Nasir bin
Salim al-Bahlani (often known as Abu Muslim), whose father had been a
judge during the Imamate of Azzan bin Qays and whom Sultan Barghash

---

[28] Anne Bang, *Sufis and Scholars of the Sea: Family Networks in East Africa, 1860–1925*
  (New York: Routledge, 2003), p. 118.
[29] See ibid., pp. 135–136.

appointed as a *qadi* in Zanzibar, where he lived for most of his life (apart from a period of about six years in Oman). He also contributed directly to the later Omani *nahda*, writing an extensive letter to Imam Salim bin Rashid al-Kharusi (as discussed later) in 1915, urging him to promote education and to make sure that the Imamate he had just established engaged widely with the wider Muslim world.[30] It was Nasir al-Bahlani who first suggested that the Imam should engage the services of the Libyan Ibadi intellectual Sulayman al-Baruni, who was, at that time, working for the Ottomans in Istanbul. In recognition of his key role in supporting the growth of the *nahda* in both Zanzibar and Oman, Sultan Barghash himself was singled out for praise as a strong supporter of the Ibadi *madhab*, by another key ideological figure of the next phase of the Omani *nahda*, Nur al-Din Abdallah bin Humayd al-Salimi.[31]

This intellectual culture was amplified by the fact that it took shape as part of a wider social and material transformation of Zanzibar, described by Jeremy Prestholdt and others as far more than a mere replication of European and American urban modernity and as a significant instance of nineteenth-century globalisation.[32] Although it involved the introduction of goods, practices and technologies associated with similar processes in Paris, London, Chicago and New York – electricity, trams, paved roads, mass consumption of luxury commodities, steamships, urban planning, proposals for a major railway, public concerts, street lighting and the Bait al-Ajaib (House of Wonders), a waterfront exhibition hall in which the products and technologies of the new economy were displayed, as in the great exhibitions of the American and European colonial capitals – it also entailed what Prestholdt calls the 'creolisation of global symbols'. Two striking examples of this were the widespread adoption of the umbrella and the erection of public clocks. Umbrellas were purchased and used as fashionable accessories, not just by business or social elites, but also

---

[30] See Ghazal, *Islamic Reform*, pp. 82–87.

[31] These approving observations are contained in his *Tuhfat al-Ayan*, cited in Bang, *Sufis and Scholars*, p. 118.

[32] See Jeremy Prestholdt, *Domesticating the World: African Consumerism and the Genealogies of Globalisation* (Berkeley: University of California Press, 2008), pp. 105–116. See also Erik Gilbert, 'Zanzibar: Imperialism and Proto-Globalization, and a Nineteenth Century Indian Ocean Boom Town', in Andreas Exenberger, Philipp Strobl, Günter Bischof and James Mokhiber (eds.), *Globalization and the City: Two Connected Phenomena in Past and Present* (Innsbruck: Innsbruck University Press, 2013) and, for an account of how this project was adapted and superseded by British colonial administrators once Zanzibar became a British Protectorate, William Cunningham Bissell, *Urban Design, Chaos, and Colonial Power in Zanzibar* (Bloomington: University of Indiana Press, 2011).

by ordinary citizens, and in Zanzibar they acquired a distinctive symbolic meaning, beyond the class and taste distinctions they signified in many other contexts, to represent a conscious participation in a shared Zanzibari identity. The public clocks in Zanzibar did not display the time as measured in relation to Greenwich Mean Time and using the standard twenty-four-hour clock, but marked instead a Zanzibar time in which one o'clock was shown at sunrise and adjustments were made every ten days to accommodate shifts in the length of the day (which does not, in fact, vary greatly because of Zanzibar's proximity to the equator). Barghash's social and cultural modernisation policies were supported by a booming economy, in which he made substantial public investment, such as the purchase of six steamships in order to set up his own steam line to challenge the dominance of the British Indian Steam Navigation Company on Bombay–East Africa routes. One consequence of this was a massive increase in trade between Bombay and Zanzibar, especially in Indian cloth whose production dated from the interruption of American cloth exports to the region at the time of the U.S. Civil War (1861–1865).[33] It is important to recognise, then, that the Omani *nahda* and many of the ideas that animated it in the later part of the nineteenth and early twentieth centuries were nurtured within and actively assisted by a process of economic and social modernisation, particularly in Zanzibar. While the *mutawiah* were critical of aspects of this process and, in particular, of the extent to which it coincided with the extension of British colonial power, they were also a part of it, and not, as some accounts would have it, merely isolated and parochial figures ignorant of the wider world in which their religion and their politics had been shaped.[34]

The period of Sultan Barghash's rule in Zanzibar coincided almost exactly with that of Sultan Turki bin Said in Muscat. Sultan Turki restored the Sultanate in February 1871, just four months after Sultan Barghash had come to power in Zanzibar, and the two men died within three months of each other, Barghash in March 1888 and Turki in June. In the first few years of his rule Sultan Turki was largely preoccupied

---

[33] Prestholdt, *Domesticating the World*, pp. 81–82.

[34] John E. Peterson's valuable account of the Imamate revival of 1913–1920 is an example of the reproduction of this limited view of the Imamate's supporters and the *mutawiah* of the period more generally when he characterises the alternative offered by the Imamate to the continuation of the Sultanate as 'fanatically religious, xenophobic and inward-looking'. John. E. Peterson, 'The Revival of the Ibadi Imamate in Oman', in R. B. Serjeant and R. L. Bidwell (eds.), *Arabian Studies III* (London: Hurst, 1976), pp. 165–188(166).

with securing his position in Muscat against various challenges. The former Imam's brother, Ibrahim bin Qays, had succeeded him in Sohar and continued to exercise influence over much of the Batinah and entertained ambitions to take back Muscat for himself and his Ibadi revivalist allies. Salih bin Ali of the Hirth continued as pre-eminent *shaikh* in the Sharqiyah, and the former Sultan, Salim bin Thuwaini, secured his support in a number of attempts to unseat Sultan Turki. Sultan Turki's position was made no easier by the economic situation, in which a continuing decline in commercial activity depleted government revenues.

This, then, was the difficult political and economic situation in which Sultan Turki responded to a renewed effort on the part of the British government to act against the slave trade. As we have seen already (Chapter 2) there had been a series of treaties between the British and Sayyid Said that were designed to restrict the trade. But these had only limited effect, and many Omanis believed that the institution of slavery had its place as a legitimate feature of an established social order, permitted according to religion and long-standing custom and practice. In 1872, Sir Bartle Frere, a former Governor of Bombay, travelled to both Muscat and Zanzibar to seek agreement on new and more effective treaties. He arrived first in Zanzibar, in January 1873, with George Percy Badger, who had recently published an English translation of Ibn Ruzayq's *History of the Imams and Seyyids of Oman*, as his adviser and interpreter. His initial negotiations with Sultan Barghash failed and he moved on to Muscat; there Sultan Turki – clearly, as we have seen, in a much weaker political and economic position than Sultan Barghash – agreed to the terms of Frere's treaty on April 14 and issued a proclamation that traffic in slaves was now 'entirely forbidden' in his 'dominions and dependencies'. In subsequent negotiations in Zanzibar, Sultan Barghash, acting under extreme duress, including the threat of British naval blockade, agreed to sign. Having done so, he successfully persuaded the British to pay the Zanzibar subsidy (agreed under the terms of the Canning Award) on his behalf, in order to compensate him for the loss of customs revenues that he claimed would follow from signing Frere's treaty. Thus, once Sultan Barghash signed, the British were able to relieve some of Sultan Turki's financial difficulties. Although this helped Sultan Turki consolidate his position, it also meant that the Sultan and his successors in Muscat would come increasingly to rely upon British support. This pattern, in which the Sultan in Muscat would have to weigh up the advantages of British support against its unpopularity among the very opposition he needed either to appease or to confront, would be characteristic of the relationship between successive governments in Muscat and the British for many years to come. For the time being, Sultan Turki was briefly able to take advantage of this development, successfully fending off the challenges of Ibrahim bin Qays and Salih bin Ali (who, as we have seen, had allied himself with the former Sultan, Salim bin Thuwaini). However, in 1875 he fell ill and withdrew for most of the following year to Gwadar, leaving his brother Abd al-Aziz bin Said to rule on his behalf. In his absence, Abd al-Aziz sought to win political support for his own claim to rule, reintroducing some of the social restrictions implemented during the Imamate of Azzan bin Qays. On Sultan Turki's return from Gwadar, Abd al-Aziz made a brief attempt to hold on to power, until Sultan Turki was able to gather a military force to drive him out of Muscat and eventually into exile.

Sultan Turki's subsequent rule established some significant basic frameworks according to which the Omani government in Muscat continued to function for almost a hundred years. These included limits on the participation in government by close and senior members of the Sultan's immediate family; the development of an administration in close cooperation with both Arab and Indian business leaders; extensive use of British advisers, especially in matters of foreign affairs, military development and finance; the incorporation of Dhofar into the territory under the rule of the Sultan (in 1879; see Chapter 5); the establishment of a permanent army staffed largely by soldiers with no significant Omani tribal affiliations (among them Baluchis, Hadramis and Africans); and the careful balancing of the Sultan's relations with major tribal leaders through subsidies and other financial inducements and rewards. Sultan Turki's rule is significant for one further reason. According the Oman's Basic Statute of the State, succession within the Al Bu Said family may now proceed only through descendants of Sultan Turki, a provision which suggests that the present Sultan, who wrote the Basic Statute himself (see Chapter 7), was convinced that the continuity in which successive direct descendants of Sultan Turki had governed (Faisal bin Turki, Taimur bin Faisal, Said bin Taimur, Qaboos bin Said) had served the interests of the Sultanate more effectively than had the frequent and sometimes violent struggles for ascendancy that preceded them.

Towards the end of Sultan Turki's rule, the British were intensifying their efforts to achieve greater control over the coastal areas of the Persian Gulf – a process that would lead, elsewhere, to the establishment of formal Protectorates (in Bahrain from 1880, in the Trucial Shaikhdoms from 1892 and in Kuwait from 1899) and to the assertion of effective control of the Persian Gulf as an exclusively 'British lake' by Lord Curzon, Viceroy of India, in 1903. In Oman, there was no Protectorate, but instead a series of understandings and agreements, including the announcement in 1886 of a guarantee by the British government in India that it would specifically support Sultan Turki against challenges to his right to rule in Muscat (formalising what had been the case in practice through much of his reign). Then, in 1891, after Sultan Turki's death in 1888, his successor, Sultan Faisal bin Turki, signed a commercial treaty with the British which included an accompanying clause in which the Sultan committed himself 'never to cede, to sell, to mortgage or otherwise give for occupation save to the British government, the dominions of Muscat and Oman or any of their dependencies'.[35] Because this agreement did not give the British exclusive rights to conduct foreign policy, as did the 'Protectorate' treaties with other regional leaders (in recognition of Oman's extensive existing foreign relations), Oman was not regarded as a formal Protectorate. In Zanzibar, however, a Protectorate had been established in 1890.

It was also during Faisal bin Turki's reign (1888–1913) that the political challenge of the Omani *nahda* entered its second principal phase. Once again, events that played out in Oman itself, while they were shaped largely by local circumstances, were also influenced by developments in Zanzibar. In 1894 a crisis developed when Salih bin Ali responded to Sultan Faisal's attempts to have him replaced as Tamimah of the Hirth by mobilising against him. Omani tribal leaders who rallied to support him sent a delegation to Zanzibar, where they secured money and arms from the Sultan to challenge Sultan Faisal in Oman. In February 1895 forces gathered by Salih bin Ali and strengthened by this support from Zanzibar approached Muscat from the Samail Gap. On entering Muscat they raised the white flag associated with the Imamate over Sultan Faisal's palace, while the Sultan himself retreated to Jalali Fort. The British adopted a position of neutrality (which may have come as a surprise to Sultan Faisal, who might reasonably have expected their support). As would be the case in the later and more significant Imamate challenge from 1913, the leaders of the opposition forces were careful to indicate that they had no quarrel with the British (here, as so often, the actual behaviour of the Omani opposition to the Sultan offers no evidence of their 'xenophobic' attitudes). After Sultan Faisal gathered his own force of tribal supporters and the two sides engaged in an indecisive

---

[35] See Landen, *Oman Since 1856*, pp. 222–223.

stand-off for several weeks, they started negotiations, which concluded in March 1895 with the departure of the tribal forces and substantial payments by Sultan Faisal to Salih bin Ali. This would be the last time that Salih bin Ali would challenge the Sultan: he died the following year. But, as we shall see, once a new generation of both tribal and religious leaders was able to organise, the challenge would return, reinvigorated by a further injection of religious and political energy from the revival in Ibadi thought across both Oman and Zanzibar. Meanwhile, in Zanzibar, Sultan Hamad's death was the occasion for a brief struggle between Khalid bin Barghash, who attempted (for a second time) to claim the succession for himself, and the British, who backed Hamud bin Mohammed, whom they considered much more amenable to their political and economic interests. The British response to Khalid's attempt was swift and overwhelming: they bombarded the palace, captured Khalid and sent him into exile in Dar es Salaam. Many of his supporters who were arrested as part of the crackdown subsequently fled to Zanzibar, where several would play active roles in the growth of pro-Imamate agitation in the period before the major Imamate challenge of 1913–1920.

In response to the British refusal to come to his aid against the 1895 attempt to take Muscat from him, Sultan Faisal briefly explored the potential for more developed relations with France, a course of action which revealed that British assurances that he enjoyed a free hand in the conduct of foreign policy might not be entirely reliable. When Sultan Faisal granted the French permission to build a coaling station at Bandar Jissah – a natural harbour just ten miles from Muscat (where today the Bar al-Jissah Hotel complex is situated and a new complex is under development) – which was announced in the French press at the end of 1898, Lord Curzon decided that this threat to British exclusivity had to be counteracted. Not only did the British force Sultan Faisal to cancel the concession, but British ships threatened to bombard Muscat itself if Sultan Faisal did not come aboard a British ship to make this cancellation a public act. Faced with this example of British 'gunboat diplomacy', Sultan Faisal had little option but to comply. For the next ten years or so Sultan Faisal managed to achieve a measure of political control, relying increasingly on a combination of British advice, the effectiveness of Sulayman bin Suwaylim, a former slave who now served as his *wazir*, and the establishment of good relations with the new Tamimah of the Hirth, Isa bin Salih. However, despite the comparative stability, a new challenge to his rule was starting to take shape in the interior.

THE IMAMATE REVIVAL

In May 1913 religious scholars and tribal *shaikhs* assembled in Tanuf to conduct an election for the position of Imam, which had been vacant since the death of Azzan bin Qays. Among the prime movers of this restoration of the Imamate were the religious scholar Nur al-Din Abdallah bin Humayd al-Salimi and the leader of the powerful tribe of the Bani Riyam, Himyar bin Nasir al-Nabhani, whose principal town was Tanuf. This assembly of *ahl al-hall wa'l aqd* (those who elect the leader of the Muslims) chose as the new Imam Salim bin Rashid al-Kharusi, a religious scholar who was descended from a family closely associated with the Imamate and from which a considerable number of previous Imams had been elected in pre-Ya'ariba Oman. At the time of his election, Imam Salim bin Rashid was about thirty years old. The role of Abdallah al-Salimi was of particular significance in the restoration of the Imamate at this time. He had been actively promoting his ideas for the reunification of Oman under appropriate Muslim leadership for more than a decade; he had established himself as the pre-eminent figure of the Omani *nahda* and a critic of what he regarded as the failures of the Al Bu Said to conform to Ibadi religious and political principles. He had in the past engaged Sultan Faisal in substantive conversations on the subject of appropriate Muslim leadership, seeking to persuade him to take up the mantle himself in 1905. Although Faisal declined this proposal, he did suggest that Abdallah al-Salimi might take responsibility for the education of his son, Taimur bin Faisal.

Although Abdallah al-Salimi was known for his strong objections to the cultural influence of Europeans on the social life, education and political arrangements of Muslims, he was by no means a merely parochial figure whose views were shaped by isolation from the rest of the world. He had encountered leading Muslim intellectuals in Mecca when he made the *hajj* in 1905–1906; his own thought and publications shared some of the key ideas of the wider *nahda*, including a commitment to the practice of *ijtihad*, and he corresponded with key figures elsewhere in the *umma*, particularly on the need for Muslim unity, and notably with the Libyan Ibadi scholar Sulayman al-Baruni, who would eventually come to Oman to work in the administration of the next Imam, Mohammed al-Khalili.[36]

By the time of the election of Imam Salim bin Rashid, the political situation in Oman had created the conditions in which a direct challenge to

[36] See Ghazal, *Islamic Reform*, pp. 32–33.

Sultan Faisal's government might succeed and in which Abdallah al-Salimi's call for a contemporary revival of the Imamate would find widespread support. In addition to the ideological force of Abdallah al-Salimi's message, Oman's economic decline had continued; the government in Muscat had become increasingly dependent upon British support; it was widely believed that under the influence of the British, the Sultan's government was permitting activities held by many Muslims to be prohibited (the sale and consumption of alcohol and tobacco) and prohibiting activities the same Muslims considered to be specifically permitted according to religious law (the sale of arms and the trade in slaves). The government of Sultan Faisal itself had been weakened following the death in 1907 of Sulayman al-Suwaylim, who had been his most effective political operator for many years. It appears that the Sultan's decision in 1912, at British urging, to set up a warehouse through which all arms and ammunition traded in Oman would have to pass, was crucial in mobilising a combination of religious and anti-colonial sentiment. This decision was seen as an inappropriate restriction on the liberties of the Omanis and also, potentially, as a measure designed to deprive them of the resources with which they might oppose the extension of British power in their territory.

Having elected Imam Salim bin Rashid, the political and religious leaders assembled at Tanuf proceeded to take immediate steps to secure the political position of the restored Imamate and to advance their objectives. Shaikh Abu Zayd Abdallah bin Mohammed al-Riyami (an influential religious leader from the Bani Riyam, who had himself been one of the four candidates in the election), speaking to the assembly after the election, formally declared that a *jihad* was now under way. Troops were assembled and moved first to take control of Nizwa, the historic capital of the Imamate, which swiftly fell to the new Imamate's forces, so that Imam Salim bin Rashid could establish it as his new seat of government. Imam Salim wrote to the Sultan shortly after his election, calling on him to join Omani Muslims in their support for their Imam: it is not clear to what extent this constituted a call for the Sultan to step down, let alone whether it should thereby be understood that the election of the Imam automatically meant the deposition of the Sultan, as has often been suggested.[37]

---

[37] See, e.g., Landen, *Oman Since 1856*, p. 394. This account is contested by Mohammed bin Said al-Hashimy, in his unpublished PhD dissertation, *Imam Salim bin Rashid and the Imamate Revival in Oman 1331/1913–1338/1920* (University of Leeds, 1994), citing Muhammad al-Salimi's *Nahdat* as his source for the contents of the Imam's letter to Sultan Faisal.

The initial success in taking Nizwa seems to have persuaded the new
Tamimah of the Hirth, Isa bin Salih, to become involved. As we have
already seen, Sultan Faisal had earlier been successful in securing his temporary support. Perhaps as a result of this his role initially included sustained efforts to bring the Imam and the Sultan to negotiations, at least
until 1915. Further tribes rallied to the Imamate as military successes
followed, with Izki, Bidbid and the vital strategic position of Samail falling to its forces. In Muscat, the British, who had already communicated
their concern about the ambitions of the new Imamate, were clearly sufficiently alarmed by the success of the military campaign in the interior to
reinforce their troops stationed at Bait al-Falaj, just inland from Muttrah
and Muscat, having already made it clear in writing to the Imam that
they would not stand by to see either of these two key assets captured.
The attitude of the new Imamate to the British presence was more complex than those accounts which routinely characterise it as 'xenophobic': the Imam corresponded with the British Political Agent in Muscat
in terms which suggest that his objections were not so much to their
presence in Oman as to the specific nature and consequences of their
influence (the permitting of the prohibited and the prohibition of the permitted). The Imam's letter to the Political Agent (Knox), informed him of
the decision 'to rise against him [Sultan Faisal] disliking the innovations
he has brought about in Islam, by contravening the Sharah [*sic*] com-
mands and committing what is forbidden therein and setting the people against one another, and thereby disturbances are rife in the country
and the order of things is disturbed, crimes have been committed, blood
has been shed, property looted, legal punishments dispensed with and
rights destroyed'.[38] In later correspondence he responded to Knox's suggestion that he might help reconcile the Imam and the Sultan, informing
him that 'I see no objection to peace being arranged between myself and
Sd. Taymur, and you are a suitable and capable person to undertake the
same.'[39] There is no indication that he demanded the withdrawal of any
foreigners from Oman. In general he seemed, at least initially, to be seeking mutual agreement on the appropriate allocation of roles and responsibilities between the Sultan, the British and himself. As far as the British
were concerned, the Imamate leadership contested their right to station
troops on Omani soil, to intervene in matters of Omani governance (over

---

[38] An English translation of the Imam's letter included in Knox's letter to Cook, October
9, 1913, cited in Peterson, 'Revival of the Ibadi Imamate', p. 170. Peterson describes this
letter as 'haughty'.

[39] Cited in al-Hashimy, *Imam Salim bin Rashid*, p. 98.

FIGURE 2. Sultan Faisal with Sayyid Taimur and Sayyid Said, 1913.
Source: Pictures from History/Bridgeman Images

arms, alcohol, tobacco and slaves, for example) and to restrict the free movement of ships to and from the Omani coast. Their concerns about the way the British claimed absolute control over the coast were exacerbated by the implementation of a blockade that prevented goods from reaching the interior and also made it impossible for people in the interior who owned coastal property to conduct business there. The outbreak of World War One in August 1914 intensified the economic difficulties experienced by Omanis at this time: this not only increased general discontent in the interior, but also threatened to weaken still further the economic position of the Sultan and his government.[40] The British, whose anxieties about the challenge to the Sultan were now heightened by the context of world war, in which both the Germans and the Ottomans were believed to be seeking to undermine British power in the Gulf, strengthened their position further with the stationing of six companies of infantry at Muttrah at the end of 1914.

---

[40] See Landen, *Oman Since 1856*, pp. 397–398.

Until this point the Imamate leaders had held off from making a direct assault on the Sultan at Muscat. This was the red line as far as the British were concerned, so they could expect British forces to be deployed in defence of the Sultan on this occasion (unlike 1895). Isa bin Salih, who still seemed to be encouraging negotiations, also clearly had reservations about the Imamate's capacity to move effectively against Muscat – especially since he would have to bear much of the cost of such a campaign. However, further funds were secured from Zanzibar, and in January 1915 the Imam's forces gathered at Bausher and Isa bin Salih's at al-Khuwayr. As they advanced towards Muscat they were met and repelled by British Indian Army forces from Bait al-Falaj and Ruwi. Over the next few years there were a series of negotiations, sometimes conducted by letter, sometimes during face-to-face meetings, in which Isa bin Salih would often represent the Imamate side. Successive British Political Agents encouraged Sultan Taimur to engage in these negotiations. In 1917, the Political Agent Major L. B. H. Haworth clearly believed that there was much substance to the Imamate's case. He noted that it was providing better government than the Sultan's administration and that, by denying the Omani people the right to be governed as they pleased, the British government risked inflaming the situation to no good purpose, just as had been the case, he observed, in Ireland. So although, as we have seen, the Imamate did not oppose the British presence as such, it is clear that at least one British official on the scene recognised in its political objectives a significant anti-colonial dimension.

In 1920 two of the leading figures of the Imamate died. Himyar al-Nabhani died in February, and in July Imam Salim bin Rashid himself was murdered (apparently as a result of some minor dispute or grievance rather than by someone motivated by political aims). The Imamate's primary intellectual inspiration, Abdallah bin Humayd al-Salimi, had died in 1914. In the last few years of Imam Salim bin Rashid's life, he had also lost some other key advisers, either to death or resignation, and his administration had to deal with rising discontent among the Omanis of the interior. A new Imam, Mohammed al-Khalili, was elected and faced some of the same problems, without the personal authority enjoyed by the previous Imam. Meanwhile, on the coast, with World War One at an end, the British were able to strengthen their position, and encouraged by what appeared to be an improving position, Sultan Taimur imposed a blockade of the interior and increased taxes on agricultural produce from the interior in what seems to have been a punitive measure designed to apply political pressure on the Imamate. It appears to have had some effect, as Omanis in the interior increasingly called upon the new Imam to reach an agreement with the Sultan. A further round of negotiations, held at Seeb, outside Muscat, in which Isa bin Salih again led the Imamate delegation, facilitated this time by another British Political Agent, Ronald Wingate, resulted in an agreement between the Sultan, on the one hand, and the 'Omanis', on the other, in which both parties effectively agreed that they would not interfere in the affairs of the other. The Seeb Agreement, the text of which was not made public at the time (nor, indeed, until it was reported in international newspapers in the 1950s, when supporters of the Imamate sought to make it part of their claim against Sultan Said), established four conditions to which each party would abide. The Sultan undertook not to impose taxes of more than 5 percent on any goods from the interior brought to the coast; to grant freedom and security to all 'Omanis' when in the coastal region; to lift all impediments to people seeking to leave and enter Muscat or Muttrah; and not to grant asylum to anyone fleeing justice in the interior (in other words, not to interfere in matters that were the proper jurisdiction of the Imam's government). For their part, the 'Omanis' undertook to be at peace with the Sultan and not to attack coastal towns or interfere in the affairs of his government; to grant freedom of travel and the right to trade to anyone with lawful business in the interior; not to give asylum to anyone fleeing the Sultan's justice; and to judge any claims made against them on the basis of religious law. The Seeb Agreement was not a full-scale treaty, and nor was it even an agreement between the Imam and the Sultan (it was agreed between the Sultan and Isa bin Salih on behalf of 'the Omanis' and subsequently ratified by other *shaikhs*, including the new Imam). It had therefore nothing to say about any competing or conflicting claims to sovereignty.

In the years following the Seeb Agreement, Oman enjoyed the suspension of hostilities between the interior and the coast. At the same time, however, the economic position of the Sultanate continued to deteriorate, and Sultan Taimur became increasingly disengaged from Omani political affairs, leaving more and more responsibility in the hands of British officials, while he spent much of his time in India. There was some development of the government apparatus, much of it carried out along lines suggested by the British, including the formation of the Muscat Levy Corps, which would be the basis for the eventual establishment of today's Sultan's Armed Forces. It was also during this period that oil exploration in Oman began, following Sultan Taimur's grant of exploration rights to the D'Arcy Exploration Company. An initial expedition failed to find

FIGURE 3. Sultan Taimur and his court, 1913.
Source: Pictures from History/Bridgeman Images

any commercially viable deposits in the western Hajar mountains, and it would fall to Sultan Taimur's successor (he abdicated in 1932), Sultan Said bin Taimur, to grant a further concession, this time to a subsidiary of the Iraq Petroleum Company, in 1937. It was this company, which undertook its exploration under the name Petroleum Development (Oman and Dhofar), that would eventually find oil in Oman in viable quantities, but not before the competition for oil resources in Arabia more generally and Sultan Said's consequent efforts to unify Oman led to a series of crises out of which the modern Sultanate would eventually emerge. That is the story to which we now turn, in Part II of this book.

PART TWO

MODERN HISTORY

4

The Sultanate as Nation, 1932–1959

Said bin Taimur had served as the President of Sultan Taimur's Council of Ministers since 1929, effectively in charge of the government during his father's prolonged absences from Muscat. When Sultan Taimur abdicated, he succeeded him, as had been planned, becoming Sultan of Muscat and Oman on February 10, 1932. In June of the same year the first oil on the Arabian side of the Gulf was found, in Bahrain. In September Abdul-Aziz ibn Saud finally succeeded in reunifying the provinces of the earlier Saudi states in the new Kingdom of Saudi Arabia. The year 1932 marks more, therefore, than the transition from one Sultan to another in Oman; it may also be seen as the moment at which a major change was inaugurated in the political and economic order of the Arabian Peninsula. As part of this broader process of change, Oman started to become, for the first time in its history, the kind of unified nation-state that has become the dominant form of political organisation in the modern world. This process of transformation owed much to external circumstances: in particular, the possibility that there might be oil to be discovered in Oman, too, led Sultan Said, the British government and the oil companies to the shared conviction that its exploitation could best be achieved within a clearly delimited territory under a single political authority. From 1932 to 1959, then, Sultan Said oversaw a complex and difficult attempt to forge a unified state, while at the same time he sought to limit the extent of its dependence upon the British, even while relying upon their political and military support to secure its unity and its independence.

UNDERSTANDING SULTAN SAID

It used to be a commonplace of historical accounts of his reign to characterise Sultan Said as a deeply conservative and intransigent figure, entirely resistant to change and responsible for maintaining his country in a state of backwardness and isolation. Much of this reputation appears to derive from the last decade of his reign, by which time he had withdrawn to Salalah, where his minimal administration was certainly responsible for widespread economic neglect, social repression and stagnation in Dhofar. Significant aspects of his image as a ruler have therefore been composed by those who opposed him politically and eventually took up arms against him (see Chapter 5). This negative image was also fuelled by the resentment of successive British officials who found him increasingly difficult to deal with and unwilling to submit to their advice, and who seem to have responded to their own frustrations by painting a distinctly 'Orientalist' picture of the Sultan as a despotic anachronism.

Recent historical scholarship has gone a long way to correcting this impression. It has done so partly by looking at the circumstances in which he found himself in order to understand why he acted as he did and partly by moving away from the kind of historical writing that seeks to attribute the course of events to the intentional actions of individual historical actors, particularly rulers. Thomas Bierschenk made an important initial contribution to this revisionist project by identifying the extent to which external factors – primarily the competition between British and American oil companies for Arabian oil – created an entirely new set of political dynamics for Oman.[1] More recently, Uzi Rabi's book-length study has added an enormous amount of detail to the revisionist picture, revealing Sultan Said to have been engaged in the negotiation of complex and interrelated internal and external pressures and developments (from tribal allegiances to neighbouring Arab states) rather than merely responding in a reactionary manner to developments he had no wish to understand.[2]

The possibility that oil might be found in Oman created the conditions for its transformation into a unified state, even if it did not determine the precise course that transformation would take. No sooner had Ibn Saud completed the establishment of the third Saudi state (the present-day Saudi Arabia) than he granted the oil concession to an American company,

---

[1] Thomas Bierschenk, 'Oil Interests and the Formation of Centralized Government in Oman, 1920–1970', *Orient* 30.2 (1989), pp. 205–219.
[2] Rabi, *Emergence of States in a Tribal Society*.

FIGURE 4. Sultan Said in 1957.
Source: Keystone-France/Getty Images

Standard Oil of California, which he favoured over a rival bid from the British Iraq Petroleum Company. It was a Standard Oil subsidiary that had struck oil in Bahrain the year before. United States oil companies were taking the lead in the race to find and bring to market Arabian oil, entering a region where until now British companies had dominated (in Iraq and Iran, for example). For the British, whose political involvement in Arabia had hitherto been largely limited to securing control of the coast in order to protect the heart of its empire in India, this required a significant change in policy as regards Oman. In order to help British oil interests compete effectively with their U.S. commercial rivals, the British government recognised that it needed to pay attention to the interior of the country as well. This realisation would eventually evolve into a policy of encouraging Sultan Said to extend his effective political reach into the interior, which is where, in all likelihood, oil in Oman would be found, if it were to be found. In doing so they hoped to secure for British companies access to territories that offered promising prospecting opportunities and, in the process, exclude U.S. companies from operating in such territories. This meant that the loose and inconclusive nature of the Seeb Agreement (at least when viewed from the perspective of people shaped by the norms of the modern nation-state) would become a problem, as it offered no basis for anyone to assert sole authority over the crucial territory in question. As we shall see, the dynamics of this new competition between Britain and the United States (slightly reminiscent of the commercial rivalry in Zanzibar in the mid-nineteenth century) would lead to conflict over sovereignty, first at the oasis of Buraimi in the Dhahirah, which, as we have already seen (Chapter 2), had in the past been the forward base for Saudi/Wahhabi expansion into Oman, and subsequently in the very interior of Oman, over which the Imamate still exercised its political authority and in whose 'internal affairs' the Seeb Agreement specified that the Sultan should not interfere (see Chapter 3).

The British Iraq Petroleum Company secured a seventy-five-year concession from Sultan Said in 1937. It did so as part of a series of acquisitions between 1933 and 1939, including ones in Qatar, Aden and the Trucial States, all on the basis of prior agreements with their rulers that no oil concessions would be made without the prior approval of the British government. The Oman concession, which led to the formation of Petroleum Development (Oman and Dhofar), subsequently Petroleum Development Oman (PDO), specified that prospecting expeditions in the interior could be made only with the Sultan's permission, but also seemed to recognise that such permission might not, in practice, be sufficient in light of the limits to his authority there. The company, therefore, also sought, unsuccessfully, to gain the permission of the Imam to explore the interior for oil. For his part, Sultan Said initially looked for ways to use the now well-established techniques of an Omani ruler to secure for himself, and by extension the company, a foothold in the interior, courting both the Tamimah of the Hirth, Isa bin Salih, and leaders of some of the main Dhahirah tribes. He was also able to use some of the money from the oil concession to bring members of the Imam's administration into his own service, a move which was consistent with his wider policy of building an administration at Muscat composed largely of Omani officials rather than relying, as had Sultan Taimur, on British personnel to manage government affairs.

He had embarked on this process from the outset, abolishing the Council of Ministers the British had encouraged his father to establish, in favour of three key offices, responsible for finance, internal affairs and justice. When the British official who had inherited the financial portfolio left Oman in 1933, Sultan Said took on the responsibilities himself. Responsibility for internal affairs became a more significant aspect of his administration once money from the oil concession started to come in and the need to consolidate his authority in the interior became a policy priority. After briefly appointing Sulayman al-Baruni to this role in 1938 (al-Baruni, it will be recalled, was the Libyan Ibadi scholar who had come to Oman to work for Imam al-Khalili), he handed responsibility to Ahmad bin Ibrahim Al Bu Said, the nephew of Imam Azzan bin Qays, who remained in the post until 1970. The justice portfolio was given to Zubair bin Ali, whose son, Mohammed Zubair, would become one of Sultan Qaboos's closest advisers. It is notable that in making these appointments he largely avoided entrusting significant power to senior members of his own family and built instead enduring alliances with prominent commercial figures, both Omani and Indian, and leading Dhofari families (he married Mazoon al-Mashani, a Dhofari woman, in 1936; she was Sultan Qaboos's mother). The contributions of members of the Khimji, Zubair, Zawawi, Rowas and Shanfari families to economic and political life in contemporary Oman can be traced to their incorporation into Sultan Said's circle of associates. It is also notable that, to this day, the Omani government is not as dominated by close relatives of the Sultan as are some of the governments elsewhere in the Gulf Cooperation Council by senior members of their own ruling families.

Sultan Said inherited a government in debt. In taking personal responsibility for its financial affairs he made it his overarching priorities, first, to eradicate the existing debt, much of which was owed to Indian merchant houses, and, second, to incur none further. He had already started work to this end before he became Sultan and through the 1930s succeeded, through cuts in public spending and improvements in customs and other tax collection, to achieve this objective. One particularly significant and lasting reduction was achieved in the share of the budget allocated to members of his own family: in 1931 this stood at nearly 34 percent and by 1968 it was down to just 2.4 percent.[3] He also limited expenditure and avoided debt by declining to invest in any capital projects that could not be funded out of existing revenues. While this may have been financially prudent, in a strict sense, it was this minimal approach to the responsibilities of government that would eventually attract so much criticism from

[3] John. E. Peterson, *Oman in the Twentieth Century: Political Foundations of an Emerging State* (London: Croom Helm, 1978), pp. 88–89 and app. G.

those who hoped to see the development of Oman's infrastructure, health and education systems.

By the 1940s, and especially after World War Two, the gradual decline in British influence in Oman, as elsewhere in the world, became much clearer. With the British withdrawal from India and the relinquishing of other colonial possessions, the rationale for the British strategic presence in the Gulf was changing. This would lead, as we shall see, to the British withdrawal from east of Suez, announced in 1966. In the twenty years between the end of World War Two and this decision, British interests in the Gulf in general, and in Oman in particular, came increasingly to focus on new priorities: competition for oil (with the United States as the main rival); oil security (where it shared U.S. interests); and more general defence of the region against the challenge of a new socialist nationalism and the related spectre of Soviet influence. In 1946, at a time when Imam al-Khalili appeared to be about to die, Sultan Said sought British support for his attempt to assert himself more forcefully in the interior, building on the political alliances he had created by bringing Imamate figures into his own administration and by occupying key interior towns. Although the British government in India expressed its support, in view of the opportunity it might afford for PDO to start meaningful explorations in areas to which it didn't at present have access (particularly Fahud), the government in London ruled it out. For Sultan Said this was a troubling development, as it meant that the British, effectively recognising that the Sultan didn't have the political authority to facilitate the exploration rights he had granted in the 1937 concession, were opening the door to attempts by interior leaders to negotiate directly with PDO and further undermine his aspirations to sovereignty over the whole of a unified Oman. Sulayman bin Himyar of the Bani Riyam sought to explore just this possibility, unsuccessfully seeking recognition from the British government as the ruler of an independent state of the Jebel Akhdar in 1950. The competition for oil was therefore one of the key factors in bringing Oman into further conflict in the 1950s: it forced Omani political leaders in Muscat and in the interior into decisions (and eventually conflict) over the right to control access to territory that the Seeb Agreement had not sought to determine and that no previous situations had demanded.

If the accession of Sultan Said in 1932 and the simultaneous events in the immediate neighbourhood marked the start of a period of transformation that would have lasting consequences for Oman, the death of Imam al-Khalili in 1954 marked the moment after which that process would accelerate into crisis. For leading figures associated with the

Imamate, the death of the Imam forced active consideration and debate over the future of their relationship with the Sultanate. It compelled them, as we have suggested, to focus on questions which had, to some extent at least, remained unaddressed in the preceding thirty years. For during the period since the Seeb Agreement the conditions in which the Sultanate and Imamate had enjoyed coexistence had changed, gradually but substantially, partly as a result of oil, as we have already seen, but in other ways, too. Most significantly, developments across the region had made it increasingly difficult to maintain the ambiguity over sovereignty which the Seeb Agreement embodied.

Anti-colonial and nationalist movements had begun to win major victories in their struggle for self-government and the end of colonial rule, a process which had accelerated after World War Two. The year of the Imam's death also saw the defeat and withdrawal of the French from Indochina and the launch of the revolution in Algeria. Only two years earlier, the Free Officers Movement in Egypt, led by Gamal Abdel Nasser and Mohammed Naguib, had overthrown the pro-British King Farouk and in 1953 had established Egypt as a republic. It was during 1954 that Nasser moved decisively to take command of the Egyptian state, replacing Naguib as President and Prime Minister. Cairo had established itself as the headquarters for Arab nationalist movements – many subsequent revolutionary and nationalist campaigns (from Algeria to Yemen) would come to depend on Cairo during this period for financial and material support and as a base for political organisation and radio propaganda activity. Oman, as we shall see, would be no exception.

But even before a nationalism inspired by the example of Egypt would emerge as a factor in Oman's political situation, one major consequence of the broader context of decolonisation would be – perhaps paradoxically – that European conceptions of the relationship between nation and sovereignty would increasingly dominate the political organisation of non-European nations. This seems paradoxical at first sight, since one might expect the influence of European systems and concepts to decline with European withdrawal and political defeat. But it seems logical enough, on further examination, since the newly independent nations of the postcolonial moment needed to establish their autonomy and legitimacy with reference to the existing system of international law and diplomatic recognition, established on European terms, which emphasised the importance of territorial integrity and clearly delimited borders. The Seeb Agreement was not an agreement between two sovereign powers, understood in this European sense, and nor did any of its participants think of it as involving a parcelling out of territory that might lead, for example, to the delineation of borders between Imamate and Sultanate. But by 1954 it would have become clear both to Sultan Said and to the leaders associated with the Imamate that their political futures would depend upon their capacity to assert and demonstrate sovereignty.

Sultan Said, as we shall see, appears to have recognised that his capacity to govern effectively would depend upon his ability to control territory as well as maintain allegiances and alliances. Although he may not have characterised this process of state-building in terms of sovereignty, let alone in relation to its historical diffusion in the postcolonial period, his actions both before and after 1954 had the decisive effect of establishing the Omani nation as a sovereign state, even though it would fall to his son, Sultan Qaboos, to complete this process after 1970. At the same time, those who assumed leadership of the Imamate following the death of Imam Mohammed al-Khalili would soon find themselves making use of the rhetoric of nationalism and the associated concepts of sovereignty to advance and defend their political position, internationally, in their struggle against Sultan Said. For both parties, of course, the prospect of major oil discoveries in Oman made the issue of territorial possession, which sovereignty would underpin, an urgent and compelling economic imperative. Thus, the politics of oil intersected with the politics of nationalism and postcolonial authority. Indeed, no one in the region could fail to grasp the significance of the relationship between oil and national sovereignty after the overthrow in a U.S.-backed coup in 1953 of the Iranian Prime Minister, Mohammed Mossadeq, who had, two years earlier, asserted national sovereignty against the interests of the British Anglo Iranian Oil Company (AIOC) in nationalising Iran's oil reserves and appropriating AIOC assets. In Oman, as we have seen, questions of who would secure the right to make money from exploitable oil reserves had for some time motivated Sultan Said's policy-making. In 1952, such questions were decisively sharpened with the seizure by Saudi Arabian forces of an Omani village at the Buraimi oasis, in support of a territorial claim apparently backed by the American oil company Aramco (formed as a result of the 1933 concession granted to Standard Oil). The circumstances of the Buraimi dispute – in which the Sultan, the Imamate leadership, the Saudi, British and American governments, as well as Aramco and the Emirate of Abu Dhabi were all involved – offers an illuminating view of the balance of these various powers in the region in the moment immediately preceding the death of Imam Mohammed al-Khalili and indispensable background for an understanding of the conflict between Sultanate and Imamate that followed.

THE BURAIMI DISPUTE

The oasis of Buraimi lies almost equidistant from Abu Dhabi to the west and Sohar to the east. Dominated today by Al-Ain, the second-largest city of the Emirate of Abu Dhabi, in 1952 it was the location of nine villages, three of which are usually reported to have considered themselves Omani, while the other six, according to most historical accounts, were under the rule of the Shaikh of Abu Dhabi.[4] However, the complexities of tribal allegiance mean that these characterisations need to be examined carefully, not least because, as we have already suggested in relation to the Seeb Agreement, local understandings of political relations and structures differed from those associated with a conception of sovereignty originating from earlier European experiences, which was now the basis for the system of international law in which nations could assert their identity and define their territorial boundaries. One significant aspect of the Buraimi dispute, then, would be the tension between local politics and the international structure – negotiations between nation-states – through which resolution was sought.

In 1949, as the U.S. oil company Aramco began to expand and intensify its operations in Saudi Arabia, the government of Saudi Arabia, eager to identify and secure new reserves for exploitation, had laid claim to various territories in some of its partially undefined border regions. Buraimi lay within one of these regions. Buraimi had been the object of Saudi interest for more than 150 years. Because it is by far and away the richest source of fresh water in this northern part of south-east Arabia and a key crossroads for traffic from the Gulf coast south into the heart of Oman and west into the centre of the Arabian Desert, Buraimi had considerable strategic importance. In periods of Saudi expansion, therefore, especially at the beginning of the nineteenth century, when Wahhabi conquest was

---

[4] Uzi Rabi describes these nine villages as 'administered in part by Abu Dhabi and in part by Oman' (*Emergence of States*, p. 70). John E. Peterson also uses the term 'administered' (*Oman in the Twentieth Century*, p. 55). Donald Hawley writes that the villages 'belong', respectively, to the 'ruler of Abu Dhabi' and 'the Sultan of Muscat and Oman'; see Donald Hawley, *The Trucial States* (London: George Allen & Unwin, 1970), p. 186). Majid al-Khalili writes that at the time of the dispute the villages were 'controlled' by the Shaikh of Abu Dhabi and the Sultan of Oman. He also reverses the more familiar allocation of six to Abu Dhabi and three to Oman; see Majid al-Khalili, *Oman's Foreign Policy: Foundation and Practice* (Westport, CT: Praeger, 2009), p. 22.

at one of its early high points, Buraimi would become a key target. It
had been seized by Wahhabi forces in 1800 and became a base for subsequent campaigns against the Sultan of Oman, until they were expelled by
Ottoman forces in 1818. The area fell under Saudi control again from the
mid-1820s until the successful Egyptian campaign of 1837–1838 drove
them out again. The withdrawal of Saudi power from Buraimi was not
complete until June 1869, at the very end of the Wahhabi period, when a
force loyal to the newly installed Imam, Azzan bin Qays (see Chapter 3
for an account of Azzan's brief attempt to bring Muscat and the Imamate
together) expelled the remaining Wahhabis from the forts at the oasis.
Buraimi was thus briefly under the control of the short-lived Imamate of
Azzan bin Qays, but when this ended, political authority in the villages
of the oasis reverted to local *shaikhs*.

From the perspective of international law, then, the key questions in
the dispute, according to Husain M. Albaharna, were whether Muscat or
Abu Dhabi had established 'effective possession' of Buraimi and whether
the Saudis had 'lost title' due to the 'lack of any effective state activities' after 1869.[5] Whether such questions could actually be answered
with the clarity required by international law seems doubtful. In practice, during the period from 1869 to 1949, when the Saudi claim was
made, the whole Dhahirah area, including Buraimi, lay outside of any
central government control (it was, in local terms, administered as part
of the *dar* of the regional *shaikhs* rather than as an element in a larger
supra-regional structure of a *dawla*, or state). In practice, political loyalties were fluid.[6] A pivotal position, at least as far as the three villages
usually claimed to be Omani are concerned, seems to have been held by
the Na'im *shaikhs*, who, according to Hawley, 'acknowledged the over-
lordship of the sultan of Muscat and Oman, and their Tamimah [para-
mount *shaikh*] acted as his representative'.[7] But 'before the turn of the

---

[5] Husain M. Albaharna, *The Legal Status of the Arabian Gulf States: A Study of Their
Treaty Relations and Their International Problems* (Manchester: Manchester University
Press, 1968), pp. 237–38.

[6] For discussions of the fluidity of political loyalties and the local understanding of such
relationships see Wilkinson (1991), pp. 259–272 (which also includes discussion of the
tensions between such arrangements and conceptions of sovereignty based on territory
and property) and Rabi, *Emergence of a State*, pp. 32–42 (which specifically concerns the
period 1920–1952). See also Dale Eickelman, 'From Theocracy to Monarchy: Authority
and Legitimacy in Inner Oman, 1935–1957', *International Journal of Middle East Studies*
17.1 (1985), pp. 3–24, for a more fine-grained account of how these relations were conducted in practice.

[7] Hawley, *The Trucial States*, p. 187.

century' the Na'im had also become dependent upon Shaikh Zayed bin Khalifah of Abu Dhabi until his death in 1909, after which Shaikh Saqr bin Sultan (who was to become the Tamimah of the Na'im) renewed professions of allegiance to Muscat and continued to receive payment as his representative.[8] Wilkinson, however, adds details which complicate this situation even further, recording that the Saudis sought to take advantage of a 'vacuum of power' in the region following the death of Shaikh Zayed and had brought several tribes of the oasis under their protection in 1925. It was in the year after this that Shaikh Saqr took over the position of Tamimah of the Na'im (murdering his brother Sultan). In order to prevent the Saudi governor of Hasa, Ibn Jaluwi, from backing Sultan's sons who had taken refuge with him, Saqr granted Ibn Jaluwi the right to collect *zakat* in the Buraimi area, and the Na'im took to describing their land as Saudi territory in discussions with outsiders such as the British.[9]

The shifting allegiances of the Na'im would be a pressing issue for Sultan Said in his attempts to assert his authority in Buraimi in 1949. In February Sultan Said sent his Interior Minister, Sayyid Ahmad bin Ibrahim, to initiate negotiations with leading *shaikhs* in the Dhahirah, including Shaikh Saqr of the Na'im and Rashid bin Hamad of al-Hamasah. This initiative eventually drew together a large meeting of *shaikhs* in Muscat (with which Shaikh Saqr, however, engaged only by letter from Buraimi) out of which emerged an agreement in which the *shaikhs* offered letters professing their loyalty to Sultan Said and formed themselves into a confederation under the leadership of Shaikh Saqr, with Sultan Said making appropriately generous payments in return. However, this confederation proved fallible and fragile. When a PDO expedition sought to take advantage of the new political situation and start activities in the Buraimi area, it was shot at while passing through Wadi al-Jizzi. Interior Minister Ahmad bin Ibrahim was summoned to clarify the situation, but found himself confronted by *shaikhs* in the confederation insisting that the letters of loyalty had been obtained dishonestly. Shaikh Saqr denied that he owed any allegiance to the Sultan and demanded further direct payments from PDO to even enter into negotiations over oil exploration.

So despite this gap of eighty years in which loyalties had shifted among the local *shaikhs*, with some involvement of both Muscat and Abu Dhabi, the history of Saudi administrative control and consequent Wahhabi religious adherence among inhabitants of some Buraimi villages

---

[8] Ibid., pp. 187–188.
[9] Wilkinson, *Imamate Tradition of Oman*, pp. 279–280.

were still among the justifications offered for the assertion of a Saudi territorial claim to Buraimi in 1949, even though oil was clearly also the key motivating factor.[10] Only fifteen years earlier a Saudi proposal for the demarcation of borders had made no suggestion that Buraimi be included within the Kingdom: it was the prospect of oil, arising with increasing salience in the intervening period, that would encourage the Saudi government to revive its expansive ambitions in this area. In 1935 there had been negotiations between the British and Saudi governments (to which neither Oman nor Abu Dhabi had been party) with a view to reaching an agreement on the basis of the Saudi proposals, but nothing had come of them. The formal revival of the Saudi claim to Buraimi in 1949 gave rise to further diplomatic activity, not least because the British government also took an interest in the possibility of oil reserves and wanted to secure a share of them for British corporate interests.

The British company Petroleum Development Oman (PDO) had been formed, as we have seen, in the context of a concession agreement between Sultan Said in 1937, in order to secure access to oil in Oman, and the British government wanted to make sure that Buraimi and similar border areas did not fall into the hands of Aramco via the terms of their concession agreement with the Saudi government. However, Saudi–British talks in Dammam and London in 1951 and 1952 left matters unresolved, with the British government determined not to give ground on an issue which would seriously undermine its oil interests in the region, especially in the context of the 1951 nationalisation of AOIC in Iran and the pressure exerted by the new Egyptian Republic, from 1952 onwards, for a British withdrawal from the Suez Canal (through which at that time about two-thirds of the oil exported from the Gulf to Europe was shipped).

---

[10] Control of oil resources is usually given as the key factor underlying the importance attached to Buraimi by all parties involved in the dispute. Wilkinson dissents from this view, however, claiming that for Saudi Arabia, at least, the attempt to secure legal possession of Buraimi was not primarily about oil, but actually part of a wider campaign to secure other territories, in both present-day Oman and Yemen, on the basis of comparable claims. If Saudi Arabia could successfully claim Buraimi on the basis of tribal allegiances established by a combination of profession and tax collection, it was hoped that similar evidence would lead to successful claims elsewhere, including claims in the Omani interior. This interpretation emphasises the continuity between Saudi action over Buraimi and the subsequent Saudi support for the Imamate insurgency led by Ghalib and Talib. Indeed, Wilkinson (and others) offer as evidence for this continuity the persistence of Saudi attempts to secure the allegiance (and the conversion to Wahhabism) of Omani tribal leaders in the interior in 1950–1951. See Wilkinson, *Imamate Tradition of Oman*, pp. 291–294.

These then were the local and international dimensions of the stand-off over Buraimi at the end of August 1952, when a detachment of Saudi armed forces entered the oasis under the command of Turki ibn Ataishan and seized the village of al-Hamasah, one of the three villages in the supposedly Omani part of the oasis (or, in other words, those over which the Na'im traditionally exercised control). He came, according to Wilkinson, accompanied by '40 or so bodyguards, vehicles and a radio receiver and transmitter'[11] and, according to Kelly, with the assistance of Aramco transport.[12] He brought with him letters for all the leading *shaikhs* 'from Dank to the north of the Buraimi oasis,[13] and also one for Imam al-Khalili himself, in which he announced that he had been obliged to establish himself as a Saudi representative in Buraimi, because Saudi subjects in Oman had asked him to do so. The message invited the Imam to unite with him to throw 'foreign' influences out of Oman. He offered a substantial financial 'gift' in return for this alliance. Imam al-Khalili declined this proposal, noting that it 'astonished me because we do not know that you have subjects in Oman'.[14]

Not only did the Imam repudiate the Saudi approach, he took active steps to make common cause with Sultan Said in assembling a military force to expel Turki ibn Ataishan from Buraimi. He cooperated in a call for tribal forces to gather in support of the Sultan. One of the two leading *shaikhs* charged by the Imam with delivering his message of support to the Sultan was Talib bin Ali (who would soon emerge as a leading figure in the opposition to the Sultan's rule in the interior, as we shall shortly see). The Sultan sent the Imam camels, guns and ammunition so that he could assemble his own force, which would meet up with the troops the Sultan himself was gathering in Sohar. Eventually a force of more than eight thousand men was assembled and set out from Sohar for Buraimi. The force reached Wadi al-Jizzi and was ready to descend upon Buraimi when the Sultan was persuaded by the British government to halt the expedition. The British government had initially characterised the Saudi action as an 'armed invasion', but under pressure from the U.S. government, chose not to support Sultan Said in his military response.[15] The British Consul in Muscat communicated this advice to Sultan Said, who,

[11] Wilkinson, *Imamate Tradition of Oman*, p. 294,
[12] J. B. Kelly, *Arabia, the Gulf and the West* (London: Weidenfeld & Nicholason, 1980), p. 71.
[13] Wilkinson, *Imamate Tradition of Oman*, p. 294.
[14] al-Khalili, *Oman's Foreign Policy*, p. 22 and n. 50.
[15] *The Times*, May 27, 1954.

calculating that he had no choice but to acquiesce, nonetheless demanded that the Consul present this message to him publicly, in front of his assembled troops, so that he could read it aloud to them and make it very clear that the military mission was being abandoned against his will and better judgement. Because Sultan Said had placed the conduct of foreign affairs in the hands of the British government, he was not even party to the standstill agreement which was then drawn up between the Saudis and the British. According to this agreement, signed on October 26, 1952, the British government agreed to 'remove all restrictions and obstacles imposed by them' (such as flying low over Buraimi, stopping the supply of provisions and imposing restrictions on normal movement). It was 'understood that the Saudis are also to desist from provocative actions. In other words life is to revert to its normal course'.[16] With both sides remaining in position at Buraimi 'discussions will be resumed between the British and the Saudis'.[17] Sultan Said then withdrew to Salalah.

This was a decisive moment. Sultan Said's credibility in the eyes of the Omani *shaikhs* was undermined. He appeared indecisive and gave the impression that his freedom of action was subject to the inexplicable whims of a foreign power. He missed an opportunity to secure a broad coalition of Omanis around a common purpose and against a common antagonist. Each of these perceptions was crucial; each demonstrated a failure or inability to exercise the political authority necessary for the maintenance of a *dawla*. Wilkinson describes the standing down of the Sultan's military force as a 'calamitous stroke' which substantially determined future developments. Wilkinson's reading of this event suggests that the political divisions which Sultan Said would later have to confront, in the interior and in Dhofar, might not have arisen had Sultan Said been permitted by the British to act as he had planned over Buraimi. He might, Wilkinson writes, 'have gained great prestige and the concerted action of the Sultan and Imam could have led to accelerated cooperation in the administration of a country whose old divisions were already beginning to break down'.[18] If we were given to counterfactual historical speculation, we might go as far as to suggest that a successful coalition between the Sultan and the Imam would have so strengthened pro-Sultan sentiment among the Omani tribal leadership that, when they met, in a little more than eighteen months' time, to agree on a successor to Imam

[16] Jane Priestland, ed., *The Buraimi Dispute: Contemporary Documents, 1950–1961*, vol. 2 (Slough: Archive Editions, 1992), p. 613.

[17] Ibid.

[18] Wilkinson, *Imamate Tradition of Oman*, p. 295.

al-Khalili, their choice might have fallen on a candidate more inclined to continued and enhanced cooperation between Imam and Sultan, and the period of armed insurgencies which are the central focus of this chapter might never have ensued. Numerous other factors contributing to the outbreak of insurgencies would still have been in place, however, as we shall see. All the same, the standing down of the Buraimi force seriously damaged Sultan Said's political position and placed the future of cooperation with the Imamate in grave jeopardy. It also left the challenge posed by the Saudi incursion (or 'invasion') unanswered.

In the period that followed the standstill agreement the Saudis engaged in vigorous diplomacy seeking to win American support for their proposal for a plebiscite, which they felt confident of winning. The British argued for arbitration, and the Americans eventually agreed, and in July 1954 the British and the Saudis agreed that their dispute over Buraimi be referred to an international tribunal which would determine both the sovereignty of Buraimi and the position of the border between Abu Dhabi and Saudi Arabia. Under the terms of this agreement, the British agreed to allow the Saudi force to remain in Buraimi and to keep the Trucial Oman Levies (Omani soldiers under British command) out of the oasis. Meanwhile the Saudis continued to work to secure the support of Buraimi's inhabitants, with large sums of money distributed to prominent *shaikhs*, leading the British to believe that the Saudis were running a clandestine operation in Buraimi to retain political control. In October 1955, the British renounced the arbitration agreement and sent the Trucial Oman Levies into Buraimi to expel the Saudis by force, an action which could be seen as a vivid recognition that their advice to Sultan Said three years earlier, to refrain from such action, had been mistaken. By this time, however, the Sultan was once again seeking to extend his political authority in the Omani interior (with the strong encouragement of PDO and in anticipation of securing oil revenues for a nascent state). The expulsion of the Saudis from Buraimi thus became a decisive move on this political front.

THE STRUGGLE IN THE INTERIOR

Mohammed al-Khalili had been elected Imam in 1920. His political authority was enhanced through much of the succeeding thirty-year period by the support of two very powerful Omani *shaikhs*, Isa bin Salih of the Hirth and Sulayman bin Himyar al-Nabhani from the Jebel Akhdar. As Imam, al-Khalili was the inheritor of a long and distinctive tradition of religious and political authority in the Omani interior, an area which includes the urban settlements of the Hajar mountains and their surrounding foothills and plains, often constructed around oases, with major towns, including Nizwa, Rustaq and Hamra.[19] Exact figures are not available (there was no central collection of data until the 1970s), but we may estimate that around half of the total population of Oman lived in this interior region in the 1950s. The Imamate is a political and religious formation in which, theoretically, life is regulated as in an ideal Muslim state, and in which divisions of ethnicity and tribe are held to be immaterial and adherence to Islam, as understood in the Ibadi tradition, is the sole criterion for participation. The Imamate must be led by an Imam who is chosen, from among the community's men of learning, by a gathering of religious scholars and 'notables' (in practice, landowning *shaikhs*), known collectively as *ahl al-hall wa'l aqd*. The process of election – which, as Eickelman notes, need not be understood as a democratic process in the specific modern Western sense – followed the principle of *shura* (consultation), according to which all decisions of collective significance were to be taken according to Ibadi thought. What this meant was that an Imam would be chosen who could be expected to secure broad approval on the basis of his religious credentials and his perceived capacity to exert political authority (including by force of arms). In practice this had meant, for a long time, that only members of certain leading families were ever chosen. Imam Mohammed al-Khalili, for instance, was the grandson of Said bin Khalfan al-Khalili, the scholar and poet, who, as we saw in Chapter 3, played a key role in the restoration of the Imamate of Azzan bin Qays (1868–1871).

The de facto capital of this region was Nizwa, Oman's traditional seat of learning and culture, and it was here that the twentieth-century Imamate had its headquarters. The Imam himself lived in the fort at Nizwa, where he retained a personal militia. His authority was enforced across the region by around forty governors and a shifting cadre of tax collectors, judges and soldiers, numbering around five hundred. On a day-to-day basis, however, most of the population would have had little or no direct interaction with the Imamate government, since most economic and social activity was regulated locally by *shaikhs*, who were, typically, the principal landowners (and thus also slave owners)

---

[19] This account of the organisation of the Imamate in the 1950s is indebted to the work of Dale Eickelman, especially his article 'From Theocracy to Monarchy'. For the most extended treatment of the history and nature of the Imamate, see Wilkinson, *Imamate Tradition of Oman*.

in their town or village. Although most of the population worked the land in these urban settlements, there were also significant populations of Bedouin. Unlike the majority of the population of the interior, who were Ibadi, the Bedouin were predominantly Sunni, but most of them tended to owe whatever allegiance they offered to the Imam. Although most of the *shaikhs* in the interior owed allegiance to the Imam, it was not unusual, writes Dale Eickelman, for 'leading shaykhs to accept gifts serially or simultaneously from the Imam, the Sultan and the Saudis'.[20] This did not necessarily indicate that they had multiple or shifting allegiances, but rather that they were free to enter into a range of political and economic relations (which did mean, of course, that rival external powers would compete for their support at times of conflict and crisis, such as that which broke out in the mid-1950s).

It is clear, as we have already seen, that Sultan Said, from his accession in 1932, had consistently envisaged and even intermittently taken action to promote the unification of Oman, which would necessarily entail a significant limitation, or even the eradication of the Imamate as a political entity. All the same, relations between the Sultan and the Imamate had been managed largely in the spirit of the Seeb Agreement, with neither party making an overt challenge to the autonomy of the other. Indeed, in 1948, when it seemed that Imam al-Khalili might be about to die, some tribal *shaikhs* are said to have proposed that Sultan Said might additionally take on the title of Imam. This proposal does not appear to have secured much wider support, either among the tribal leaders in the interior or with Sultan Said himself, who is said to have been fully aware that he lacked the religious qualifications to be a serious candidate for Imam.

When the Imam did die, in May 1954, there appear to have been three divergent strands of opinion among the tribal leaders who gathered in Nizwa to elect his successor. It is clear that these discussions were not simply about the identity of the next Imam, but also concerned the political future of the Imamate as such. One group, presumably connected in some way to those who had proposed the idea that Sultan Said might become Imam in 1948, advocated the effective termination of the Imamate as a political entity and the unification of the Omani people under the leadership of Sultan Said. This group did not participate in the election of the Imam that ensued. Another group simply argued for the maintenance of the status quo, which for them meant minimal interaction with external powers. A third, and ultimately successful faction, was the group,

---

[20] Eickelman, 'From Theocracy to Monarchy'. p. 8.

including Talib bin Ali al-Hinai, his brother Ghalib and Sulayman bin Himyar, which argued that the Imamate's political future could best be sustained with support from Saudi Arabia and, by implication, resistance against any attempt by Sultan Said to advance his unification project. The success of this last group was confirmed by the election of Ghalib bin Ali as Imam.

It was believed by some that Ghalib bin Ali, a *qadi* with strong religious credentials but limited political authority, was the preferred choice of the deceased Imam al-Khalili. An alternative view is that the deceased Imam had preferred Abdallah bin Salim al-Kharusi, but that his candidacy had apparently been compromised by his being seen as too close to Sulayman bin Himyar. The election of Ghalib was thus an attempt to avoid vesting too much power in the hands of a single leader. His brother Talib provided his leadership with its initial political dimension. Sulayman bin Himyar had previously been a political opponent of Talib's, and following Talib's election he continued to keep his options open, spending time in Muscat apparently contemplating a renewed alliance with Sultan Said. But both Talib and Sulayman had already been working to build political ties with the Saudi government, apparently travelling between Oman and Riyadh via Buraimi on several occasions since 1952. Their success in securing the election of Ghalib as Imam marks the extent to which the Saudis had gained ground in the competition for tribal allegiances with Sultan Said that had begun in the late 1940s.

Sulayman bin Himyar's political position had been strengthened considerably on the death of Salih bin Isa of the Hirth in 1946, who had been his principal competitor for influence among the tribes of the interior. Since then he had started to enhance his political position still further by trying to persuade a range of external powers to back him in a bid to have himself recognised as an autonomous ruler under the title of King of the Jebel Akhdar. He variously approached Sultan Said, with a view to securing agreement on a partition of territory between them, representatives of the British and American governments and, following the death of Imam al-Khalili, rulers elsewhere in the Gulf. Eventually, however, he came to see that his best interests might be served if he threw in his lot with his erstwhile opponent, Talib bin Ali, now that Talib's brother had been elected Imam and since he and Talib were both capable of securing Saudi backing. It is worth noting here, then, that the key political alliance at the heart of the Imamate rebellion and insurgency, between Talib bin Ali and Sulayman bin Himyar, was of very recent formation and that the objectives of the rebellion were confused and even, perhaps, contradictory.

Among the potentially very contradictory objectives that seem to have motivated the leaders of the Imamate rebellion, we may include Sulayman's ambitions for independence, a struggle *over* the leadership of the Imamate as well as *for* the preservation of the Imamate against the incursions of Sultan Said and, finally, the possibility of the incorporation of the Omani interior into an expanding Saudi state. It is perhaps unsurprising, then, that a rebellion launched on such a self-contradictory basis would lead to the decisive end of the twentieth-century Imamate. That it happened at all, and that it commanded both the local popular support and the international profile that it did, is evidence, perhaps, of just how uncertain and difficult Sultan Said's tentative project of state formation and unification was at this time.

The election of his brother Ghalib as Imam allowed Talib bin Ali to intensify efforts he had already been making to gain recognition for the Imamate as a state, such as issuing passports and seeking admission to the Arab League.[21] As we have seen, the Seeb Agreement was not an agreement between sovereign powers or states in the modern European sense. While the Sultanate had to a very significant degree been integrated into the modern system of states and international law, the political authority of the Imamate had not previously been dependent upon this system. As we shall see, a contradiction was soon to emerge right at the heart of the new Imamate project. The political and religious legitimacy of the Imamate and its place in the popular imagination depended upon ideas and practices that were barely compatible with the sovereign state system and, crucially, quite incompatible with the Arab nationalist cause with which the leaders of the Imamate were increasingly to associate themselves. In the process of gathering political support for preserving the Imamate by turning it into a modern nation-state, the leaders of the Imamate movement found themselves caught between two incompatible regimes of legitimation. In noting this contradiction we might also pause to ask whether there might actually have been some underlying consistency at work here, too. What potential might there have been for a synthesis of local ideas about collective social organisation, Ibadi austerity and *shura*-based decision-making, on the one hand, with the anti-monarchical socialism articulated by nationalists such as Nasser? In other words, was there a base in the popular imagination which might

---

[21] The Imamate had not traditionally issued passports, which could be acquired at Muscat by anyone who needed to travel abroad from within the Imamate. Efforts to secure Arab League recognition had begun even during Imam al-Khalili's lifetime. See Wilkinson, *Imamate Tradition of Oman*, p. 310.

sustain a political movement? This question will arise again, in the third section of this chapter, when we come to explore the social and economic circumstances of the war in Dhofar.

In mid-1954 both the leaders of the Imamate on one side and Sultan Said on the other were preparing to make decisive moves in the new situation created by the death of Imam al-Khalili. On Sultan Said's side, the first move was to authorise a PDO expedition to prospect for oil in Fahud. Fahud had been surveyed from the air in 1948 and the chief geologist of the Iraq Petroleum Company had noted it as an exceptionally promising site. This assessment eventually proved correct, and today the Fahud field is the largest in Oman, holding reserves of more than 6 billion barrels of oil.[22] But until 1954 geologists had not visited it on the ground. To reach Fahud meant travelling through territory generally considered to be part of the Imamate, and Sultan Said had strongly opposed PDO requests to send an expedition there. Earlier in the year PDO had established a coastal base at Duqm, an act which aroused opposition from within the Imamate, including an order from Sulayman bin Himyar that local villages raise the white Imamate flag and a formal complaint from Imam al-Khalili to the Sultan. PDO had also contemplated the idea of making a 'wild dash' to Fahud in March 1954, but refrained from doing so.[23] Fahud lay within the territory of the Duru tribe, which had not been party to the Seeb Agreement and whose status in relation to the Imam and the Sultan was uncertain. One might perhaps summarise a complex and shifting situation by saying that while the Imam had held some influence here, the Sultan enjoyed very little. The knowledge that PDO entertained expectations of significant oil discoveries in this region can only have intensified political competition over this territory: tribes already ill-disposed towards Muscat would certainly have wished to secure economic benefits for themselves and saw continued independence from the Sultan as crucial in this respect. Indeed, many of their leaders almost certainly took the view that the Sultan had no right to grant PDO any rights to prospect in the interior, or even to enter their territory. But dissension among the Duru had recently created a situation in which the Sultan thought he might be able to persuade some of the *shaikhs* from the region to pledge their allegiance to him, in return for promises that he would provide them with military assistance if they were attacked by

---

[22] Cees Corsten, Said Mahrooqi, and Peter Engbers, 'Good Vibrations in Fahud', *Leading Edge* 24.8 (August 2005), pp. 827–830.

[23] See Wilkinson, *Imamate Tradition of Oman*, p. 298.

Imamate forces. In August 1954 an agreement on this basis was reached, after negotiations between PDO and the Duru, which was facilitated in Muscat by the Sultan's Interior Minister, Ahmad bin Ibrahim, and which also involved cash payments by PDO to the paramount *shaikh* of the Duru. This prepared the way, politically, for PDO to make its move into Fahud, in spite of the fact that the company had secured no agreement from either the Imam or other tribal leaders that it could do so.

Meanwhile, however, the new Imamate leadership was also seeking to reaffirm its authority. In addition to the external diplomacy which aimed at recognition by the Arab League (and would eventually lead to the 'Oman Question' being tabled at the United Nations), they also started to take action on the ground, especially in the contested area of the Dhahirah, south of Buraimi. In September 1954 Imamate forces made a move to seize Ibri, about a hundred miles from Buraimi, which was the town at the centre of the area controlled by the Duru *shaikhs* with whom the Sultan had just concluded an agreement. Their aim was to force the Duru to pledge allegiance to the Imam. With Imamate forces on the outskirts of Ibri, the leading *shaikhs* fled to Sharjah. PDO then assembled its expedition and, accompanied by a detachment of troops from the Muscat and Oman Field Force, left the PDO base at Duqm for Fahud. This military unit had been assembled a year earlier, at the request of PDO's parent company, the Iraq Petroleum Company (and at its expense).[24] It comprised local men, mainly recruited from the Batinah, under the command of British officers. By the end of October, as geologists conducted the first on-the-ground survey of possible oil reserves, this military force had succeeded in restoring pro-Sultan tribal leadership in Ibri (the *shaikhs* who had fled at the Imamate advance had been brought back from Sharjah and had accompanied the expedition) and was gradually securing the loyalty of surrounding villages for the Sultan.

At the end of 1954 we can observe, with retrospect, several processes under way: the extension of the Sultan's influence to parts of the interior in which he had not previously held sway; the persistence of Imamate ambition directly to contest control of the interior in the name of a potential independent state; and initial steps, on the Sultan's part, towards the establishment of a standing army, conventionally one of the key attributes of a modern state. The balance of power in the interior seemed to be shifting

---

[24] The agreement between the Iraq Petroleum Company and the Sultan involved an initial payment to the Sultan of £230,000 and subsequent annual payments of £150,000 to equip and maintain the MOFF. See John E. Peterson, *Oman's Insurgencies: The Sultanate's Struggle for Supremacy* (London: Saqi Books, 2007), p. 58.

quite decisively in the Sultan's favour. The Sultan, however, was reluctant to press his advantage, despite encouragement from the British, now more clearly than ever in favour of Omani unification under the Sultan, that he seize the opportunity to press home his advantage by moving on to take control of both Adam and Dank. For nearly a year neither side attempted decisive action. Talib bin Ali continued to seek external political support for an independent Imamate. This was the context in which, in October 1955, the British government unilaterally renounced the arbitration agreement on Buraimi and sent Trucial Oman Levies under the command of British officers in to force the withdrawal of Saudi forces from the oasis.

The capture of Buraimi prepared the way for decisive action against the Imamate as a means, not simply of extending the Sultan's rule over a unified Oman but, perhaps just as important, of defending Oman against any further Saudi incursions or expansionist moves. A plan for a military operation to take Nizwa – symbolic capital of the Imamate and Oman's foremost seat of religious learning – had been under discussion between the Sultan and the British from early 1955, and following the consolidation of the successful capture of Buraimi, it was put into effect in December. Forces from the Muscat and Oman Field Force (MOFF) and the Trucial Oman Scouts combined with Royal Air Force reconnaissance flights to capture, seemingly with almost no resistance, Adam and Firq on December 14. Having been unable to raise any force to oppose the Sultan's action, Ghalib bin Ali fled Nizwa that night and was reported to have publicly stepped down as Imam. The following day the Sultan's forces entered Nizwa, meeting no resistance at all. Ghalib bin Ali retreated to his family home at Bilad Sait, and Sulayman bin Himyar was detained in Nizwa before being permitted to return to his own home in Tanuf. The only significant resistance to the Sultan's operation was in Rustaq, where Talib bin Ali and his followers held out for four days, before surrendering on December 18 to a tribal force brought in from the Batinah. Talib bin Ali managed to evade efforts to prevent him from leaving Oman and found his way to Dammam in Saudi Arabia, where he resumed his political activities in support of an independent Imamate. Sultan Said appointed his own *wali* in Nizwa to replace the Imam's. The Sultan then carried out a rapid tour of the interior, receiving pledges of allegiance from key tribal *shaikhs* in Nizwa, Ibri, Buraimi (where he also met Shaikh Shakhbut of Abu Dhabi) and other key locations.[25] After visiting Muscat, he then withdrew once again to Salalah.

[25] In fact, he set off for this tour some days before news of the fall of Nizwa became known. Jan (then James) Morris wrote an account of travelling with Sultan Said on this expedition, published as *Sultan in Oman* (London: Faber & Faber, 1957).

In this moment of apparent success for his long-term policy of securing a unified Oman, however, Sultan Said did not move to impose the kind of direct and unmediated political authority generally considered consistent with the establishment of a modern nation-state. Although he clearly believed and repeatedly claimed at this time that the Imamate no longer existed, he took no significant steps to replace the structures, or even in many cases the people, through which its leaders had exercised their power. Instead he appears to have preferred to exercise political control through the patronage of key clients among the tribal leadership, often precisely those who had been key players in the Imamate's own administrative structure. Some commentators have attributed this apparent failure to assert himself politically to his personal weakness as a leader.[26] His choice might alternatively be explained by the only very limited extent to which so-called modern conceptions of sovereignty had taken hold in the Omani political consciousness.[27] Neither Sultan Said nor, it seems, many of the people he ruled saw sovereignty in such terms, even though, as we have seen, several factors (including oil, Saudi incursions, postcolonial nationalism) were creating conditions in which it might have seemed judicious to adapt to such norms. We might additionally speculate that Sultan Said's reluctance to adapt his mode of government according to modern conceptions of the nation-state might

---

[26] See, e.g., Wilkinson, *Imamate Tradition of Oman*, pp. 316–317, where the Sultan, in this moment, is described as 'autocratic, unforgiving, lazy and mean'. For some time this sort of characterisation of Sultan Said was fairly ubiquitous in historical scholarship on Oman, sometimes, it seems, reflecting the frustrations of British officials with actions that they found difficult to understand or that did not conform to their own, culturally informed conceptions of how sovereign rulers should behave. Today it is more common for historians to seek explanations beyond personal foibles and to detect more continuity between Sultan Said's reign and that of Sultan Qaboos, whereas previously a narrative of 'renaissance' succeeding 'dark ages' had tended to prevail.

[27] We use the term 'modern' here with qualifications, in recognition that the idea of a process of progressive development from 'traditional' forms of political association and government to 'modern' ones is a myth, largely manufactured in support of colonialism, although often sustained by postcolonial nationalist regimes. For significant critiques of this mythology see Dipesh Chakrabarty, *Provincializing Europe: Postcolonial Thought and Historical Difference* (Princeton, NJ: Princeton University Press, 2000); Partha Chatterjee, *The Nation and Its Fragments: Colonial and Postcolonial Histories* (Princeton, NJ: Princeton University Press, 1993); and Ranajit Guha, *Dominance Without Hegemony: History and Power in Colonial India* (Cambridge, MA: Harvard University Press, 1998). Chatterjee's reflections on nationalism may be particularly helpful for thinking about the character of the Imamate rebellion: he argues that nationalism is not merely a modern political form but also, in colonial contexts, a way of defending what he calls 'spiritual' conceptions of belonging against the encroachments of an alien power.

also have been motivated by a desire not to emulate the rhetoric of the nationalism promoted in Cairo, to which his opponents in the Imamate leadership had begun to express their commitment. He may also have considered caution preferable to any risky overreaching, bearing in mind that it was only three years earlier that his supposed allies, the British, had so damagingly prevented him from asserting himself over Buraimi. Sultan Said was rightly wary of placing too much trust even in his close British advisers. Dale Eickelman summarises this aspect of the situation: 'In the 1950s and 1960s the Sultan often repeated to his foreign advisers this observation: "If Oman's little rulers are all right, then so is Oman." ... Reliance on tribal shaykhs provided an inexpensive means of governing in the interior, but at the cost of maintaining an administrative system with neither the capacity nor the resources to undertake development projects of any sort or to access local needs in any significant way.'[28] Probably the most significant changes to life in the interior were those occasioned by the intensification of PDO activities at Fahud, through the employment of local people (primarily from the Duru) and the development of some infrastructure, such as a new access road to Fahud, to support this expanding operation. We may also note, once again, that Sultan's Said's approach to government continued to be very strongly shaped by a reluctance to incur further debt: expanding government functions to include either economic stimulus or social provision of any kind was therefore out of the question, from his perspective, whether or not he even considered it desirable.

In setting his face against any project of nation-building (development of new administrative structures along with material infrastructure) and relying instead on maintaining consensus among the key *shaikhs*, however, Sultan Said was also ignoring two further constituencies that would come to exert increasing influence in the Omani political sphere. The first of these comprised ordinary Omanis, who did not normally concern themselves very much with questions of who controlled and shaped the *dawla* but who would increasingly come to look beyond their tribal leadership for economic and social benefits, particularly now that they had seen the Sultan assert himself as their ruler. The second constituency involved external powers, both regional and international, some of which, at least, would come to offer alternatives to either local leaders or the Sultan as sources of economic and social improvement for ordinary Omanis, and particularly for Dhofaris in the 1960s. While it is

[28] Eickelman, 'From Theocracy to Monarchy', p. 17.

unclear how much the thoughts and aspirations of ordinary Omanis were caught up in the nationalism to which Imamate leaders would increasingly adhere in the middle to late 1950s, it is very clear that economic and social disadvantage would be a major factor in the insurgency against the Sultan that would start to take shape in the 1960s. It is probably fair to say that local support for the Imamate leadership derived from a combination of cultural and political factors. These would have included an understandable and socially conservative resistance to anything that might disrupt familiar patterns of everyday life: the Imamate leadership certainly took advantage of justifiable anxieties that the Sultan, if allowed to do so, would bring unwanted and unnecessary innovations, along with his unwelcome foreign supporters (the British). Under such circumstances the Sultan's reluctance to engage in any kind of political innovation is understandable, even if, in Dhofar in the 1960s, this same reluctance can be shown to have had disastrous consequences.

While Sultan Said sought to do little to alter the situation, his leading opponents continued to develop their own plans for an independent Imamate of Oman. An ambassador of the self-proclaimed independent Imamate had already been appointed to the Arab League. Talib bin Ali had set up an Imamate office in Cairo. As a result of its representations, the Arab League agreed in July 1956 to send an investigative committee to Oman, but Sultan Said denied them entry to the country. Talib, back in Dammam, started to assemble and train the Oman Liberation Army (OLA), which he had recruited largely from the growing diaspora of Omanis who had been forced by poverty at home to seek work elsewhere in the Gulf (where oil revenues were transforming local economies). His plan was to return to Oman to rally Imamate supporters in an attempt to reverse the Sultan's takeover of the interior. Meanwhile, the Cairo office of the Imamate maintained contact with the former Imam Ghalib, presumably to share information on how the external diplomatic environment might combine with conditions on the ground in Oman in such a way as to provide propitious circumstances for a further rebellion. In the final months of 1956, Britain's military intervention in Egypt over Nasser's nationalisation of the Suez Canal substantially increased the intensity of international hostility to continued British attachment to colonialist policy, especially in the Arab world. The political case presented by the Imamate leaders, in Cairo and elsewhere, depended upon their presentation of the Sultan's capture of the interior and the denial of Imamate autonomy as indicating his connivance in continued British colonial domination, and even expansion. The British action over Suez

gave such claims considerable credibility, with the British action in support of the Sultan over Buraimi, just a year earlier, conforming readily
to a narrative in which Britain sought to strengthen rather than withdraw from colonial possessions and the political relationships which
had helped sustain them in the past. The fact that Sultan Said publicly
expressed his support for the British action over Suez would not have
helped anyone seeking to present a convincing alternative account of the
situation.

Although there were sporadic incidents in the interior during 1956
which required the intervention or mediation of the Sultan's appointees,
the first more substantial sign that the Sultan's rule might be challenged
afresh was apparent in the Sharqiyah, where Ibrahim bin Isa, who was
the brother of the exiled pro-Imamate leader Salih bin Isa (by this time
moving between Egypt and Saudi Arabia) and the uncle of Ahmad bin
Mohammed, the current Tamimah of the Hirth and the new Wali of
Nizwa, led his followers in an attempt to enforce his claim to leadership
of the Hirth. It appears that this local action may have been planned in
concert with Talib bin Ali's intended return to Oman via the Batinah
coast. Ibrahim bin Isa's forces incorporated some men who had received
OLA training in Dammam, and another ally, Mohammed bin Abdallah
al-Salimi (the historian of the *nahda* and son of Abdallah al-Salimi), who
had been in exile with Salih bin Isa, soon joined them. In this limited
mobilisation it is again difficult to disentangle intra-tribal struggles for
supremacy (in this case for the position of Tamimah of the Hirth) from
the broader struggle for the Imamate. In such cases it seems that armed
followers can best be mobilised into at least temporary alliances when
there is a locally comprehensible and almost personal contest through
which the pursuit of broader objectives can be channelled. Whatever
the precise motivations of the parties to the Sharqiyah action, most analysts of the Imamate rebellion suggest that Ibrahim bin Isa's actions were
indeed designed to coincide with Talib bin Ali's arrival, but that Talib's
return to Oman was delayed because his boat had initially run ashore on
a sandbar when leaving Ras Tanurah.[29] The absence of the support anticipated from Talib left Ibrahim bin Isa unable to secure a decisive advantage, so he settled for negotiations with the Sultan's brother Sayyid Tariq.
He then travelled to Muscat, where he surrendered himself to Sultan
Said, in the hope that his claims to leadership over the Hirth would at
least be heard. He was disarmed and imprisoned in Jalili, to be released

---

[29] See, e.g., Peterson, *Oman's Insurgencies*, p. 80.

only under the terms of the general amnesty announced on the accession of Sultan Qaboos in 1970. At this point (June 14, 1957) Talib finally did arrive back in Oman, landing at Khor Diyan near Suwayq, from where he and his OLA force, gathering additional troops to their camp, made their way into the interior to join Ghalib bin Ali. The former Imam then started dispatching messages to other local *shaikhs*, once again signing himself as Imam and requesting that they back further action in support of the Imamate. Talib's forces harassed the communication lines of the Oman Regiment (as the MOFF was now called), inflicting casualties and forcing its withdrawal from the area. The news of this reversal persuaded the Sultan's *wali* in Nizwa to flee the town, and the remaining Oman Regiment garrison in Nizwa then surrendered to Imamate forces. By this time Talib had also taken the fort at Bahla. As the Oman Regiment retreated, Sulayman bin Himyar left Muscat to rejoin his erstwhile allies in the interior. On July 16, 1957, Sultan Said made a formal appeal for British military assistance.

British action initially came in two phases. The first involved RAF Venom aircraft, brought into Sharjah from their regular base at Aden, to launch rocket attacks on forts held by Imamate forces: Nizwa, Izki, Birqat al Mawz, Firq, Tanuf and Bahla. The second, beginning in early August, involved the introduction of ground troops, with two forces assembled to approach Nizwa from opposite directions: one from Fahud and one from Muscat. With continued air support this ground operation succeeded in capturing Nizwa by August 12. The last town held by the Imamate forces – Birqat al Mawz – surrendered the following day, and the Imamate leaders, accompanied by perhaps as many as a thousand men, withdrew into the Jebel Akhdar. Tribal forces loyal to the Sultan spent the last week of August trying to capture them in the villages of Sayq and Shrayjah, but without success. As the British wound down their ground operation, the Sultan ordered the demolition of all the forts associated with Sulayman bin Himyar, including Tanuf, which was razed and remains a ruin today. By September 1957 most of the interior had been recovered for the Sultan, but the continued presence of the Imamate leaders on the Jebel Akhdar remained a real threat to the political stability the Sultan had hoped to restore. It would be another eighteen months before they would be dislodged.

The Jebel Akhdar (Green Mountain) is a high massif in the Hajar mountains. Its highest point, Jebel Shams, is, at about 3,000 metres, the highest point on the Arabian Peninsula. In its upper reaches the cool climate supports the cultivation of fruit (including pomegranates, peaches

FIGURE 5. Nizwa after its capture by Sultan Said in 1957.
Source: Central Press/Getty Images

and apricots) and the rearing of livestock, mainly goats, with extensive use made of *aflaj* (irrigation channels) and terrace agriculture. Its people live in small villages scattered through the area, much of which is remote and inaccessible from the plain below, with steep wadis cutting into the mountainside. The Jebel Akhdar therefore provided a sanctuary in which the Imamate forces could receive hospitality and support from a self-sufficient local community and from which they could also sustain a campaign of sabotage and disruption, attacking PDO operations and local leaders thought to be loyal to the Sultan. As well as enjoying support from the local community, Talib and his followers could also count on a continued supply of weapons smuggled in from Saudi Arabia. Talib was also able to maintain the loyalty of many local leaders with financial incentives, presenting himself and the Imamate generally in a more favourable light than Sultan Said, who was then regarded by most of the people of the Jebel Akhdar as a remote figure from whom they received little or no material benefit.

The practical obstacles to a military assault on the Jebel Akhdar were compounded by the external political situation. International opinion was increasingly hostile, post-Suez, to any action on the part of the British that might look like an attempt to assert new colonial powers. The withdrawal of British ground troops from the area in September 1957 was clearly motivated, at least in part, by the need to avoid a prolonged military presence that could be construed abroad as a form of occupation. In October 1957 the British government agreed that greater coordination among the various British-led Omani military units was required and that, while the political climate prohibited substantial bombing of the Jebel Akhdar, a blockade, supported by air power, would be implemented. In practice, however, this decision also seemed to permit fairly extensive shelling of suspected Imamate positions on the Jebel Akhdar and the destruction of agricultural infrastructure, clearly designed to intimidate the local population in the hope that they might abandon their support for the Imamate forces. It may have had the opposite effect.

During 1958, Sultan Said reached an agreement with the British government on the establishment of his own permanent armed forces, bringing together the various units, most of them temporary, which had been mobilised in recent years. This reinforcement of his position in Oman appears to have been facilitated partly by the income derived from the sale of Gwadar to the government of Pakistan for the sum of £3 million, after months of intensive negotiations mediated by the British government.[30] The Sultan's Armed Forces (SAF) were established as part of an agreement between the two governments, signed in London in July 1958, which also provided for British assistance with a civil development programme (involving roads, agriculture, health and education). The exchange of letters in which the agreement was made public also extended 'present arrangements regarding civil aviation and the use by the Royal Airforce of the airfields at Salalah and Masirah', which had been the subject of earlier agreements in 1934 and 1947.[31] The SAF

---

[30] See John E. Peterson, 'Britain and "The Oman War": An Arabian Entanglement', *Asian Affairs* 7.3 (1976), p. 291. Pakistan had been seeking the return of Gwadar since gaining independence in 1947, and it seems that the British government's sudden interest in facilitating this sale may well have arisen from the expediency of providing Sultan Said with additional resources so that the campaign in the interior would no longer make such a substantial demand on the British budget.

[31] See Peterson, *Oman's Insurgencies*, p. 103, and Fred Halliday, *Arabia Without Sultans* (Harmondsworth: Penguin, 1974), p. 302, n. 27.

would be under the command of a British officer, one of twenty-four who were to be seconded to it.

Plans had been drawn up for a large-scale operation (Operation Dermot) involving substantial British forces, beyond even those currently stationed in the Gulf and Kenya. However, a combination of practical and political considerations led to its being abandoned. In the Gulf itself, the nationalist military coup led by Abd al-Karim Qasim in Iraq in July 1958 had weakened the British political position and meant that British forces stationed in Kuwait could not easily be diverted to Oman. More generally, in the aftermath of Suez, public opinion in the UK and the Arab world would be hostile to such an operation. A lower-key solution was called for, much to Sultan Said's disappointment. He did not believe that a political approach, involving economic development and the enhancement of his government's social and administrative provision, was an appropriate response to a tribal rebellion. It was at this point that both the British and the Imamate leaders took separate initiatives in which they started to explore the possibility of a negotiated settlement. For most of November 1958 air operations over the Jebel Akhdar were suspended as preliminary negotiations got under way. The Imamate leaders appear to have sought prior agreement that negotiations would seek to restore some version of the Seeb Agreement. In their engagement with the Arab League and the United Nations, they had made the Seeb Agreement the basis for their claim for an independent state, representing it as a treaty between two autonomous states. Since the Sultan had already in effect repudiated the Seeb Agreement by asserting his authority in the interior since 1954 and, did not, in any case, regard it as a treaty between states, this precondition was most unlikely to be acceptable. Indeed, Peterson suggests that it may have been 'designed deliberately to break off negotiations'.[32] This is not entirely consistent with the earlier indications that Talib and Ghalib had offered a deal in which they would accept the authority of the Sultan in return for being allowed to live in peace on the Jebel Akhdar. On the one hand, it seems unlikely that Talib and Ghalib (or, for that matter, Sulayman bin Himyar) would have imagined they could achieve much more than a debilitating stalemate with the Sultan's forces, preventing the full assertion of his power without restoring their own. On the other, it seems entirely plausible that they believed they could sustain their current resistance more or less indefinitely, since the

[32] Peterson, *Oman's Insurgencies*, p. 110.

FIGURE 6. Imam Ghalib and Sulayman bin Himyar with President Nasser in 1959.
Source: Picture from History/Bridgeman Images

Sultan and the British seemed unable to act decisively to expel them from the Jebel Akhdar.

During the planning and preparation for Operation Dermot (which had been abandoned in early October 1959) it appears that some consideration had been given to the inclusion of the British Special Air Service (SAS) regiment, which was, at that time, in the final stages of a counter-insurgency operation in Malaya.[33] Once Operation Dermot had been abandoned, the idea of using the SAS alone, rather than as part of a larger operation, seems to have emerged. The first detachment arrived in Oman in December 1959 and carried out reconnaissance around the base of the Jebel Akhdar, concluding that a second squadron would be needed for a successful operation. This request was approved by the British government, and a second squadron arrived in Oman on January 12, 1959. In the event, after much careful planning of an operation to take the Jebel Akhdar, the final phase of the rebellion was something of an anti-climax

---

[33] David Smiley recalls that the deployment of at least one squadron of the SAS to Oman on its return from Malaya was discussed with him at the War Office in August 1958. See David Smiley with Peter Kemp, *Arabian Assignment* (London: Leo Cooper 1975), p. 67.

FIGURE 7. The ruins of Sulayman bin Himyar's house at Birkat al Mowz.
Source: Middle East Centre Archive, St Antony's College, Oxford (Charles Butt Oman 2584)

(despite the wealth of memoir material by British participants celebrating it as a great military success). The SAS met some limited resistance from the couple of hundred Imamate forces on the mountain, but more frequently confronted local non-combatant villagers. The leaders of the Imamate forces managed to slip away, undetected. Smiley's account of the operation, while celebrating the success of both the SAF and the SAS in taking the Jebel Akhdar, in effect acknowledges that a major objective of the operation was not achieved: he recalls reminding the SAS commander that 'from our point of view – that is, from the Sultan's – the capture of Talib, Ghalib, and Suleiman is very nearly as important as the capture of Beercan [the operation's code word for the top of the Jebel].'[34] Some prisoners were taken, and large quantities of documents (including details of secret Imamate sympathisers), arms and ammunition were found in the caves where the Imamate forces had sheltered. Under the supervision of Sayyid Tariq, people displaced by the conflict returned to their home villages.

[34] Ibid., p. 78.

Sultan Said remained in Salalah, and although the Jebel Akhdar was now effectively back under his control, sporadic acts of sabotage took place on roads and in Muscat. These were directed, to some degree, by the Imamate leadership, now gathered again in Saudi Arabia and shifting their focus from the defence of the Imamate as such to a more general campaign, increasingly articulated as an anti-colonial struggle, for which they therefore sought to win support from the new Arab republics, such as Iraq and Egypt. This political reorientation would achieve genuine resonance among an Omani diaspora, particularly in the Gulf, where men unable to secure a livelihood in Oman had sought work in the fast-growing oil-based economies of the region and among whom a new political consciousness, combining labour solidarity and Arab nationalism, was taking shape. Unlike the Imamate, which, rather than offer an alternative to the status quo, sought to mobilise its supporters in defence of old ways of life, the emergent political organisation of Omani opposition to Sultan Said had the advantage of addressing contemporary conditions with a promise of an alternative mode of 'modernisation' to that offered by the British and the oil companies. Sultan Said's resistance to even the kind of economic and political 'modernisation' recommended by the British as a way to combat the Imamate rebellion would make him particularly vulnerable to this new mode of opposition to his rule. The political struggle between the Sultan and this new opposition is the subject of the next chapter.

5

Dhofar

The subsequent phase of political opposition to the rule of Sultan Said played out primarily in the southern region of Dhofar. It was not, however, merely a local problem. Like the struggle in the interior, it had international dimensions and, especially after 1967, as we shall see, quite serious implications for both sides in the Cold War. Within Oman, too, the armed uprising against the Sultan in Dhofar extended, primarily through clandestine networks, to Muscat and other key locations in the north of the country. But since this phase of political conflict originated in Dhofar and was shaped by the particular social and economic characteristics of the region, we begin this chapter by describing the region and its people and the circumstances from which armed rebellion emerged in the 1960s.[1]

[1] The most thorough account of the diversity of the people and cultures of Dhofar is John E. Peterson, 'Oman's Diverse Society: Southern Oman', *Middle East Journal* 58.2 (2004), pp. 254–269. In addition to sources already cited in the preceding chapter (Peterson, *Oman's Insurgencies*; Halliday, *Arabia Without Sultans*), significant aspects of the Dhofar conflict are discussed in David Lynn Price, *Oman: Insurgency and Development* (London: Institute for the Study of Conflict, 1975); J. B. Kelly, 'Hadramaut, Oman, Dhufar: The Experience of Revolution', *Middle East Studies* 12.2 (1976), pp. 213–230, later adapted to form part of ch. 3: 'Tribal Rebellion, Marxist Revolution', in *Arabia, the Gulf and the West* (New York: Basic Books, 1980), pp. 104–163; Fawwaz Trabulsi, 'The Liberation of Dhuffar', *Pakistan Forum* 3.2 (1972), pp. 8–13; John E. Peterson, 'Guerrilla Warfare and Ideological Confrontation in the Arabian Peninsula: The Rebellion in Dhufar', *World Affairs* 139.4 (1977), pp. 278–295; John Newsinger, *British Counterinsurgency: From Palestine to Northern Ireland* (Houndmills: Palgrave, 2002), ch. 6: 'The Unknown Wars: Oman and Dhofar', pp. 132–151; Geraint Hughes, 'A "Model Campaign" Reappraised: The Counter-Insurgency War in Dhofar, Oman, 1965–1975', *Journal of Strategic Studies* 32.2 (2009), pp. 271–305; Clive Jones, 'Military Intelligence, Tribes, and Britain's War in Dhofar, 1970–1976', *Middle East Journal* 65.4 (2011), pp. 557–574; Marc DeVore, 'The United Kingdom's Last Hot War of the Cold

RULING DHOFAR

Dhofar is the southernmost region of Oman, with Yemen at its western border, and is effectively cut off from the rest of Oman by a desert region, the Jiddat al-Harisis karst, inhabited mainly by Bedouin.[2] Most travel between Dhofar and the rest of Oman, until the opening of passenger air travel between Muscat and Salalah (the regional capital), was by sea. The main urban settlements in Dhofar are on the coastal plain. In addition to Salalah, Taqa and Mirbat are significant towns east of the capital, while Rakhyut, Dalkut and Mugsayl lie to the west, along the coast towards Yemen. The coastal plain is surrounded by three ranges of mountains, beyond which the Nejd eventually gives way to the sand desert of the Rub al-Khali (the Empty Quarter). Dhofar is the only part of the Arabian Peninsula to experience the Indian Ocean monsoon, which produces the *khareef* season between June and September, during which mist hangs over the mountains, rain falls and a startling profusion of green vegetation transforms the landscape.

The physical distinctiveness of the region is compounded by strong cultural differences between Dhofar and the rest of Oman, of which perhaps the most striking is language: a number of non-Arabic languages are spoken by the inhabitants of Dhofar. The Arab population of the region is almost exclusively Sunni, with no significant presence of the Ibadism associated with the north of the country. Many are members of the various branches of al-Kathir, inhabiting Salalah itself, stretches of the coastal plain, as well as areas of the Nejd. The Dhofari *jebel* is home to a number of non-Arab groups, whose members are usually referred to, collectively, as *jabbalis* (mountain people). The largest such group comprises the Qara, who speak their own South Arabian language and whose traditional livelihood has been the raising of cattle and goats. Other groups include the Shahra, conventionally regarded as the earliest inhabitants of the mountains, and the Mahra, a northern branch of a larger linguistic group spread across Dhofar and, in larger numbers, Yemen. Both speak their own South Arabian languages (there are in fact two, mutually intelligible Mahra languages). The Mahra leadership considered themselves

War: Oman, 1963–1975', *Cold War History* 11.3 (2011), pp. 441–471; and Abdel Razzaq Takriti, *Monsoon Revolution: Republicans, Sultans and Empires in Oman, 1965–1976* (Oxford: Oxford University Press, 2013). Memoirs of serving British officers also offer useful perspectives on some aspects of the situation. See, in particular, Tony Jeapes, *SAS Secret War: Operation Storm in the Middle East* (London: Greenhill Books, 2005).

[2] For details of the nomadic inhabitants of the Jiddat al-Harisis, see Dawn Chatty, *Mobile Pastoralists: Development Planning and Social Change in Oman* (New York: Columbia University Press, 1996).

sufficiently autonomous from any of the relevant governments (in Yemen, Oman or Saudi Arabia) to issue their own passports in the 1960s, but the larger group accepted incorporation into the People's Republic of South Yemen on its establishment in 1967. Other socially distinct groups include people of African descent, many of whose ancestors came to the region (and to Salalah in particular) as slaves and who were generally known in Arabic as *khuddam*, and the Bahhara, a community traditionally associated with fishing (and whose name identifies them with the sea), whose origins are uncertain. The Hawashim, an Arab group also known as *sada*, descendants of the Prophet, constitute a religious elite who trace their origins to the Hadramaut. There are strong hierarchies in place both between and within these various groups: those considered *da'if* (weak) conventionally do not carry arms; some groups prohibit intermarriage with members of groups they consider to be of inferior social status. These caste-like distinctions have diminishing significance today. Their abolition was part of the political programme of the radicalised Dhofari political movements of the late 1960s, and the social and economic development instituted in Dhofar from the 1970s has included government interventions to minimise social tensions and conflicts arising from tribal differences and hierarchies.

Although Dhofar is now very much a constituent of contemporary Oman, its inclusion within even an imagined sense of an Omani nation dates only from the late nineteenth century. It was annexed in 1829 by Sultan Said bin Sultan after Qara forces had overthrown a local leader, Sayyid Mohammed bin Aqil, who had taken control of Salalah. Mohammed bin Aqil is represented in some British and American historical accounts as a pirate responsible for multiple criminal acts, including the massacre of the entire crew of an American ship. This sort of characterisation seems to be typical of early British (and some American) accounts of this period, in which merchants and political leaders whose actions brought them into conflict with the norms of British commercial practice are routinely described as pirates. Sometimes, such designations tended to overlap with allegations that such figures were in league with colonial rivals, such as, in Mohammed bin Aqil's case, the French.[3]

---

[3] The debate on the true nature of 'piracy' in the region in the early nineteenth century can be traced in, inter alia, Charles E. Davies, *The Blood-Red Arab Flag;*, Patricia Risso, *Oman and Muscat;* Mohammed Morsy Abdullah, 'The First Saudi Dynasty and Oman, 1795–1818', *Proceedings of the Fourth Seminar for Arabian Studies* (1970), pp. 34–40; and Sultan bin Mohammed al-Qasimi, *The Myth of Arab Piracy*. See also Chapter 2, this volume.

In Lorimer's *Gazetteer*, however, it is acknowledged that after an earlier life as 'a buccaneer and slave trader', he 'governed the district in an
enlightened manner'.[4] After the assassination of Mohammed bin Aqil,
the Sultan's forces withdrew, and in practice the region reverted to an
earlier state of affairs in which multiple local leaders held sway over
their various tribal populations. A more lasting assertion of Omani rule
in Dhofar followed another local uprising, in 1879, this time to expel
Sayyid Fadhl bin Alawi, a religious leader from the Malabar coast who
had been expelled from British India for his participation in a Muslim-led
uprising against British rule and had established himself in Salalah four
years earlier on the basis of his capacity to mediate between tribes in
conflict with one another (tribal feuds continued to be a significant factor in Dhofari social and political life and contributed to the dynamics of the uprising against Sultan Said in the 1960s). It was not simply
his identity as a known opponent of British rule in India that made the
British view Sayyid Fadhl's role in Dhofar with suspicion. It was also the
fact that he sought political backing from the Turks, which could have
led to the incorporation of Dhofar into the Ottoman Empire, that concerned the British and led them increasingly to offer practical support to
Omani efforts to control Dhofar. In the final decades of the nineteenth
century the Sultan's Governor in Dhofar had to contend with local Qara
uprisings and received some British military assistance to do so, motivated by the fear that these uprisings against the Sultan's continued rule
would lead to Dhofar's falling under Turkish control. We may detect,
in the events of the 1960s, some of the legacy of these earlier struggles
between the inhabitants of Dhofar, their various local leaders (some of
whom came from outside Dhofar), the Sultan in Muscat and the British.
At the very least, there endured a widely held perception that Dhofar
was an unstable polity, potentially disruptive to both Omani and British
colonial interests. From the perspective of both Muscat and the British,
this perception would certainly have encouraged a defensive reaction to
expressions of Dhofari political identity. From the point of view of at
least some Dhofaris, it would have contributed to a latent political consciousness of the region being subject to a double colonial regime.

Sultan Said bin Taimur was the first Omani Sultan to devote substantial energy to Dhofar, beyond the occasional military campaign. From
the 1940s onwards he spent much of his time in Salalah, gradually

---

[4] John Gordon Lorimer, *Gazetteer of the Persian Gulf, Oman, and Central Arabia*, II
(Calcutta: Superintendent Government Printing, 1915), p. 589.

establishing the al-Hisn palace as a residence and developing a number of private estates in the vicinity. From 1958 onwards he made Salalah his permanent home. He had earlier married a woman from the Mashani, one of the largest tribes of the *jabbali* Qara (and, after her death, married her cousin, Mazoon al-Mashani, who was Sultan Qaboos's mother). Sultan Said's interest in Dhofar was a distinctly mixed blessing for its inhabitants, however. In northern Oman, as we have already seen, Sultan Said could conduct domestic policy on the basis of a shared understanding with the leadership groups of the key tribes. Even when this involved conflict, it always required engagement, the balancing of interests and, often, the provision of subsidies, as we have seen from the way in which he managed relations with the Imamate, for example. In Dhofar, by contrast, and despite his marriage with a woman from the Mashani, which may be presumed to have involved some political intent, such long-standing relations did not exist. Furthermore, many of the most significant political groups, especially the Qara, understood themselves to have a historical pre-eminence in the region that long preceded that of the Sultan of Muscat. Rather than seek the kind of quasi-consensual and delegated power that he exercised in northern Oman, therefore, Sultan Said seems to have regarded Dhofar as a region over which a direct, almost colonial power had to be imposed. In this respect he was largely continuing a pattern in which those who sought to establish political control over Dhofar did so through a combination of taxation and mediation, in which the fact that they stood outside the intertribal relations of the region enabled them to mediate between opposing tribes, while encouraging them to use the region primarily as a source of direct tax revenue rather than as a territory to be developed or incorporated into their own economic, social or political structures.[5]

FROM REBELLION TO REVOLUTION

In the early 1960s the long-standing tensions attendant upon this form of government were exacerbated by new factors. Employment prospects for Dhofari men were very limited, with a taxation regime that discouraged both agriculture and fishing (the two primary sources of livelihood for most Dhofaris). One out of every five goats had to be given as tax annually. The Governor of Rakhyut, a major fishing location, imposed

---

[5] See Jörg Janzen, *Nomads in the Sultanate of Oman* (Boulder, CO: Westview Press, 1986), pp. 44–50.

stringent and often, it seems, arbitrary taxes on all catches. Dhofar's limited exports, such as ghee, were also subjected to much higher levels of taxation than were imposed elsewhere in Oman.[6] In effect, and as had been the case for many years, the population of Dhofar was subject to a regime which appropriated nearly all surplus value through taxation, making economic development more or less impossible. Many Dhofaris therefore started to seek work elsewhere, particularly in those countries in the Gulf where development based on oil was transforming economies and generating a significant demand, even for unskilled labour. Although it was extremely difficult and often impossible for Dhofaris even to obtain a passport (it would, at the very least, involve an often hazardous journey by sea to Muscat), let alone obtain permission to leave the country, it is clear that many thousands did so and that, given the lack of the kind of education and training that would prepare them for skilled work elsewhere in the Gulf, when they did, it was mainly manual and low-skilled employment which they found. The quasi-legal nature of this migration and the almost complete lack of any government statistics from this period make it hard to give a precise account. However, some sense of the scale of this labour migration (which was not exclusively from Dhofar, of course) is given by figures which show that, in 1965, for example, there were nearly 20,000 Omanis working in Kuwait, that by 1971 (after some significant returns, following the accession of Sultan Qaboos), more than 10,000 were working in Bahrain, where they constituted 28 percent of the expatriate workforce, and that even in 1975, by which time the Qaboos-era programme of oil-led development was starting to turn Oman into a labour importer as well as a labour exporter, there were still more than 38,000 Omanis (28 percent of the total Omani workforce) employed abroad.[7] Not only did this process indicate levels of economic hardship almost certain to generate some measure of political opposition, it also facilitated the organisation of that opposition, by bringing Omani labour migrants into contact with fellow workers and allowing them to participate directly in political movements where they worked.

In explicitly political terms, the most significant of these movements was the Movement of Arab Nationalists (MAN). This had begun in Beirut as a student organisation led by George Habash, initially

[6] Halliday, *Arabia Without Sultans*, p. 326.
[7] J. S. Birks and C. A. Sinclair, 'The International Migration Project: An Enquiry into the Middle East Labor Market', *International Migration Review* 13.1 (1979), pp. 122–135.

committed to the cause of Palestinian statehood, and had evolved by the 1960s into an organisation with branches in numerous Arab countries, all generally committed to a pan-Arabist and socialist politics. Some branches identified more strongly with Nasser, while others developed a more distinctively Marxist position. It was within MAN that a number of Dhofaris encountered these ideas and made common cause with like-minded contemporaries from elsewhere in the Arab world, including, significantly, Yemenis who were later to play leading roles in the National Liberation Front revolution that established a socialist republic in South Yemen, across the border from Dhofar, in 1967. Furthermore, through their associations with political activists from other countries in the Gulf, some Dhofaris started to understand their own local situation as part of a larger political movement of opposition to the British colonial presence. Others made contact with exiled supporters of the Imam, with whom they found common cause in their opposition to the government of Sultan Said. Although the Imam's supporters had identified themselves with the Arab nationalist cause, as we have seen, their primary objective remained the establishment of an independent Imamate of Oman rather than the development of a pan-Arab front against British colonial power. Similarly, some Dhofaris emphasised the idea of an independent state in Dhofar above the wider nationalist agenda. The Dhofari exiles who established the Dhofar Liberation Front (DLF) in 1962 embodied both tendencies: nationalists associated with MAN and separatists with an exclusively Dhofari perspective. They were also joined by Musallim bin Nufl, a *shaikh* of the Bait Kathir, who had previously been dismissed from the Sultan's Dhofar Force and who was responsible, in 1963, for what is now considered the first armed action of the Dhofar rebellion. This was an attack on an oil company vehicle on the Salalah–Thamrayt road, in which one Omani was killed. Musallim recruited mainly from within his own tribe and seems to have received both arms and military training for his recruits from Talib bin Ali al-Hinai (presumably with Saudi support). Other recruits from the Bait Kathir were believed to be receiving military training in Iraq. During 1964 sporadic incidents of sabotage and attacks on oil company assets, the Dhofar Force and the Royal Air Force (which operated out of an airfield just to the north of Salalah) persuaded Sultan Said that he needed to bring the larger and more developed Sultan's Armed Forces to Dhofar to counter what was beginning to look like the first phase of a coordinated uprising.

It was in 1965, however, following the First Congress of the DLF, held in Dhofar's Wadi al-Kabir on June 1, that the armed struggle began in earnest. The DLF Congress elected an executive committee of eigh-teen, of whom Yusuf bin Alawi, the main DLF representative in Cairo, and Mohammed Ahmad al-Ghassani were two of the leading figures. The previous month Iranian intelligence had intercepted a dhow carrying a group of Dhofaris who had been training in Iraq down the Shatt-al-Arab with a consignment of arms destined to contribute to the DLF's struggle. Following their transfer to Muscat and interrogation, a further thirty-five arrests were made in and around Salalah on June 18. Although this episode had been a shock for what it revealed about the scale and intentions of the Dhofari militants, both the capture of the group in the dhow and the arrests in Salalah encouraged the Sultan and his advisers to believe that they had struck a decisive blow against the nascent rebellion. But by this time the DLF had begun its campaign proper. Their first action had been on June 9, and, like Musallim's first action, it involved an attack on traffic using the Salalah–Thamrayt road, which the DLF sought to make impassable as part of their initial efforts to establish control of the central Dhofari *jebel* from their bases in three of its valleys and to cut off road links between Dhofar and the rest of Oman. This and subsequent DLF actions in 1965 soon brought them into direct military confrontation with the SAF, in Dhofar at this time in only limited numbers as a supplement to the small Dhofar Force.

In April 1966 Sultan Said survived an assassination attempt. He was inspecting the Dhofar Force at its camp outside Salalah, and as he prepared to take the salute from a ceremonial guard, two members of the guard, including its commander, took aim at him and fired. Their shots missed their target and the Sultan was escorted from the scene. In the confrontations that ensued, several members of the Dhofar Force and some of the Sultan's personal servants were killed and wounded, as it became clear that it had been substantially infiltrated by members of MAN (as it turned out this infiltration had begun as early as 1962). Out of a total of about one hun-dred soldiers, thirty-five were held in custody following this episode, and around twenty either fled or were on leave at the time and did not return. The remaining soldiers, mainly *khuddam* rather than *jabbali* in origin, were kept on, but the Dhofar Force did not subsequently play a significant role in the developing conflict. Sultan Said himself did not appear in public again after the assassination attempt, giving rise to persistent rumours that he was actually dead. In fact, the DLF issued a communiqué in June 1966 announc-ing that the Sultan was dead and that the British had covered up the fact while they found a suitably pliant successor.[8] Meanwhile, through 1966 and

---

[8] FO 371/185364.

FIGURE 8. Lieutenant Said Salim with Said Musalim Said al-Mahri.
Source: Middle East Centre Archive, St Antony's College, Oxford (Charles Butt
Oman 6359)

1967 the DLF continued to limit the Sultan's control over central Dhofar,
while both British and Omani military forces sought to block the DLF's
supply lines for ammunition, closing off access to both Saudi Arabia to the
north and Yemen to the west, where, just across the border in the village
of Hauf, the DLF had established a key base for operations in the western
sector of Dhofar. A barbed wire fence was erected around Salalah. The SAF
tended to respond to DLF actions with indiscriminate reprisals against the
local population rather than with targeted efforts to identify and interdict
the perpetrators. These actions, especially the reprisals and the fence around
Salalah, seem to have amplified local hostility to both the Sultan and the
British and to have encouraged active collaboration with the DLF among
the local population. Significant numbers of young men, prohibited from
travelling abroad, began to leave Salalah for the *jebel*, where some of them
swelled the ranks of the DLF militants.

A key event in the development of the conflict in Dhofar was the departure of the British from Aden and the establishment in November 1967 of
the People's Republic of South Yemen (PRSY), which would later (1970)
become the People's Democratic Republic of Yemen (PDRY), under the
leadership of the National Liberation Front (NLF), the more radical of

the two nationalist organisations that had been fighting a guerrilla war against the British. The British exit from Aden was forced and hasty, following the government's failure to secure a compliant successor regime in the form of the Federation of South Arabia. In addition to their role in forcing the rapid departure of the British from Aden, the NLF had also led an uprising against the traditional rulers in the inland areas beyond Aden. This meant that, from the foundation of the new independent state, the DLF would benefit from the active support of a neighbouring government for their campaign to expel the British and overthrow the Sultan. The new Yemeni Republic was unique in the extent to which it proclaimed and sought to implement a socialist politics modelled on the political experiments led by Communist parties in the Soviet Union and China, rather than on the basis of the Nasserist Arab nationalism, which had until this point been the dominant form in which socialist and republican politics had been articulated in Arab contexts. However, although no other regional state declared itself so unambiguously for Communism, the political orientation of the PRSY was in keeping with a broader 'radicalisation' in Arab politics following the disastrous and symbolically very damaging defeat of Arab forces under (Nasser's) Egyptian leadership in the Six-Day War against Israel in June 1967.[9]

INTERNATIONALISATION: DHOFAR AND THE COLD WAR

Both the Soviet Union and China moved quickly to develop good relations with the PRSY, some of whose leaders identified more strongly with the Soviet Union and some with China. For the Soviet Union the PRSY represented a valuable addition to the list of independent states, such as Angola, Ethiopia, Mozambique and Nicaragua, in which it saw potential long-term allies in the Cold War. Military, economic and political support (including attempts to influence the direction of Yemeni government policy) soon became key elements in the Soviet–Yemeni relationship. With American troops fighting a losing battle against Vietnamese Communism, the emergence of a Soviet-backed regime in the strategically essential Arabian Peninsula was naturally regarded by the other side in the Cold War (the United States and Britain most particularly) as a direct

---

[9] For an account of the various political consequences of this defeat, see Adeed Dawisha, *Arab Nationalism in the Twentieth Century* (Princeton, NJ: Princeton University Press, 2003), especially ch. 10: '1967 and After: The Twilight of Arab Nationalism', pp. 252–281.

threat to key interests in the region. This meant that the Dhofar rebellion, however threatening it may have been as a local challenge, took on an ominous new dimension in the eyes of Cold War planners in Washington and London. The 'domino theory', according to which one country 'falling' to Communism might almost automatically lead to the 'collapse' of neighbouring pro-Western regimes, predicted, in the eyes of some of these planners, that, unless the Dhofar rebellion were checked, the whole of Oman, and then the Emirates of the British Trucial States (which became the federal state of the UAE only in 1971) could pass from the Western sphere of influence into the Soviet 'camp'. In the case of Dhofar the falling of the domino would be facilitated by military assistance for the DLF through Yemeni channels, as well as by the military and political training of revolutionary Dhofari cadres in China and the Soviet Union.

While both Soviet and Chinese weapons and ammunition were essential to maintaining and enhancing the DLF's military capacity, the Chinese connection also provided a distinctive ideological framework through which the DLF would come to understand the grassroots aspects of their struggle. The Chinese Revolution of 1949 had taken place in a largely preindustrial and only partially capitalist setting, with the result that the Chinese Communist Party placed a far greater emphasis on the political role of the rural population than had the Communist Party of the Soviet Union, which had emphasised the key political role of a mainly urban industrial working class. This perspective meant that the Chinese experience could more readily be applied to Dhofar. The Chinese Cultural Revolution, launched by Mao Zhe Dong in 1966, had already attracted the attention of numerous radical movements in Europe, and the Maoist emphasis on the revolutionary task of changing an entire culture from the ground up would clearly come to shape the political perspectives and conduct of the DLF in the late 1960s.[10]

In its initial public pronouncements associated with the launch of the armed struggle proper in 1965, the DLF had emphasised the Arab and Dhofari nature of its struggle, reflecting its analysis of the situation in terms of a fight against a double colonialism comprising British imperial rule over Arab lands and people, and the Arab Omani rule over Dhofar, both of which would have to be overthrown in order for the Dhofari people to achieve their freedom. From 1965 to 1968 this public position effectively

---

[10] For an account of both Soviet and Chinese relations with the PRSY/PDRY, see Fred Halliday, *Revolution and Foreign Policy: The Case of South Yemen* (Cambridge: Cambridge University Press, 1990).ch. 6: 'In Search of Allies: the USSR and China', pp. 178–227.

masked and contained a division within the DLF between those who saw their struggle as a local one and those who regarded it as just one front in a wider revolutionary struggle in the region. In 1968 it was the latter group which assumed a dominant role in the organisation. At its Second Congress, held in Hamrin in September 1968, the original eighteen-member committee was replaced by a twenty-five-member General Command. Ahmad al-Ghassani, a Qara and MAN activist, assumed the position of Secretary General, while other leaders such as Yusuf bin Alawi and Musallim bin Nufl, who had been prominent in the movement before 1968 and who did not share the wider revolutionary aspirations now being articulated, were sidelined (and would eventually transfer their allegiance to Sultan Qaboos following his accession in 1970). The movement renamed itself the Popular Front for the Liberation of the Occupied Arabian Gulf (PFLOAG) and started to set out a revolutionary programme based on explicitly Marxist-Leninist conceptions of political action. This emphasised organized armed struggle, led by a People's Liberation Army (PLA), rather than the sporadic and quasi-spontaneous resistance that had characterised the earlier phase of DLF operations. The aim would be gradually to seize control of territory and, in the areas captured, to implement a radical political transformation in which slavery would be abolished, tribal affiliations transcended, the rights of women affirmed (with the abolition of polygamy and the bride price) and new modes of (non-religious) education introduced. As the new name for the organisation suggests, the struggle in Dhofar would be extended not only into northern Oman, where the National Democratic Front for the Liberation of Oman and the Arabian Gulf (NDFLOAG) would soon be developing a network of militants, but through all the Trucial Shaikhdoms, Bahrain and Qatar as well. The NDFLOAG arose from the coordination of a number of opposition groups and was organised into two main groups, one in the interior, one in the Sharqiyah. Its members had trained for guerrilla warfare in Iraq, Yemen, and Palestinian refugee camps.

Within a year PFLOAG could claim substantial successes. Above all, its military operations had resulted in control of the western sector of Dhofar, with the last SAF position, in the coastal village of Rakhyut, falling to the PLA. This meant that its cadres could start to implement the new political programme in the newly liberated zone and that both political and military operations would now enjoy unobstructed interaction with supporters across the border in Yemen. Arms and ammunition could be brought in; wounded combatants could be evacuated for medical care; training and education for young Dhofaris could be organised at Hauf. This was also the route through which Chinese support for PFLOAG could be channelled: arms shipments were supervised by Chinese soldiers based in Mukalla, and Dhofari activists could leave via Yemen for training in China. Maoist ideas about how to carry out a 'peasant' revolution gained popularity with PFLOAG leaders and militants, as translations of key texts, including Mao's 'Little Red Book', were distributed in translation. In early 1970 the RAF base outside Salalah started to come under regular rocket and mortar attack. By March 1970 the PLA had also largely secured the eastern sector, and, apart from the area of the coastal plain immediately around Salalah, nearly the whole of Dhofar was under PFLOAG control. It is clear that the British government was increasingly concerned that Sultan Said had neither a political response to the PFLOAG challenge nor a military strategy to resist its territorial advance. Anxieties about the wider consequences of this situation can only have been exacerbated in June 1970 when militants of the NDFLOAG attacked SAF positions at Nizwa and Izki, and a wave of arrests in Muscat and Muttrah led to the discovery of arms and ammunition supposedly amassed in order to facilitate the opening of a northern front in the attempt to overthrow Sultan Said and advance revolutionary change in Oman. British accounts suggest that key officials in Muscat, in the region and in London were increasingly concerned that Sultan Said was now incapable of responding effectively to this challenge. His brother, Sayyid Tariq bin Taimur, had, however, made his views very clear. After playing a prominent role in the campaign against the Imamate rebellion in the late 1950s, Sayyid Tariq had left Oman in 1962, disappointed by his brother's failure to capitalise politically on this success. After several years in exile he appears to have decided to work actively against Sultan Said, exploring political alliances with both Talib bin Ali al-Hinai and members of the DLF. In 1967 he had sent proposals for a new political direction in the Sultanate to potential supporters, but his ideas remained at odds with those of his potential allies. Nonetheless, the prospect of an alliance between Talib and Tariq appears to have concerned the British sufficiently for Malcolm Dennison, Chief Intelligence Officer with the Sultan's Armed Forces, to meet Tariq to advise him that a British-backed plan to secure the succession of Sultan Said's son, Sayyid Qaboos, was in train and that he should hold off from making any plans to move against the Sultan.[11]

---

[11] Peterson, *Oman's Insurgencies*. p. 234.

FIGURE 9. *Jabbalis* at the Salalah perimeter fence, 1968.
Source: Middle East Centre Archive, St Antony's College, Oxford (Charles Butt Oman 4162)

THE COUP IN SALALAH: SULTAN QABOOS
TAKES OVER

Dennison's meeting with Tariq is just one piece of circumstantial evidence to support the widely held belief that the British government either took an active part in or at the very least knew in advance about the palace coup in which Sultan Said was deposed. It was certainly a contentious issue at the time, and even today there is some debate over the question. For some commentators the question concerning the nature of British involvement matters primarily because of what it would tell us about the nature of the British–Omani relationship in this late colonial moment. Direct British involvement, and especially British initiative, could be understood as an act of colonial interference and might lead to questions as to the legitimacy of Sultan Qaboos's accession. Since Sultan Qaboos, as we shall see, moved rapidly and effectively to secure the legitimacy of his rule, this aspect of the question is of very little contemporary significance. Evidence that has come to light quite recently tends to confirm that the British government was probably more directly involved than has been officially acknowledged.[12] British participation in the planning and execution of the coup appears to have been managed in such a way as to permit deniability. British involvement in its execution was limited to contract officers, while British officers seconded to the SAF were not to be involved. But both Colonel Hugh Oldman, a British officer serving as the Sultan's Defence Secretary in Muscat, and David Crawford, the British Consul General in Muscat, who was conveying messages from the Foreign and Commonwealth Office (FCO) in London, appear to have instructed Brigadier John Graham, the newly arrived Commander of the SAF, that, in the event that the coup launched by Qaboos looked like it might be failing, he and his fellow seconded officers in the SAF should intervene to 'restore the situation in his favour'.[13] As events turned out, no such intervention was required, and the FCO was able to maintain plausible deniability. In short, the British government knew that the coup would happen, believed it, in the words of Antony Acland, then head of the Arabian Department at the FCO, to be 'inevitable and desirable'[14] and would have authorised action to support it by force had that been necessary. It is also clear that, with or without direct British involvement, the coup would not have happened at all had it not been for the initiative of Sayyid Qaboos himself and the support he was able to gain from his associates, both British and Omani, in Salalah.

The coup itself took place on the afternoon of July 23, 1970, in the Sultan's palace at Salalah. Sayyid Qaboos, the Sultan's only son, had been living a largely secluded life at the palace since his return in 1964 from a period of education in the UK at the Royal Military Academy, Sandhurst and a subsequent year's service with a British Army infantry regiment, the Cameronians, in West Germany. In the summer of 1970 he was twenty-nine years old. It appears that he had shared his concerns about his father's capacity to govern with some of his close confidants, including a British intelligence officer stationed in Salalah, Tim Landon, who had been a friend at Sandhurst. As the idea of taking action to depose the Sultan started to take shape, a number of other key figures were involved: one was Shaikh Buraik bin Hamood al-Ghafiri, son of the Wali of Dhofar; another, responsible for organising the Omani soldiers

---

[12] See DeVore, 'United Kingdom's Last Hot War', and BBC Radio 4 *Document*, November 23, 2009. DeVore's account, on which the BBC radio programme is largely based, is itself based on the accidental release to DeVore, in 2005, of an FCO file which has since been withdrawn from public access.

[13] John Graham, interviewed on BBC Radio 4 *Document*, November 23, 2009.

[14] Acland, interviewed on BBC Radio 4 *Document*, November 23, 2009.

involved in the action, was Said Salim al-Wuhaybi. The Commander of the Desert Regiment, Teddy Turnill, was also apprised of the preparations. Shortly before the appointed date, Said Salim recruited eleven soldiers from the Northern Frontier Regiment (currently stationed in Dhofar), but without informing them as to the nature of their mission. On the afternoon of July 23, Said Salim, accompanied by Harib bin Sayf al-Hawasini and Said bin Ghiyah Bayt Qatn (an Omani intelligence officer who had been working with Landon), Turnill and the eleven soldiers drove to the palace, where they were met at the gate by Shaikh Buraik. Shaikh Buraik, Said Salim, Harib bin Sayf and the eleven soldiers entered the palace and were allowed to pass a series of gates by the slaves guarding them, whose acquiescence they may well have been secured in advance. They eventually located the Sultan in the north tower of the palace. After an initial exchange of fire, in which the Sultan shot at the intruders with a pistol, Shaikh Buraik was wounded and had to fall back. In a second exchange the Sultan wounded himself in the foot. He soon surrendered to Turnill and signed a document announcing his abdication which had been brought to him by Sayyid Qaboos's secretary.[15]

News of the coup was not made public in Oman until three days later, when a proclamation was issued by the new Sultan, Qaboos bin Said, announcing his father's departure from the country and his own dedication to 'the speedy establishment of a modern government'.[16] The establishment of this modern Omani government and its work will be discussed

---

[15] This narrative of the events on July 23 is based on the fullest published account to date, in Peterson's *Oman's Insurgencies* (2007). It is notable that this account is more detailed than that offered nearly thirty years earlier by Peterson, in *Oman in the Twentieth Century* (1978), which does not mention Landon by name. This later and more detailed account does not refer to the presence in the group entering the palace of either Landon or the British contract officer Ray Kane, who other accounts, including Kane's own, in the *Mail* on Sunday, July 7, 2002, report as having been wounded in the operation. Our conversations in Oman largely corroborate Peterson's 2007 account, in which the role of Said Salim is, we believe, rightly emphasised.

[16] Peterson *Oman in the Twentieth Century*, p. 203. This translation follows the English version of the announcement in FCO 8/1425, Telegram 46, July 26, 1970. The official English text of this announcement used in Omani government publications translates his words as follows: 'I promise you to proceed forthwith in the process of creating a modern government.' See, e.g., the 'Extracts' from this speech on the Web site of the Ministry of Information, http://www.omanet.om/english/hmsq/hmsq3.asp?cat=hmsq (accessed July 31, 2014). It is regrettable that the account of life in Oman given on this Web site errs, in its enthusiasm for the achievements of Sultan Qaboos, in perpetrating some of the widely circulated myths about the nature of Sultan Said's rule. It affirms, for instance, that 'radios were banned as they were considered the work of the devil' See http://www.omanet.om/english/government/hmspage/tribute.asp (accessed July 31, 2014).

FIGURE 10. Eid al-Adha at Muscat, 1969 (Sayyid Ahmed bin Ibrahim, Sayyid Nadir, Sayyid Sultan, Sayyid Thuwaini, Sayyid Abbas and Sayyid Malik).
Source: Middle East Centre Archive, St Antony's College, Oxford (Charles Butt Oman 0250)

FIGURE 11. Sultan Qaboos's accession to the throne, with Sayyid Shihab officiating.
Source: Middle East Centre Archive, St Antony's College, Oxford (John Graham, 9/1/57)

FIGURE 12. Shaikh Buraik.
Source: Middle East Centre Archive, St Antony's College, Oxford (Charles Butt Oman 0042)

in much greater detail in Chapter 5, while only those aspects of the process that contributed directly, and in the next five years, to the effective resolution of the conflict in Dhofar will be treated here. Following the departure of Sultan Said from RAF Salalah, via Bahrain, to London, where he lived until his death in 1972 in the Dorchester Hotel, Sultan Qaboos established a temporary council in Salalah, whose key members, in addition to the Sultan himself, were Shaikh Hilal bin Sultan al-Hawasini, Sayyid Hamad bin Hamood Al Bu Said (who had been his father's private secretary) and Said Salim al-Wuhaybi, along with Tim Landon and John Graham. A key priority was to establish that the new Sultan would be the ruler of the whole country, to which end it was essential that he appear formally in Muscat, that he begin to establish his own administration in the capital and that he visit key towns and villages in the Omani interior to present himself to the people and their local leaders. He arrived in Muscat on

July 30 for an accession ceremony on August 2. His uncle, Sayyid Tariq, returned from exile to be appointed Prime Minister and started establishing the first new central government ministries (Education, Health, Interior, Justice). Sultan Qaboos made a series of visits throughout August to Nizwa, Rustaq and many of the other key towns in the interior. A crucial symbolic change, with implications for both domestic and foreign policy, was the decision, announced in a radio broadcast (Sultan Qaboos's first) on August 9, that the country should henceforward be known not as the Sultanate of Muscat and Oman (a name which evoked political divisions which the new government was eager to consign to the past) but instead, simply, the Sultanate of Oman. It was as representatives of the Sultanate of Oman that the new leadership, including the Sultan himself, very actively, would now seek international recognition.

THE END OF THE DHOFAR CONFLICT

Back in Dhofar, as a result of the coup and the direction established by the new government, there was a comprehensive change in the approach taken to the military conflict. This change had military, ideological, political and social dimensions. Various claims have been made both by and on behalf of those who participated in this new strategy. Some emphasise the military dimension. These tend to point to such events as the successful defence of Mirbat against a PLA attempt to seize the town in June 1971, which thus becomes a turning point in a struggle understood in terms of territory and position, in which the heroic efforts of a small number of British troops are celebrated. Since most of these accounts are informed by the experience of British military personnel, they pay less attention to later military contributions, most notable among which was the participation of Iranian troops in the final years of the campaign. More numerous, however, are those accounts, from both historians and British military memoirists, which claim the eventual success of the new strategy as a 'model counter-insurgency'. In such accounts, the emphasis is on the deployment of special troops (in this case the British SAS) in an operation that combined military force with a 'hearts and minds' campaign, in which the local population was persuaded to abandon its support for the rebels and to back the new Sultan. This 'hearts and minds' story often emphasises a combination of the military and the social, pointing to practical action such as the provision of wells, health clinics and other facilities designed to improve the lives of ordinary Dhofaris (or, more pertinently, those ordinary Dhofaris whose leaders had offered their allegiance to the

FIGURE 13. Sultan Qaboos, Shaikh Zayed of Abu Dhabi and Sayyid Tariq in Muscat, 1970.
Source: Middle East Centre Archive, St Antony's College, Oxford (Charles Butt Oman 1238)

new Sultan). The purely military accounts tend to overemphasise events such as Mirbat, and although the 'model counter-insurgency' story offers a more sophisticated explanation, it, too, tends to neglect ideological and perhaps, crucially, purely political dimensions of the new approach. It also overemphasises the impact of social and economic development, inasmuch as it seems to have been the promise of such development rather than its substantial implementation that contributed to the new government's success. The 'model counter-insurgency' account is influential because Dhofar has been extensively used as a case study in military education on counter-insurgency. Like the purely military British accounts, it downplays the involvement of the Iranian (and Jordanian) troops, which has to be understood as a significant political achievement on the part of the new government (in making new allies). It also tends to neglect the related political dimension contributed by the diplomatic successes of the early 1970s, in which nearly all Arab countries (with the exception of PDRY and Iraq) established diplomatic relations with the Sultanate of Oman. This effectively annulled any political threat to the new Sultanate from the supporters of the former Imamate: by achieving international political recognition for the Sultanate of Oman, the new government effectively removed the 'question of Oman' from the international political arena. It also limited significantly the range of external support to which the PFLOAG could turn for financial and military assistance in its campaign against the Sultanate. In the following account of the concluding phase of the Dhofar conflict, we will focus accordingly on the political dimension, emphasising that military, ideological and social aspects of the strategy were all significant but that, without sustained attention to both local and regional politics, the strategy is unlikely to have succeeded to the extent that it did.

Local politics involved securing the support of key Dhofari political leaders, starting with some of the nationalist-separatists who had been sidelined by the Marxist turn from DLF to PFLOAG in 1968. Both Musallim bin Nufl and Yusuf bin Alawi aligned themselves with Sultan Qaboos before the end of 1970, concluding, pragmatically, that many of the objectives for which they had originally gone into opposition were now more likely to be achieved through cooperation with the Sultan and his plans for modern government. But the most sustained efforts of political persuasion had to be directed towards those who were still actively engaged in the struggle on the ground and the local population who helped protect them. According to a programme conceived by officers in the SAS, who started to participate significantly in the conflict after 1970, *jabbali* combatants would be encouraged to defect, leave the *jebel*, and then start to work actively to secure further defections. These defectors were very important: they were intelligence assets who could provide information on the disposition of the remaining PLA forces; they could communicate secretly, and, crucially, in their own language, with former comrades still active in the PLA: they could interact directly with the local *jabbali* population in a way that the Omanis from the north, their Baluchi counterparts in the SAF, let alone the British officers of the SAF and SAS, could not. There was a military aspect to this programme of recruitment, too, starting in September 1970 when the surrender of a more or less intact PLA military unit enabled the SAS to convert the defectors into a new military unit in support of the Sultan. This was the first of the *firqat*: irregular military units trained to work alongside a small number of SAS soldiers.[17] The first of these, Firqat Salahadin, was trained at Mirbat, under the leadership of Salim Mubarak, and first participated in a military operation against the PLA in February 1971, playing a key

---

[17] Significant portions of Tony Jeapes's *SAS: Secret War* are devoted to his account of the organisation of the *firqat*.

role in the capture of the coastal village of Sadh. This operation also led directly to the surrender of a further large group of PLA combatants, who were surrounded by soldiers from the Firqat Salahadin in a wadi outside Sadh. Compelled to talk by their former comrades, they agreed to come over to the Sultan's side. Their leaders, like Salim Mubarak of the Firqat Salahadin, would prove to be key allies in the subsequent development of the pro-Sultan *firqat*.[18] The military contribution of the *firqat* was not always as decisive as this first success: reports from British officers suggest significant cultural differences, which the British tended to understand as a lack of discipline that betrayed an unacceptable (to them) focus on local, tribal and even personal considerations. It is clear, all the same, that the very fact that surrendered PLA militants were able to find a role for themselves once they had come over to the Sultan's side, that they were fed, clothed and given weapons, was an important factor in securing their support. It also meant that they served as an increasingly visible alternative to the PLA, both for PLA militants and for the Dhofari population more broadly. The development of the *firqat* was accompanied by a propaganda campaign, involving leaflet drops and radio broadcasts (in support of which transistor radios were placed on sale in the souk at Salalah), many of which sought to exploit local religious sentiment, which was at odds with the sometimes fiercely anti-religious ideology promoted among the population by the PLA and PFLAOG hard core. A key slogan in this campaign was 'Islam is our way. Freedom is our aim.'

Regional politics involved a sustained campaign of visits to key capitals with the aim of establishing diplomatic relations and securing Omani admission to both Arab and international organisations. This diplomatic and political activity began as early as August and September 1970 with visits to Muscat by the Shaikhs of Abu Dhabi, Dubai, and Sharjah, all of whom were shortly to participate in the formation of the United Arab Emirates (UAE) in 1971. In October 1971 at the Cairo Summit of the Arab League, Sayyid Tariq argued forcefully for Oman's membership in the face of opposition from representatives of PDRY and the Imamate, his efforts being rewarded with a vote in Oman's favour on October 6. Almost simultaneously, and as a consequence of equally effective Omani diplomatic efforts in New York coordinated by Sayyid Tariq, the UN Security Council voted to recommend Oman's application to join the United Nations on October 4. This recommendation was approved at a meeting of the General Assembly on

[18] See Ibid., pp. 71–81.

FIGURE 14. A Dhofari rebel commander, 1971.
Source: Keystone-France/Getty Images

October 7, with Cuba and PDRY voting against and Saudi Arabia abstaining.[19] In December 1971, Sultan Qaboos met King Faisal of Saudi Arabia in Riyadh, bringing to an end the state of intermittent hostility between their two countries and marking the end of Saudi Arabia's residual support for the remnants of the Imamate opposition. The Sultan Qaboos–King Faisal summit secured diplomatic recognition for the Sultanate of Oman from the

---

[19] See Minutes of the 1,957th Plenary Meeting of the United Nations General Assembly, October 7, 1971. It is worth noting that both the Soviet Union and China voted in favour of Oman's admission to the United Nations. The first speech of congratulations was made by the representative of Tanzania (not without its significance given the history of Zanzibar). The Egyptian representative welcomed Oman on behalf of the group of Arab states at the UN. The American representative who also spoke at the General Assembly to congratulate Oman on its accession was George H. W. Bush, later to become President of the United States (1989–1993). Sayyid Tariq responded on behalf of Oman, affirming Oman's identity as an Arab nation and concluding with a statement of support for the people of Palestine.

FIGURE 15. Sayyid Thuwaini attending Oman–UAE border demarcation work.
Source: Middle East Centre Archive, St Antony's College, Oxford (Charles Butt Oman 3420)

Kingdom of Saudi Arabia and, with it, its full political support. Along with the recognition also achieved in talks with other Gulf states, including, of course, the newly formed UAE, this represented a significant consolidation and external ratification of Oman's national statehood. The integration of the Sultanate of Oman into the legal and institutional framework of the postcolonial international system effectively completed, at a formal level, the process of state-making which had been under way, however slowly and intermittently, through much of the preceding fifty years. It confirmed a new political situation, in which the conflict in Dhofar could be presented with increasing credibility as a struggle between a legitimate government and a campaign of subversion sponsored by hostile external powers. From 1965 to 1970 the PLFOAG had broadly benefitted from the 'internationalisation' of their struggle; from 1971 onwards it would be the Sultanate that would enjoy the preponderant measure of external support, especially, but by no means exclusively, from among those nations allied with the United States in the Cold War.

The development of the Sultanate's relationship with Iran was a key priority at the start of the 1970s and was to make a significant contribution to the final phase of the government's campaign in Dhofar. Sultan

Qaboos attended the Persepolis Festival in October 1971, a lavish and spectacular event which commemorated the 2,500th anniversary of the Persian Empire. Shaikh Zayed of Abu Dhabi, about to become President of the UAE, also attended, along with the Emirs of Bahrain, Kuwait and Qatar. The King of Jordan and the brother of the King of Morocco were the only other Arab leaders to attend an event which was viewed by many in the region as an unwelcome expression of Iranian power. Concerns about Iran's ambitions in the region were exacerbated the following month when Iranian naval forces seized the islands of Abu Musa, Greater and Lesser Tunb, all of which were at that time administered by Emirates on the verge of forming the UAE (Ras al-Khaimah and Sharjah). Oman carefully maintained a measure of public distance from the fierce condemnation of this action led by Iraq and other Arab states, seeking to balance its relations with the emergent UAE with the priority now also attached to securing appropriate relations (including a fully demarcated maritime border) with Iran.[20] In December 1971 Sultan Qaboos and Mohammed Reza Shah Pahlavi met in Tehran and reached agreements on security cooperation, which included arrangements for Iranian troops to be sent to Dhofar to support the SAF against the PLA. Iranian planes flew supplies into Oman from August 1972, helicopters were introduced the following month and in November the first detachments of Iranian ground troops commenced rotating tours of duty in Dhofar. Oman, Iran and Britain sought to keep the Iranian presence a secret and continued to issue denials to journalists after PFLOAG had made it public in 1973. The Iranian military contribution was both materially and symbolically important, despite the political difficulties associated with it: many suspected that the Shah was hoping to use the involvement of Iranian troops in Dhofar as part of a wider expansionism signalled earlier by the occupation of the islands. In material terms Iranian ground troops contributed substantially to major operations in the concluding phase of the conflict, including the capture of Rakhyut in January 1975, while Iranian air power, including anti-aircraft batteries, significantly strengthened the SAF-led forces. The scale of the Iranian contribution reflects another aspect of the final phase of the military campaign: the development of an overwhelming numerical and technological advantage over the PLA. The number of PLA fighters was dwindling, due in no small measure to the political efforts to secure and

---

[20] For a more detailed account of these diplomatic activities, see Jones and Ridout, *Oman, Culture and Diplomacy*, pp. 155–160.

retain defectors. Supply lines from PDRY were seriously compromised by a series of fortified lines of control traversing both the coastal plain and the *jebel*. With a larger number of troops and increasingly intimidating air power, the SAF and its various British, Iranian (and for a while Jordanian) allies gradually established and extended territorial control, opening up the road from Salalah to Thamrayt at the end of 1973 and forcing the PLA into diminishing pockets of mountainous territory in the west.

The military campaign was supported with a massive increase in resources, made possible largely by oil revenues. Production had begun in 1967, following the discovery in 1964, as anticipated, of substantial exploitable reserves at Fahud. By 1973 production was running at 293,000 barrels a day, with total exports for the year reaching 106 million barrels. Although production did not increase significantly the following year (it actually declined slightly), the price rose from slightly more than $3 a barrel to more than $5 in late 1973, as major Arab producers raised prices and cut production in their attempt to use the 'oil weapon' against the United States and its allies for their continued support of Israel. This was precipitated by the 'October' or 'Yom Kippur War', launched by Egypt and Syria against Israel, in an attempt to reverse the defeat of 1967. This escalated into an oil embargo against states that continued to back Israel. Although the Arab–Israeli military confrontation was formally suspended in early 1974, the effects of the 'oil weapon' persisted. By January 1974 Oman's oil exports were earning more than $12 a barrel, and this price was maintained throughout this and the two following years. It was in the economic circumstances transformed first by oil production as such, and subsequently by this quadrupling of revenue as a result of the price rise, that a quarter of the country's 1971–1975 development budget was allocated to Dhofar. Although much of this was destined for military or military-related projects, it was also used to support the Dhofar Development Programme, announced by Sultan Qaboos in October 1972, with a budget dedicated primarily to the creation of a government-funded social infrastructure for the people of Dhofar in general and the inhabitants of the *jebel* in particular.[21]

The development of this infrastructure was of considerable political significance, because, beyond the social and economic benefits that

---

[21] A detailed account of this infrastructure and the benefits it provided to the population can be found in Jenzen, 1986, pp. 181–231.

it provided, it established the Omani state as a meaningful presence in the day-to-day lives not just of local leaders but of the population as a whole. In Dhofar, as we have already seen, there had been a long history of rulers of various kinds whose role had been limited to mediating conflicts between rival local groups and extracting revenue from the population by taxation. Through the Dhofar Development Programme the new government did something very different, by making itself both a consistent presence and a provider of rather than a drain upon local economic resources. This was achieved through the creation of 'government centres', organised throughout the region and concentrated in those parts of the *jebel* where the population was densest. Each of these combined a range of basic facilities, including a well, water troughs for livestock, a school, a medical facility, a mosque and a shop. Government employees lived in accommodations on site. The direction of each centre was aligned with the local tribal leadership, so that the government effectively recruited traditional leaders as state representatives, enabling the new state structures to be integrated with familiar conventions of social organisation. In this respect, and although the general tendency of the new government's policy towards tribes was to seek to reduce their influence, its engagement with Dhofari tribal structures in the early 1970s was in clear distinction to the approach of the PFLAOG, which had consistently worked to encourage the population to transcend tribal affiliations in favour of class solidarities. Like its promotion of a version of Marxism acquired elsewhere and its hostility to the religious practices of the Dhofari population, PFLOAG's attitude to tribal relationship was a political liability which contributed to its loss of popular support through the early 1970s.

By mid-1974 the PFLOAG leadership was fully aware that its position was deteriorating on all fronts: military, political, social and ideological. With its advances in Dhofar now substantially reversed, its ambition to play a leading role in a wider regional revolutionary movement had to be tempered, if not abandoned altogether. The organisation changed its name to the Popular Front for the Liberation of Oman (PFLO), a change which reflected not only the fact that it no longer sought revolution in 'the Arabian Gulf', but also, perhaps, a desire to open up an alternative front in the struggle within Oman. In October 1974 a routine check on a vehicle that had entered Oman from Dubai led to the discovery of a PFLO recruitment and sabotage mission that seemed to be designed to do just that. The arrests of the key participants in this mission effectively brought

FIGURE 16. A Dhofari dancer at Sultan Qaboos's wedding.
Source: Middle East Centre Archive, St Antony's College, Oxford (Charles Butt Oman 0237)

an end to PFLO activities in the north. In Dhofar, following the capture of Rakhyut in January 1975, the PLA (with the exception of some small units still active in the central and eastern sectors) had been forced into an area between the Damavand Line (set up by the Iranians and running from the coast at Rakhyut into the *jebel*) and the border with PDRY. PLA forces, augmented by troops from the army of PDRY, probably numbered around five hundred men, with about one hundred or so additional PFLO militia in support. Even with the advantage of difficult terrain, which tends to give guerrilla forces some advantage over the more conventional forces seeking to dislodge them, this depleted force was no match for a series of ground and air assaults from the now vastly superior forces of the SAF and its allies. By November 1975 the number of active PLA soldiers in Dhofar may have fallen to less than one hundred, with surrenders and flight accelerating as conditions made their lives increasingly intolerable. On December 11, after having been informed that the last remnants of the PLA had been forced out of Dhofar, Sultan Qaboos announced the end of the Dhofar War, even though the remaining PLA units in the central and eastern sectors continued to offer some sporadic resistance. In March 1976, PDRY agreed to a ceasefire, calling a halt to its cross-border activities and effectively abandoning its support for the PFLO. At the same time PDRY and Saudi Arabia inaugurated diplomatic relations. Thus two neighbouring countries, both of which had, for very different reasons, challenged Oman's existence as a nation-state and actively supported internal opposition to its consolidation, now cemented, in this act of preliminary cooperation, the final phase of the establishment of the Sultanate of Oman in its contemporary form.

6

Oil, Government and Security, 1955–1980

The future success of the new Omani state would depend upon both social and political development. This was the advice repeatedly offered to Sultan Said and with increasing insistence from at least 1955. At that time it came primarily from British military and political sources, and especially from those directly or indirectly involved in the Sultan's campaign against the Imamate. In order to secure the newly, but perhaps provisionally unified state, the Sultan would have to replace traditional tribal political structures, in which people looked to tribal leaders for all their basic needs – employment, justice, education – with a new administration organised around his own power. This would require a new conception of government: rather than an ultimate source of authority, to whom quasi-autonomous tribal *shaikhs* might turn at times of crisis or need, the Sultan himself would have to become a provider of services, offer a responsive and day-to-day involvement in the lives of people scattered across extensive territories. This would obviously require resources.

Many commentators, both at the time and subsequently, have noted the Sultan's failure or reluctance to act on this advice, and some of these have attributed his failure or reluctance, as we have already seen, to the Sultan's personality and upbringing, his resistance to change, his aversion to financial risk or his lack of interest in the political challenge. Others note, more sympathetically, that the Sultan's aversion to financial risk was strongly motivated by his desire to maintain and enhance Oman's independence from the kind of foreign political influence (particularly British) that he associated with debt. From Sultan Said's perspective, as we have seen, one of the aims of the intervention in the interior from 1954 was to create the conditions in which the commercial exploitation of oil might transform the country's financial position. This would provide the resources that would make social and political development possible. But until this basic condition for development was met, there was no incentive to embark on a programme of major change and some considerable risk involved in disrupting existing modes of government and social life.

The idea that the role of government might be to encourage or promote economic growth and progress derives from a set of economic and political relations – normally called capitalism – which were not to be found in Oman, in spite of long-standing mercantile activities which had become increasingly integrated with a world economic system during the nineteenth century.[1] Those who advised Sultan Said that development was the way forward came, of course, from a culture in which the benefits of capitalist development appeared more or less self-evident. British advisers who urged the Sultan in this way spoke from within an emergent post–World War Two consensus in which economic prosperity was understood to be the basis for a welfare state. It is hardly surprising, then, that, confronted with widespread poverty, most visible in its effects on the health of the population, such expatriate advisers should have, in all good faith, believed that the progress their own country had already enjoyed could solve the problems that surrounded them in Oman. It is equally understandable that many of them should have responded to the Sultan's apparent repudiation of this supposedly self-evident logic with dismay. This basic cultural misapprehension has helped shape accounts of Oman's modern history in which all that is premodern, backward-looking and opposed to the largely capitalist concepts of 'progress', 'development' and 'modernisation' is attributed to Sultan Said, and all credit for the success of subsequent projects is awarded to his more enlightened successors. Such accounts have also been informed, as Marc Valeri argues, by the emphasis placed in official Omani accounts of recent history on the decisive character of the events of 1970, which are routinely understood in some quarters to have been solely responsible for the 'dawn' of a 'new era' in Omani history.[2]

---

[1] It is important not to conflate mercantile activities, even on a large scale, with capitalism as such. Omani mercantilism of the eighteenth and nineteenth centuries did not depend upon the staples of a capitalist economy – wage labour and financial speculation. In some respects certain aspects of Oman's economic and social relations, even today, are decidedly non-capitalist in nature. The processes of Oman's entry into the World Trade Organization and other global systems of the neoliberal period are the latest in a series of engagements in which Oman negotiates its participation in capitalism. The entry of Omanis in Zanzibar into global flows of consumer commodities in the mid-nineteenth century constitutes an earlier example, as we have discussed in Chapters 2 and 3.

[2] See, e.g., Marc Valeri, *Oman: Politics and Society in the Qaboos State* (London: Hurst, 2009), pp. 71–72. In spite of this, Valeri repeats the idea that Sultan Said was 'hostile

While the events of 1970 were clearly of enormous significance for the Sultanate of Oman – indeed, it is possible that without them the country might not have survived in recognisable form – it is wrong to draw the simplistic conclusion that social, political and economic development is associated solely with the post-1970 period. On the contrary, as we shall see, it is clear that Sultan Said himself believed that a 'new era' was to be inaugurated on the basis of oil revenues. In 1964 PDO announced that oil discovered that year in Fahud (as well as earlier, in Jibal and Natih) constituted commercially exploitable quantities and that exports would begin in 1967. A pipeline was constructed to a terminal at Mina al-Fahal just outside Muttrah and exports began, as planned, in mid-1967. By 1970 these had risen from 20.9 million barrels to 121.3 million.[3] As Valeri exclaims, even by 1969, 'this godsend represented forty times the total annual revenue of the Sultanate in the early 1960s!'[4] As we have already seen in Chapter 5, the Sultanate's capacity to deploy new and unprecedented resources (including military resources made possible by the new income) played a huge role in its victory over the PFLO in Dhofar, especially in the final phases when the 'force multiplier' of the post-1973 oil price rise took effect. That Sultan Said recognised the implications of this new situation is clear from a text he wrote, dated January 1968, in which he set out the general direction of his plans for Oman's oil-funded development:

God willing, 1968 will be the start of a new era for our country which will see the beginning of various plans which will be executed under the supervision of qualified technicians and experts. Firstly we shall begin building offices for various Government Departments; then houses for officials who will come from abroad; then step by step will come various projects such as hospitals, schools, roads, communications, and other necessary works including the development of fisheries, animals and agricultural resources etc. until modern projects spread over the whole of the Sultanate, to each area according to its needs. So long as oil flows the Government will match its flow with continuing development for the welfare of the country.[5]

to the development of health services and education' (67), even though he earlier notes that large-scale projects were in fact launched under Sultan Said's rule almost as soon as oil revenues were ensured. These included, Valeri notes, three hospitals and a girls' school (66).

[3] Mohamed bin Moosa al-Yousef, *Oil and the Transformation of Oman* (London: Stacey International), p. 29.

[4] Valeri, *Oman: Politics and Society*, p. 72.

[5] 'The Word of Sultan Said bin Taimur, Sultan of Muscat and Oman, about the history of the financial position of the Sultanate in the past and the hopes for the future, after the export of oil', published as app. 1, in John Townsend, *Oman: The Making of a Modern State* (London: Croom Helm, 1977), pp. 192–198. It is not clear for whom this text was

In practice, as Peterson notes, Sultan Said's experience of the state's 'chronic poverty had taught him to be careful about spending money', and by the time he was overthrown in 1970 only the very first stages in the process of development to which he seems to have been committed had been accomplished.[6] It is important, nonetheless, to recognise that a commitment to development was in place before 1970 and that it was the income from oil that had made this possible. In this chapter we offer an account of the subsequent phase in Oman's economic, social and political development. Just as it is important to recognise the origins of those processes in events that preceded 1970, it is vital to understand that what happened after 1970 was not simply the automatic consequence of Sultan Qaboos's taking power that year. Historical causality, however we construe it, is invariably more complicated than that.

BUILDING GOVERNMENT: NATIONALISATION

Sultan Said's actions in the 1950s may have done much to lay the foundations of a unified nation-state. But quite apart from the fact that this state continued to face a serious challenge to its territorial integrity through the 1960s, little had been done to give this emergent nation-state the kind of government structure necessary to ensure that the benefits of its new income from oil would be managed in the interests of its citizens.

---

intended or how it was used. Valeri refers to it as a 'speech', which seems unlikely, as accounts of the Sultan's mode of life in 1968 do not indicate any public appearances. See Valeri, *Oman: Politics and Society*, 66. Peterson, *Oman in the Twentieth Century*, reports this text as having been 'issued' (85). Townsend indicates that he possesses a copy in his 'archives', which he presumably acquired in the course of his consultancy work in Oman in 1969 and 1970. It may have been developed in consultation with British and other advisers and seems to have been the basis upon which a Development and Planning Board, a Public Works Department and a Currency Board were subsequently set up. Townsend himself notes that, despite his own conclusion, after twelve months in Oman, that 'there was no more to be achieved in Oman' (12), there had in fact already been notable progress: 'In the field of development, it is not generally known (or perhaps is conveniently forgotten) that plans for the new harbour and airport near Muscat were drawn up by consultants [presumably Townsend's own team] during the reign of Sultan Said bin Taimur. At the same time, plans for two hospitals had been completed and work had begun. The first major road contract, from Muttrah to Sohar, was being negotiated when Sultan Said was ousted. The first girl's school was completed in 1970. All this meant that, when Sultan Qaboos came to power, so much ground work had been completed that dramatic development progress was seen in the first two years of his reign' (Townsend, *Oman: The Making of a Modern State*, p. 170). It might be added that these infrastructural developments were taking place while a major military campaign was also being waged.

[6] Peterson, *Oman in the Twentieth Century*, p. 85.

What followed, through the 1970s, were processes of infrastructure- and institution-building. Both of these processes are often called 'development', and we will use that term here, for convenience, even though, as we have already suggested, it does carry some misleading connotations. Foremost of these is the idea that there is a condition of 'modern' developmental maturity, which is defined in advance and to which the 'underdeveloped' nation must somehow 'progress'. In the context of twentieth-century capitalism, into whose 'world-system' the Sultanate of Oman was emerging, political 'development' and economic 'development' were often supposed to go hand in hand: in its most typical form this developmental model assumed that a productive economy would be accompanied by a secularising government bureaucracy supported by institutions of citizen representation. As we shall see, 'development' in Oman in the 1970s achieved a great deal in a short time. But while it certainly involved elements of the standard developmental model, it also showed marked divergences from it. From the outset aspects of economic activity, political organisation and the function of religious authority were managed in distinctive ways in response to the particular demands of the local historical situation. In some respects Oman's development during this period conforms to the model of the 'rentier state', in which government derives its revenue directly from a single resource (in this case, oil) and bases its political authority on its control of this resource and its income (rent).[7] However, this descriptive term only partially captures the nature of Oman's development, in that it tends to exclude any consideration of how such states might be differentiated from one another by their adaptation of older modes of social and political organisation

---

[7] See, e.g., Marc J. O'Reilly, 'Omanibalancing: Oman Confronts an Uncertain Future', *Middle East Journal* 52.1 (1998), pp. 70–84. O'Reilly draws on F. Gregory Gause III, *Oil Monarchies: Domestic and Security Challenges in the Arab Gulf States* (New York: Council on Foreign Relations, 1994), who in turn draws on the original formulation of the concept in the context of the twentieth-century Arab world, by Hazem Beblawi, 'The Rentier State in the Arab World', in Giacomo Luciani (ed.), *The Arab State* (London: Routledge, 1990), pp. 85–98. For Beblawi, the rentier state in the Arab world is one in which 'rents' (income from the exploitation of assets rather than production as such) come primarily from outside the state, in which these rents are collected by the state and in which only a few of the state's citizens are involved in their generation. Beblawi is careful to note that his adoption of the term is 'not to reach an abstract notion of such a state but to help elucidate the impact of recent developments, in particular the oil phenomenon, on the nature of the state in the Arab region' (87). He also seeks to distinguish his use of the term from its pejorative use by both 'liberal' and 'radical' economists, for whom those who live off rents tend to be viewed as parasitic and unproductive. At the same time, however, his essay does end up taking a moral position, in which the absence of any relation between work and reward is lamented.

alongside the creation of institutions to manage and distribute oil (or other rent) incomes.

In the account that follows we will suggest that a third term, 'nationalisation', might be used to describe the processes for which 'development' and 'the rentier state' are normally used. Oman's was a process of nationalisation in several respects. The government sought not just to derive income from oil, but to acquire ownership of it, in the name of the nation-state. The government also sought to direct economic activity through mechanisms of state planning. Outside the economic sphere, in which the term 'nationalisation' is reasonably familiar (denoting the taking of assets and production into state ownership), the newly established Omani government of the 1970s also sought to nationalise social allegiances and, to some extent, religious practices. The influence of tribal leadership on the conduct of national politics was significantly diminished. The reduction of tribal power had, of course, begun with the defeat of the Imamate in the mid-1950s (in which leaders of powerful tribal groups, the Hirth, the Bani Riyam and the Bani Ruwaha and their allies among the al-Khalili family had been key participants).[8] But during the 1970s a whole set of new structures, whose personnel owed their authority to central government in Muscat rather than to their local tribe, were established throughout the country and came to replace tribal leadership as the providers of employment, justice and welfare for an increasing number of the new state's citizens. This process was replicated, to some extent, in the religious sphere, as government started to take an active role in determining the nature of the religious education to be provided in schools and brought the organisation of mosques and the administration of *awqaf* (property held in trust for general benefit) under its jurisdiction.

As we have already seen, a key priority in the first half of the 1970s was the conflict in Dhofar. Substantial economic and military resources were devoted to this effort, and some of its underlying social and political assumptions (such as that government provision of basic resources might help secure popular commitment to the state) clearly applied to the approach taken elsewhere in the country. The need to focus on Dhofar may have contributed to the fact that in the first half of the 1970s key decisions about the organisation of government and the investment of resources seem to have been taken in a fairly ad hoc way. There was no government-in-waiting with a programme in place ready to be implemented upon the accession of Sultan Qaboos in 1970.

---

[8] See Peterson (1978), pp. 118–132.

One of the first decisions regarding the character of a new government illuminates the extent to which its construction was initially improvisatory rather than planned, responsive rather than programmatic. This was the appointment of Sayyid Tariq as Prime Minister. Sayyid Tariq, who, as we have seen in Chapter 4, had left Oman in 1962, returned to Muscat from Dubai just days after Sultan Qaboos arrived in Muscat after assuming power. It is not entirely clear who was responsible for inviting him to return: it is fairly clear that Malcolm Dennison, who had been in contact with Sayyid Tariq earlier in the year, played a role, and it seems likely enough that the British should have advised the new Sultan to include his uncle in his new administration from the very beginning. Nor is it clear precisely what role he was intended to perform. The title of Prime Minister was without precedent in Oman, and there was no constitutional basis upon which to determine a division of responsibilities between Sultan Qaboos as head of state and Sayyid Tariq as head of government. In addition to these uncertainties the two men seem to have held different ideas about how the Sultanate of Oman might be organised politically. In his eight years of exile Sayyid Tariq seems, unsurprisingly, to have developed an Arab nationalist perspective, which might, in other circumstances (had he not been a member of a royal family, for example) have led him to a republican orientation. His appointment as Prime Minister might have suggested that Oman would move towards a constitutional monarchy.[9] There is no indication that Sultan Qaboos would have shared such a view at this time: he appears to have been much more inclined to assume the traditional role of an Al Bu Said Sultan, as his father had done before him, than to experiment with new forms of sovereignty. Such differences were subsumed, for the time being at least, by the urgent priority of establishing and consolidating the new government. For those who participated in or supported Sultan Qaboos's move to depose his father, it was vital that Sayyid Tariq – who had, let it not be forgotten, only recently been associated with the NDFLOAG, a movement dedicated to the overthrow, not just of Sultan Said, but of Sultani rule as such – should be included. What he might contribute, and how, could be determined in due course.

In the event, Sayyid Tariq's most significant contribution was the one we have already described in Chapter 5: his extensive diplomatic efforts to secure Oman's admission to the Arab League and the United Nations.

---

[9] See Ian Skeet, *Muscat and Oman: The End of an Era* (London: Faber & Faber, 1974), p. 40, and Townsend, *Oman: The Making of a Modern State*, p. 93.

In this role he was assisted by Omar Barouni, a Libyan who had worked as a diplomat for King Idris, two associates of Barouni (Ghassan Shakir, a Saudi businessman, and Yahya Omar, another Libyan) whose connections in the Arab political world helped Sayyid Tariq and Sultan Qaboos develop constructive relations with key Arab states, including Egypt, Jordan and Saudi Arabia. It was the increasing involvement of Ghassan Shakir, Yahya Omar and their American associate, Robert Anderson, in the commercial sphere in Oman, including the oil sector, that led to the dissatisfaction of former British advisers, who felt they were being edged out of positions of economic advantage, and also, it seems, to the resignation of Sayyid Tariq as Prime Minister in December 1971. Although Sayyid Tariq himself did not succeed in establishing the role of Prime Minister as an enduring feature of political life in Oman – all accounts suggest that he was unable to gather around him the administrative infrastructure that might have allowed him to coordinate government activity – it was during his tenure that the first steps were taken towards establishing ministries which would take responsibility for the economic and social reforms that the Sultan had announced on his accession. By the end of 1970 Sayyid Tariq had appointed Ministers of Health, Education, Interior, Justice, Information, Social Services and Labour, and Economy. Sultan Qaboos kept control of Finance, Foreign Affairs and Defence, although in practice he shared responsibility for both these latter portfolios with Sayyid Tariq and, in the case of Defence, with Hugh Oldman, who remained in the country as Defence Secretary until 1973. In the absence of clear coordination, government ministers (all of whom were in positions which required them to maximise expenditure) focussed on approving projects for which they could see and demonstrate social and economic need. Because they had at their disposal a level of financial resource the like of which they had never before experienced, neither they nor indeed, it seems, Sultan Qaboos himself saw the need at this time to establish the kind of priorities that a more coordinated and resource-limited government would ordinarily set.

While Sayyid Tariq oversaw the establishment of an embryonic system of government ministries, whose ministers were formally constituted as a Council of Ministers (a body which seems not to have really operated collectively in these early years), Sultan Qaboos also developed two government departments which seem to have been intended, in the first place at least, to offer the new head of state scope for acting outside the conventional structures of the 'modern' government of ministries over which Sayyid Tariq initially presided. It was in the Palace Office and the Diwan that several of Sultan Qaboos's closest and most trusted political allies were appointed. These included Colonel Said Salim, who, as we have seen, was a key actor in the coup, Sayyid Hamad bin Hamood al bu Saidi, formerly the secretary to Sultan Said who had immediately committed himself to Sultan Qaboos and who then became Minister of the Diwan, and Tim Landon, the intelligence officer who had been Qaboos's crucial ally in the organisation of the coup. The establishment of political structures whose leading figures enjoyed the personal confidence of the Sultan is one of the ways in which the new government would come to be distinguished from both the 'modernised' ministerial system and other kinds of 'traditional' systems associated with tribal power-balancing (of the kind preferred by Sultan Said) or the kind of 'family'-dominated administrations which developed in some other Gulf states.

Sayyid Tariq's appointment as Prime Minister had been announced in Sultan Qaboos's inaugural radio broadcast to the nation on August 9, 1970, in which he also announced the new name of the state, its new flag and the implementation of social reforms and economic development. It was also in this speech that the Sultan called on Omanis abroad to return to the country to take part in these new processes. No doubt the fact that this appeal to the substantial Omani diaspora – which included by this time significant numbers who might be considered political refugees, dissidents or opposition figures by the lights of Sultan Said's regime – was backed by the presence and political prominence of Sayyid Tariq so soon after the coup was intended to communicate the extent to which the political climate had already changed and to encourage even the most implacable opponents of Sultan Said to return and contribute. The appeal to Omanis abroad to return also involved the effective removal of obstacles which had for some time prevented Omanis in Oman from leaving the country, too (many of those who had left the country, even for purely economic reasons, had technically done so illegally).[10] Thus one of the effects of this was actually to stimulate a new wave of economic migration, at the same time as it succeeded in securing the participation in government service of a large number of able and well-educated Omanis who had been living abroad. Among those who returned and made a major contribution from the very beginning was Yusuf al Alawi, a former leader of the DLF and its Cairo spokesman; he, along with Ahmad Macki, who

[10] See J. S. Birks and C. A. Sinclair, *The Sultanate of Oman: Economic Development, the Domestic Labour Market and International Migration*, no. 179611. (International Labour Organization, 1978).

was also later to take a senior ministerial role, joined a small circle of Omanis who worked informally as diplomats in the early years of the new government. Another prominent former opponent of the Sultanate, the former Imam Ghalib bin Ali, was invited to return and, indeed, apparently offered the position of Mufti (a new government role as the official leader of the national religious community), which he declined.

Perhaps the most significant group of returning Omanis, however, comprised those of Zanzibari origins, many of whom were not actually returning at all, since, although they could trace their family lines back to the Omani interior and more particularly, in many cases, the Sharqiyah, many of them, born and brought up in Zanzibar, had never before set foot in Oman. In 1964 the new revolutionary government that seized power in Zanzibar ordered Zanzibaris with Omani backgrounds to leave. It is estimated that around 3,700 who did so eventually took up residence in Oman, while others were compelled to seek refuge elsewhere in the Gulf (Dubai, Kuwait) or as far abroad as Cairo. After 1970 a large number of those who had initially fled Zanzibar to destinations other than Oman were welcomed to the Sultanate with an enthusiasm very different from the suspicion with which their predecessors had been received. Many had received good educations, had achieved literacy and possessed technical and administrative skills, and although they did not, in general, speak good Arabic (their first language was almost always Swahili), many of them also spoke English, which was a prized ability in a context where commercial activities involved regular interactions with British and Indian partners and colleagues. Having never spent any time in Oman before, these Zanzibaris were regarded as politically reliable, since they were largely free from tribal or other political allegiances that might compromise their commitment to the national government. As a result many Zanzibaris were able to find employment in sensitive areas, such as security, intelligence, defence and the oil industry, areas in which they still contribute significantly today.

A further indication of how much Oman in the 1970s initially owed to those who had acquired education and expertise abroad can be found in the membership of the Interim Planning Council set up in March 1972. Although this was a short-lived body, soon to be superseded in a series of organisational changes before government structures were consolidated in the interests of the first Five-Year Development Plan (1976–1980), it appears to have been an attempt, following Sayyid Tariq's resignation, to establish some coordination over government projects and to strengthen Omani rather than expatriate participation in key decision-making.

John Townsend, who was soon to be employed as the Sultan's Economic Adviser, describes it as 'the first genuinely Omani vehicle of government' and notes that it was created at the instigation of its own members, among whom Abdul Hafidh Salim Rajab, who held two ministerial portfolios (Economy and also Communications and Public Services), was the dominant figure. Like Rajab, who was a Dhofari, five other members of this Council had been educated either in the Soviet Union or in Eastern Europe. Of the remaining members, two were Zanzibaris who first arrived in Oman in 1970 and one had only recently returned from working in Bahrain.[11] Thus the impulse to 'nationalise', and, in particular, to limit the visible British influence over the conduct of government and the expenditure of oil resources, revealed the importance of high-level education and training – an issue which remains one of the most pressing challenges facing the Omani government forty years later.

In addition to Omani citizens of diverse origins and eclectic educational experiences, a major contribution to Oman's development during the 1970s was made by various groups of expatriate workers. Some of this represented a continuity with past practices: key roles in defence and intelligence continued to be held, either officially or informally, by British officers; the armed forces continued to benefit from the presence of a significant number of Baluchis (while some of these were Omanis, others were direct immigrants from Baluchistan). But the development of Oman's physical infrastructure – roads, hospitals, schools, government offices, new housing – called for a large number of unskilled labourers, the majority of whom came from India and Pakistan. This was an entirely new development. Thus, as Birks and Sinclair note, Oman in the mid-1970s was in the unusual position of being both an importer and an exporter of labour. Relatively unskilled Omani men tended to seek at least temporary employment (for periods of several years in many cases) elsewhere in the Gulf, particularly in Abu Dhabi (which absorbed more than half of Oman's outward labour migration at this time), where they could earn higher wages than in Oman.[12] Another significant and essential group of expatriates were teachers: in 1975–1976 more than half of the teachers employed in Oman were Egyptian, and nearly one-fifth were Jordanian. Of the Omanis employed in education, most had themselves been educated in Zanzibar. Although the distribution of employment between Omanis and expatriates today is very different, it is clear

---

[11] Townsend, *Oman: The Making of a Modern State*, pp. 128–129.
[12] Birks and Sinclair, *The Sultanate of Oman*.

that some key problems persist: a shortfall in the number of highly qualified Omanis in key sectors, accompanied by the presence of numerous unskilled expatriate workers – a combination which leads to high levels of under- and unemployment among young Omanis without substantial professional or vocational qualifications. This is a long-standing structural problem for Oman, to which the protests of 2011 can be attributed at least in part (see Chapter 8). It is hard to see, however, how this problem could have been avoided at this early stage, short of forcing unskilled Omanis into construction labour by refusing them permission to leave the country, an intervention which would have been entirely out of keeping with policies aimed at lifting restrictions on the choices and movements of Omani citizens.

Therefore, Oman's 'nationalisation' under Sultan Qaboos had a cosmopolitan dimension which ensured that everyday life, most obviously in Muscat, came to be characterised over time by visible signs of a range of cultural influences, as well as by the gradual development of a more self-consciously Omani 'look'. The long-standing involvement of Indian and European commercial interests gave the fabric of the city a distinctively hybrid feel, with the signs on shops and businesses combining languages and typographies, and with residential areas developing their own micro-cultures based on the socialisation of a variety of immigrant groups. At the same time, a kind of retrospective 'Omanisation' of public space started to take hold, most notably in the development of a style of public architecture in which features such as fort crenellations, old-style windows and doors and low- rather than high-rise development were to the fore. In Muscat this style is visible both in the growth of residential neighbourhoods with villa developments, such as al-Qurum, and in the construction of a dedicated 'ministries' district in al-Khuwayr. The establishment of commercial malls as the key sites for popular consumption – and now probably the main spaces for everyday sociability – added the full range of global consumer brands to the feel of city life.

In the first years of the new government, then, Sultan Qaboos had gathered around him in various governmental institutions a mixture of Omanis (some, but by no means the majority, from within his own family) and expatriates (either British or, in the case of those more recently recruited, Arab): those with formal educations were, by default, men who had spent substantial amounts of time, and in some cases, their entire lives, outside Oman. After a few years he also started to introduce into the structures of government a category of senior advisers and ministers who would come to constitute one of the most significant axes of power in the Sultanate, all of whom would be Omanis. Depending on whether one wishes to emphasise the continuity of this decision with previous Al Bu Said government practices or, alternatively, to stress its novelty, one might call them either merchants or businessmen. While previous Omani rulers (most notably Sayyid Said bin Sultan) had combined government and mercantile activity in such a way that non-Omanis could effectively take quasi-governmental positions, the nationalisation imperative of the 1970s meant that only prominent Omani merchants or businessmen could participate officially in government (although significant Indian merchants would still enjoy powerful economic positions). Foremost among this new group of Arab businessmen, many of whom started to take positions in Omani government from the end of 1973, was Qais Zawawi, who was appointed Minister of State for Foreign Affairs in December 1971. Zawawi was a successful businessman, whose grandfather had emigrated from the Hijaz to Muscat and set up business there, where he became an adviser to Sultan Faisal bin Turki. Qais Zawawi's father had maintained this connection with the Al Bu Said, serving both Sultan Taimur bin Faisal and Sultan Said bin Taimur. Qais Zawawi himself had moved to Muscat in 1967 and he was a participant in the small Interim Council convened by Sultan Qaboos between his accession to power and the appointment of Sayyid Tariq as Prime Minister.

The appointment of Qais Zawawi as a government minister brought what had for a long time been a standard but informal practice of successive Sultans into the more formal frameworks of government that were being developed at the time. The presence and influence of such figures, whose political credibility derived neither from their membership of the Al Bu Said family nor from their positions within tribal leadership structures, was an important counterbalance to other traditional power centres in the country. As Sultan Qaboos worked gradually to reduce both the actual and formal influence of expatriate British officials and advisers, the Omani business community would become an increasingly important alternative source of post-traditional political support. We use the term 'post-traditional' here in an attempt to capture the fact that the participation of merchant-businessmen was not a non-traditional innovation, but rather the adaptation of a long-standing political tradition in changing circumstances: The appointment of Qais Zawawi also brought his brother, Dr Omar Zawawi, closer to formal government structures, consolidating his position as a key source of advice and support for the new Sultan. It was followed, in November 1974, by the appointment of two further businessmen, Said bin Ahmad al-Shanfari as Minister for Petroleum, Minerals, Agriculture and Fisheries and Mohammed Zubair (whose father, as we have seen, was Sultan Said's Justice Minister) as Minister of Trade and Industry. All four men would play leading roles in Omani government for many years. Qais Zawawi would become Deputy Prime Minister for Economic and Financial Affairs until his death in a car crash in 1995. His brother Omar is still a Special Adviser to the Sultan. Mohammed Zubair (whose father and grandfather, like the Zawawi brothers', had served previous Sultans in business capacities since the nineteenth century) is also an influential adviser today. Said bin Ahmad al-Shanfari retired after twenty-three years as Minister for Petroleum in 1997. At the time of the appointment of Zubair and Shanfari, two new councils – for Finance and for Development – were established to work alongside the existing Natural Gas and Petroleum Council. Both new councils had exclusively Omani membership, with the Sultan as Chair and with Qais Zawawi as Vice Chair in both cases. The membership of the Natural Gas and Petroleum Council changed at this time, so that it, too, had only Omani members, with the Sultan as Chair and the new minister, Shanfari, as Vice Chair.

Here again, therefore, it is important to emphasise that this incorporation of business interests and expertise into government did not (as it would in many countries today) signal an embrace of conventional free-market capitalist economic policy. Indeed, in some respects it involved a very different approach to the economy: one which was to emphasise state planning and control. It also involved the recruitment of a large number of Omanis into government employment, a process which may be seen as simultaneously political in a fairly traditional sense (in that a nascent state can secure the commitment of those who depend upon it directly for their livelihood) and in an economic one, in that it is a mechanism for the distribution of government revenues through wages. In an economy dominated by oil in which productive labour is of subsidiary significance in wealth creation, the classic capitalist relationship between wages and productivity barely obtains: thus for many Omanis in the 1970s it seems likely that government employment – and indeed, employment more generally – would have been understood in terms shaped by previous patterns of allegiance and subsidy. Omani nationalisation therefore built upon and adapted for its purposes existing understandings of social relations rather than securing popular support for a logic of development and modernisation driven by capitalist conceptions of progress from productivity.

These appointments, the establishment of the councils in which the new ministers took leading roles and the emergence of the state as a major employer were, taken together, important, perhaps even central, components of the process of nationalisation which we have identified as characteristic of Omani politics across the board at this time. They led, following a substantial review by Morgan Grenfell of government expenditure (which, as we have seen already, was not entirely coordinated, nor strictly controlled), to the establishment of the country's first Five-Year Plan in 1976. That Oman should have adopted as a core element of its economic policy a state mechanism so readily associated with the economies of the Soviet Union and the socialist bloc – and at a time when so much of the capitalist world was in the process of turning, perhaps decisively, against a state role in the economy – is an important indicator of how little Oman's 'development' at this time was capitalist in nature. Indeed, the state–business partnership forged through nationalisation presided over the implementation of policies – at least in the spheres of education and welfare – that much more closely resembled socialism. Nowhere was this more decisively and successfully the case than in the field of health, where Oman's health service, established on a decentralised foundation of primary health centres, achieved the World Health Organisation's top ranking for the efficiency with which it 'translated expenditure into health' in the World Health Report of 2000.[13] It was this achievement that the Minister for Health at the time, Ali bin Mohammed bin Moosa once described, jokingly in conversation, as 'communist'.[14]

One final dimension of this process of 'nationalisation' has been the incorporation of religious and thus also legal authority into the structures of the state. This involved the formation of a government Ministry for Endowments and Religious Affairs (1971) and the creation of a new position of Grand Mufti (1973), a position taken on its establishment, and still occupied at the time of writing, by Ahmad bin Mohammed al-Khalili, a prominent member of the family from whom many Imams, including the last but one (his father), had been drawn. The Ministry for Endowments and Religious Affairs added Judicial Affairs to its remit in 1981, but in 1997, as part of a reorganisation of government after the

---

[13] World Health Organisation, *The World Health Report*, 2000, p. 150 and annex table 10; Health System Performance in all Member States, pp. 202–203.
[14] Interview with the authors.

promulgation of the Basic Statute of the State (1996; see Chapter 7), a separate Ministry of Justice was created, and all judges were thereafter expected to demonstrate appropriate competence in both religious and non-religious legal codes. Thus religious legal practice has been preserved within what might typically be described as a more 'modern' judicial system but, more important, has become subject to the supervision of government.

This process was further reflected in the development of the religious curriculum in schools, which did not seek to emphasise Oman's Ibadi traditions but rather to present what Marc Valeri has called a 'generic' Islam, in which sectarian distinctions are wholly absent. Mandana Limbert observes that education in Oman makes a priority of cultivating Omani citizenship and that the teaching of religion contributes substantially to this process, by abstaining from an emphasis on regional and religious differences in the country: 'Oman's religious studies textbooks and their important counterparts – classrooms, officially recognized study circles, and private study groups – navigate through the pitfalls and dangers of these contesting and overlapping identity politics.'[15] The Ministry of Education, established in 1971, made religious studies compulsory from first to twelfth grade. In the first six, elementary grades, this involved six weekly sessions, with the number of sessions slightly reduced in subsequent years but remaining a significant presence in the timetable. In so doing it set the terms for religious education and started to provide a standard and accessible alternative to the religious education previously provided in specialist schools and informal settings. At the same time the government sought to exercise influence over these other sources of religious education, especially schools associated with mosques, which were brought under the administrative authority of a dedicated department for the study of Islam within the Ministry of Education. The government also established four institutes for Islamic studies, which taught specialist programmes at the elementary- and secondary-school levels and also offered four-year degree programmes. By 1998 these degree programmes were brought to an end, as similar programmes were now available within Oman at Sultan Qaboos University. The schools offering this specialist religious education were closed in 1995, as part of the government's response to the arrest and conviction of activists accused of

---

[15] Mandana E. Limbert, 'Oman: Cultivating Good Citizens and Religious Virtue', in Eleanor Abdella Doumato and Gregory Starrett (eds.), *Teaching Islam: Textbooks and Religion in the Middle East* (Boulder, CO: Lynne Rienner, 2007), pp. 10–124.

forming an Islamist organisation dedicated to overthrowing the Sultanate (see Chapter 7 for more on this episode). The Sultan Qaboos Centre for Islamic Culture, associated with the Sultan Qaboos Grand Mosque in Muscat, which supervises what remains of the mosque-based religious education, may be understood today as devoted to the general preservation of religious tradition, and, indeed, Omani intellectual culture more generally, rather than playing a central role in shaping the kind of religious education offered to Omani citizens. In 2012 it was renamed the Sultan Qaboos Higher Centre for Culture and Science. A noted Omani scholar, Abdulrahman al-Salimi (great-grandson of Abdallah al-Salimi, whose role in the Imamate of 1913 is discussed in Chapter 3), analyses the aims and effects of this overall process:

These changes represent a larger trend in Omani society that has allowed it to address competing ideologies and incorporate diverse religious opinion in the development of the country. Such change could have represented a challenge to formal religious representation and created unease between religion and state, but this was not the case in Oman. As in many other Muslim states developing in the wake of independence from colonialism, Oman created a Ministry to deal with religious matters and encouraged a class of *ulama* to be the official spokespersons of Islam. In Oman, however, these religious scholars work within the framework of the government, inhibiting the emergence of a class of staunchly political Muslim thinkers and activists, which tends to characterise Islamic states where unique space within the governmental framework is not carved out for religious scholars.[16]

Nonetheless, as Mandana Limbert shows, many Omanis look elsewhere, in private study groups and the like, if they are serious about pursuing a specialist religious education. Teachers of religious education in state schools are frequently regarded as less authoritative than private scholars and other religious figures. Thus there remains some scope for divergent and competing interpretations of Islam and its relation to the nation of Oman. No project of national-identity formation is ever likely to be ideologically watertight.

SEEKING SECURITY: REGIONAL AND INTERNATIONAL RELATIONS

We have seen so far how during the 1970s the consolidation of Oman as a nation-state was accomplished across a range of military, diplomatic,

---

[16] Abdulrahman al-Salimi, 'The Transformation of Religious Learning in Oman: Tradition and Modernity', *Journal of the Royal Asiatic Society* 21.2 (2011), pp. 147–157 (151).

administrative and infrastructural activities, a process financed almost exclusively by oil exports. Each of these processes required new kinds of organisation, requiring government agencies to work at a new, much larger scale and involving operations of ever greater complexity, whether the task in hand was the construction of a primary health care service or the suppression of armed insurrection. One particularly significant aspect of this new scale and complexity was the extent to which domestic policy and foreign policy became increasingly interdependent upon one another. In this section of the chapter we offer an account of Omani foreign policy in the 1970s, emphasising the Sultanate's various efforts to establish its own position in a changing regional and global situation, as well as its attempts to help shape that environment.[17] In all these efforts a key consideration – intimately bound up with Oman's sense of itself as a nation – would be its strategic position at the Strait of Hormuz, through which tankers were transporting more than 50 percent of world oil trade in the early 1970s. This was viewed as both an asset and a responsibility. Considered as an asset, the Strait of Hormuz brought immediately into play the question of Oman's borders and territorial integrity.

The rocky outpost of Arabia which constitutes the southern side of the Strait is now shared by Oman and the United Arab Emirates, with the very tip of the Musandam Peninsula belonging to Oman. As the British government prepared its decisive but hasty withdrawal of military and administrative functions from the Gulf in the late 1960s, the eventual jurisdiction of this territory remained uncertain. Oman's own stability was still jeopardised by outright civil war in the south and the possibility of insurgency in the north (including Musandam). The Emirates which made up the Trucial States were moving towards independence as a federation. But given the failure of a similar plan, brokered by the British in Yemen in 1967, the reluctance of at least one Emirate (Ras al-Khaimah) to enter the new state, not to mention Iranian territorial claims to islands at the western end of the Strait, it was by no means clear how the Arabian side of the Strait of Hormuz would eventually be administered, nor how any new political arrangements would be viewed on the northern, Iranian shore. Oman's interests would lie in affirming its position at the Strait, securing its borders and thereby its sovereignty. Thus Oman's position

---

[17] For a more detailed account of Omani foreign policy in this period, see Joseph A. Kechichian, *Oman and the World: The Emergence of an Independent Foreign Policy* (Santa Monica, CA: RAND, 1995), and for an account which also seeks to explain the interaction of foreign policy at this time with Oman's historical culture and its domestic social life, see Jones and Ridout, *Oman, Culture and Diplomacy.*

at the Strait would become a vital strategic asset. With this asset would come responsibilities, including, most crucially, that for the security of tanker traffic through the Strait. Oman's responsibility for the security of the Strait of Hormuz required that the Sultanate be able to guarantee its own territorial integrity, maintain good relations with its immediate neighbours on the Arabian side, develop effective cooperation with Iran and work towards a reliable regional arrangement for maritime security. Inevitably, given the global importance of the oil trade, taking responsibility for the security of the Strait of Hormuz meant taking a position in the Cold War. It was predominantly, although not exclusively, oil destined for the West that passed through the Strait of Hormuz, and so the security of this trade came to be seen as a crucial factor in the Cold War politics of the Gulf region. Thus the various levels or dimensions of state policy – from oil-financed social and economic 'development' to participation in Western global security strategy – became locked into increasingly complex interaction. Thus, too, Oman's key foreign policy priorities were shaped at this time: good relations with all neighbours, including Iran; collective responsibility for regional security; strong pro-Western sympathies underpinning a commitment to an anti-Communist strategy both regionally and internationally.

As a distinctive and articulable foreign policy, this set of interests and positions really achieved coherence only in the 1970s, but it had both recent and distant antecedents. Iran has been a constant presence for all Omanis seeking to engage with the world beyond its shores, and long-standing habits – not least among them commercial contacts – encouraged cooperation with a large and ever present local power. More recently, however, the realisation by the mid-1960s that another power (Britain) would no longer be present, at least in quite the same way, created new circumstances to which Oman would have to respond. The decision by the British government to withdraw all its forces from military bases east of Suez, articulated as policy from 1966 and expressed in a legislative proposal in February 1967, effectively brought to an end a period of more than 150 years in which Britain had been the major external power with whom rulers of Oman had consistently engaged. Indeed, the terms of Omani–British cooperation through most of the twentieth century had involved most of what passed for foreign policy being conducted first by the British government in India and subsequently by the Foreign and Commonwealth Office in London. Thus the announcement that the British were withdrawing from the Gulf would have made it clear that Oman would need simultaneously to develop its own foreign policy, engage with unpredictable new political developments among its neighbours in both the north and the south and consider how best to manage relations with the United States, which would, in many respects, come to replace Britain as the dominant external power in the Gulf. However, in developing its relations with the United States, which would become the Sultanate's key strategic ally up to and including the present day, Oman would also make sure to develop its relations with Iran. After all, one day the Americans, like the British, might withdraw. The Iranians would not. So even when, after 1979, Iran ceased to be a friend and ally of the United States, Oman would continue to maintain and enhance its good relations with both. In the passage between British withdrawal and the establishment of a strategic alliance with the United States, Oman not only maintained and enhanced its relationship with Iran, but did so under circumstances which would require very careful management of its relations with the Emirates of the Arabian Gulf, many of which regarded Iran as perhaps their most powerful external threat. The development of Omani policy from 1967 onwards has to be considered, therefore, in relation to the establishment of the United Arab Emirates and the regional aspirations of Iran.[18]

It is worth recalling that the political formation which preceded the United Arab Emirates – the Trucial States – had been established on the basis of a peace treaty of 1820, designed by the British to repress the maritime activity of the Qawasim, and that the Qawasim, who had their political base at the Port of Ras al-Khaimah, had been keen rivals of the Omanis for power and trade in the lower Gulf (see Chapter 2). At the same time it may be recalled that the Trucial States were also frequently known as Trucial Oman (which was routinely distinguished from the separate entity known as Muscat and Oman). As John Wilkinson notes in a 1971 paper on the political geography of this south-eastern part of the Arabian Peninsula, 'The name common both to the full title of the Sultanate and to Trucial Oman (a collective name formerly much used

---

[18] For an historical account of the formation of the United Arab Emirates, see Frauke Heard-Bey, *From Trucial States to United Arab Emirates: A Society in Transition* (London: Longman, 1982); Rosemarie Said Zahlan, *The Origins of the United Arab Emirates: A Political and Social History of the Trucial States* (London: Macmillan, 1978); and Abdullah Omran Taryam, *The Establishment of the United Arab Emirates, 1950–85* (London: Croom Helm, 1987). For an analysis of Iranian foreign policy at that time, see Shahram Chubin and Sepehr Zabih, *Foreign Relations of Iran: A Developing State in a Zone of Great Power Conflict* (Berkeley: University of California Press, 1974). John B. Kelly's *Arabia, the Gulf and the West* is a detailed history of the British withdrawal from the point of view of someone who regarded it as an historic betrayal.

for the seven Trucial States) is the clue which indicates that what we are dealing with is the political geography of south-east Arabia in some form of territorial unit called Oman … its dismemberment must have been based on highly variable and inconsistent criteria.'[19] In other words there are deep underlying cultural and historical affinities between the people of northern Oman and those who were on the point of becoming citizens of the UAE. A close study of the map of the present-day UAE confirms this in the sometimes bewildering division of territory between Oman and the various Emirates: in one case there is an Omani enclave, Madha, within the territory of Fujairah, and within Madha itself, there is a further enclave, belonging to Sharjah, named Nahwa. Cultural affinity permitted social interactions and allegiances, such as the employment of tens of thousands of Omani men in the armed forces of the various Emirates, especially in wealthy and powerful Abu Dhabi, which would not normally be possible in circumstances shaped by clear borders and fixed national identities. Suffice it to say that in the late 1960s relations between Oman – itself by no means a clearly defined territorial entity – and the Emirates that were to become the UAE involved a high degree of fluidity and overlapping identities. The questions of how these Emirates would proceed to define themselves, their identities and their boundaries were therefore of immediate and material concern to Oman. From Oman's point of view it was significant that it had historically enjoyed good relations with Abu Dhabi, which was now, as the financial sponsor and pre-eminent power among the Trucial States, seeking to shape the post-British political order. Shaikh Zayed had been the only head of state to visit Sultan Said bin Taimur in Salalah (in 1968), presumably to brief the Omani Sultan on his plans for federation, which at that time envisaged a state that would include not only the seven Trucial States (Abu Dhabi, Dubai, Sharjah, Ras al-Khaimah, Ajman, Fujairah, Umm al-Qwain), but also Bahrain and Qatar. Oman certainly supported the idea of federation under the leadership of Abu Dhabi: such an arrangement would maintain the beneficial economic relationship with Abu Dhabi and would continue to contain any resurgence of Qawasim hostility towards Oman that might undermine its administration of Musandam. In many respects it would offer Oman the most viable and potentially stable neighbour and should, in principle, make the management of relations much easier because it would presumably involve dealing primarily with a single government

---

[19] John C. Wilkinson, 'The Oman Question: The Background to the Political Geography of South-East Arabia', *Geographical Journal* 137.3 (1971), pp. 361–371 (362).

in Abu Dhabi rather than with numerous individual Shaikhdoms. From Oman's perspective this would be particularly helpful when it came to determining territorial boundaries.

While Oman, under both Sultan Said and, then, after July 1970 under the rule of Sultan Qaboos, supported moves towards the establishment of the United Arab Emirates, Iran, with whom Oman also wished to maintain and develop good relations, did not. When the seven Trucial States, Bahrain and Qatar signed their first agreement on federation, in Dubai in February 1968, Iran announced that it 'reserves all its rights in the Persian Gulf and will never tolerate this historic inequity and injustice ... The British Government cannot relinquish and give away land which according to history was taken away from Iran by force.'[20] This is an example of what Shahram Chubin and Sepehr Zabih characterise as the 'shrill defensive diplomacy' typical of Iran's statements and actions in relation to the Arabian states of the Gulf at that time.[21] During the 1960s Iran had placed a renewed emphasis on the development of the south, including its 900-mile Gulf littoral. It had been developing its ports and its oil installations, and its foreign policy priorities in the region focussed strongly on the need to preserve free navigation and to counter a range of perceived threats to its interests arising from the Arab states, some of which, such as Iraq, it feared as potential agents of Soviet expansion and subversion (the fear of Russian interference is a long-standing feature of Iranian approaches to international relations). Iran also sought to limit wherever possible the influence of Nasser's Egypt in the region. In this respect Iran appears to have shared the view of the British government, that the British departure from the Gulf would make the small Emirates or Shaikhdoms very vulnerable to the influence of Nasser and Nasserism. It is likely, given Egypt's role in supporting Dhofari rebels, that many Omanis also shared this anxiety. Iran's participation in the Dhofar conflict on the side of the Sultanate would have been partly motivated by Iran's desire to counter the support offered by Egypt and then Iraq to the PFLOAG and the PFLO. In fact, the Iranian involvement in Dhofar may be understood as a step beyond the 'shrill defensive' posture Chubin and Zabih attribute to the pre-1967 period. After 1967, the defeat and political decline of Nasser, the rise of the Marxists in Yemen and the announcement of the impending British withdrawal from the Gulf, Iran appears to have adopted a much more proactive stance. Not that this would have

---

[20] Cited in Heard-Bey, *From Trucial States*, p. 345.
[21] Chubin and Zabih, *Foreign Relations of Iran*, p. 204.

pleased the Arab Emirates seeking federation: from their perspective, Iran was about to move from a hostile and defensive refusal to engage into a potentially aggressive series of unwelcome interventions.

As we shall see, many of Oman's Arab neighbours would view Iran's involvement in Dhofar with grave suspicion, fearing that the presence of Iranian troops on the Arabian Peninsula might be the first step in an expansionist campaign. For Iran the main priority was to check the possible advance of pro-Soviet Arabism and also, as a crucial and related corollary, to help Oman secure the kind of long-term stability that would make it a viable partner in keeping the Strait of Hormuz, and with it Gulf navigation, free from disruption. But Iran's concerns, substantially shared by Oman, almost inevitably appeared to the Arab Emirates on the verge of federation as evidence of hostile intentions. These fears were exacerbated when, on the eve of the formation of the UAE, on November 30 1971, Iran landed military forces on three islands in the Gulf, over which it had long-standing territorial claims against Sharjah (Abu Musa) and Ras al-Khaimah (Greater and Lesser Tunb). The dispute over ownership of the islands had simmered in the background as the Emirates moved towards unification. Iran had formally renounced a long-standing claim to Bahrain, but appeared determined to press its claims to the islands. An agreement had been reached the day before between Iran and Sharjah over the division of Abu Musa, and the Iranian landing on Abu Musa was therefore unopposed, but Ras al-Khaimah refused to compromise and some armed resistance was mounted to the Iranian intervention, which resulted in some deaths and casualties on both sides. The dispute over these islands remains unresolved to this day and is still a potential source of tension between the UAE and Iran. Oman, keen to retain good relations with both neighbours, has sought to prevent the question of the islands arising as an issue in its bilateral relations with either side. In 1971 Oman avoided taking sides in the dispute by not joining public condemnations of the Iranian action nor following Iraq's attempt to lead the Arab world in severing its diplomatic relations with Iran.[22]

---

[22] There is an extensive literature dealing with the islands issue. See, e.g., Kourosh Ahmadi, *Islands and International Politics in the Persian Gulf: Abu Musa and the Tunbs in Strategic Perspective* (London: Routledge, 2008). An analysis of Oman's position, based on materials from the archive of the Ministry of Foreign Affairs in Muscat can be found in Jones and Ridout, *Oman, Culture and Diplomacy*, pp. 156–158. The legal foundations for the competing territorial claims are examined in Hussein Albaharna, *Legal Status of the Arabian Gulf States*.

The issue of the islands and, more broadly, that of the security of the Strait of Hormuz as it emerged with renewed salience at the time of the British withdrawal from the region and the formation of the UAE indicates why Oman has consistently, since the early 1970s, been the strongest advocate of collective regional security in the Gulf. Given the political circumstances of the early 1970s, it is perhaps inevitable, and certainly entirely logical, that Oman should initially have pursued this objective most thoroughly in the context of its relations with Iran. Geography determined that Iran shared Oman's responsibility for the Strait of Hormuz. With the British withdrawal, Iran became the largest power in the Gulf. Oman's Gulf Arab neighbours had either actively supported armed opposition within Oman or refrained from intervening on the side of the Sultanate. Iran, on the other hand, as we have seen, was playing a significant role in support of the Sultanate in Dhofar. A sound basis for cooperation with Iran was therefore already in place as Oman began to think about how best to secure its position in the immediate neighbourhood. At a meeting between Sultan Qaboos and the Shah in Tehran in December 1971 (that is, at precisely the moment at which tension over the islands and the formation of the UAE had reached a crisis), Oman and Iran agreed to establish joint maritime patrols of the Strait of Hormuz. This agreement was later extended to include joint inspection of shipping passing through the strait. This security cooperation was accompanied by talks which led, in 1974, to a bilateral agreement on the delineation of the maritime border between Oman and Iran.[23] Therefore, when the states of the Arab Gulf started to discuss how they might work together on regional security, Oman started to advance the view that any collective arrangement should include Iran.

Discussions about the possibility of collective regional security in the Gulf began in earnest in 1975, following the Algiers Agreement of that year. This was the treaty in which Iran and Iraq settled, at least temporarily (it would be unilaterally abrogated by Saddam Hussein in 1980) their border dispute over the Shatt al-Arab, the waterway formed from the confluence of the Tigris and Euphrates which flows into the Gulf past Basra in Iraq and Abadan in Iran. The apparent solution to this long-standing dispute encouraged states in the region, including Iraq, to think that a wider collective security agreement might be possible and

---

[23] Details of this agreement and some useful historical context for Oman and Iran's shared interest in the Strait of Hormuz can be found in Asghar Jafari-Valdani, 'The Geo-Politics of the Strait of Hormuz and the Iran-Oman Relations', *Iranian Review of Foreign Affairs* 2.4 (2012), pp. 7–40.

that this could be a welcome local replacement for the security functions previously performed in the region by the British. Iran made one
of the first moves in this direction, when the Shah visited Saudi Arabia
in April 1975 seeking Saudi support for a collective security agreement
(which had been briefly discussed more than fifteen years earlier but not
pursued). Although the Saudis did not make any commitments at this
stage, they did agree to place the issue on the agenda for the forthcom-
ing meeting of the Organisation of the Islamic Conference (the OIC, set
up in 1972 as a Saudi initiative) due to take place in Jeddah in July that
year. At the Jeddah meeting of the OIC the Foreign Ministers of all eight
Gulf countries met for the first time and discussed a Saudi proposal that
any collective security agreement should be based on five principles: the
exclusion of both superpowers (the United States and the USSR) from
the Gulf; the denial of military bases to either superpower; military
cooperation between the regional states on the security of the Strait of
Hormuz; the peaceful resolution of conflicts between regional states; and
a mutual guarantee of territorial integrity between them.[24] In November
1976 Oman hosted a conference of all eight Gulf countries in Muscat
to discuss a series of proposals for collective security arrangements.[25]
The meeting was also attended by the Egyptian Vice President, Hosni
Mubarak, as Egypt was interested in consolidating its own position after
its recent agreement with Saudi Arabia and Sudan over the security of the
Red Sea. Perhaps predictably no progress was made at this meeting. The
Omani Minister of State for Foreign Affairs, Qais Zawawi, announced at
the end of the meeting that 'no positive decisions were taken. The atmo-
sphere was not suitable for reaching a formula on mutual cooperation.'

Two very distinct proposals had been presented. Iran had offered a
plan for a united Gulf army, navy and air force under a joint command,
which would have effectively closed the Gulf to outside shipping except
where the collective created by the eight Gulf states had given permission.
For many participants in the meeting this proposal looked worryingly
like an Iranian bid for a dominant position in the region. Iraq was particularly strongly opposed to this proposal. Iraq was, of course, especially sensitive to fears of Iranian regional domination, but it had also
signed a 1972 pact with the Soviet Union which involved military cooperation based around the port of Umm Qasr. The Iranian plan would

---

[24] See M. H. Ansari, 'Security in the Persian Gulf: The Evolution of a Concept', *Strategic
Analysis* 23.6 (1999), pp. 857–871.
[25] A contemporaneous account of the proposals tabled at the Muscat meeting can be found
in *Foreign Report*, no. 1466, December 1, 1976 (London: Economist Newspapers, 1976).

have jeopardised this, damaging Iraq's important political relationship with the Soviet Union and surrendering power in the Gulf to an Iran with ambitions to establish itself as the political and military representative in the region of the United States. Iraq offered a rather minimalist counter-proposal to Iran's ambitious proposal: a defence treaty between the eight littoral states and free navigation for international shipping, which barely amounted to a collective security arrangement at all.

Whatever the merits of these two opposed proposals, it was clear that there was no way Iraq was going to agree to any arrangement that would include Iran, while at the same time it seemed unlikely that Iran would participate in any structure which did not lock the other regional states into real cooperation on the Strait of Hormuz. So although the Algiers Agreement had been optimistically welcomed as a sign that Iran and Iraq might be able to cooperate, even over the sensitive issue of Gulf security, it turned out, after all, that their mutual suspicion and their opposed Cold War affiliations would make their participation impossible. Omani policy subsequently turned, therefore, to an exploration of alternative collective solutions, including a significant role for the United States, while never quite relinquishing the ambition for a collective security agreement that might also include Iran. Of course, after the Iranian Revolution of 1979 had transformed the political dynamics of the region, this idea of an agreement to which both Iran and the United States might be party would become even more difficult to realise.

We will consider the development of the Oman–U.S. relationship and its security dimensions as a process which ran alongside Oman's participation in discussions with its neighbours about Gulf security. These two lines of diplomatic activity resulted in two distinct achievements from an Omani perspective: the conclusion of a substantive agreement with the United States in 1980 and the formation of the Gulf Cooperation Council (GCC) in 1981. Although the founding documents of the GCC make almost no reference to regional security, the circumstances of its foundation, as we shall see (in the context of both the Iranian Revolution and the Iran–Iraq War), suggest that concern about security among its six founder members was at the very least a major motivating factor in the decision to create the organisation. It is also clear that Oman viewed the GCC primarily in terms of what it might be able to contribute to collective regional security and, indeed, that to this day it continues to believe that the organisation has much greater potential as a security alliance than it does as an economic organisation, let alone a more advanced political union (see Chapter 8). This much is clear, for example, from a

Ministry of Foreign Affairs policy review of Oman's GCC membership conducted in 1989, which begins its analysis by affirming that '[s]ince the challenges it faced were first and foremost challenges to the security and political integrity of the six member states, it is appropriate that the emphasis over the first nine years of the GCC has been placed on finding solutions to problems of regional security'.[26] That Oman in the 1970s was simultaneously pursuing prospects of security cooperation with Iran, with its Gulf Arab neighbours and with the United States indicates the extent to which the Sultanate's emergent foreign policy emphasised this issue, with Dhofar, PDRY and Hormuz, as well as the British withdrawal all shaping the Omani perspective. Having considered Oman's efforts to develop cooperation with Iran, we turn now to its participation in the formation of the GCC, before giving an account of the diplomacy which led to the conclusion of the Sultanate's first bilateral security agreement with the United States.

The formation of the GCC by Oman, Bahrain, Kuwait, Qatar, Saudi Arabia and the UAE can be seen as the logical consequence both of some long-term shared historical characteristics and experiences and of the immediate circumstances created by British withdrawal from the Gulf, on the one hand, and the impossibility of accommodating both Iraq and Iran in a single organisation, on the other. All six states are Arab monarchies, with social and political systems which retain strong characteristics of tribal and personal power. Oman and Saudi Arabia were not formally part of the British imperial protectorate system in the Gulf in which Kuwait, Bahrain and all seven of the Emirates had participated. But all six were at the time of the formation of the GCC broadly pro-Western in their political orientation (notwithstanding Kuwait's reasonably friendly relations with the Soviet Union). As we have seen, they had identified, from at least as early as the announcement of British withdrawal in 1966, and with some urgency thereafter, that both their internal and external security would require them to cooperate among themselves. With the exception of Saudi Arabia, all of them were too small on their own to be confident of standing up to challenges from the larger regional powers. Although Iran had renounced its claim to Bahrain in 1970, it still clearly entertained territorial ambitions in the UAE, and Iraq had by no means abandoned its claim to Kuwait, which it had articulated very forcefully the moment Kuwait had become independent in 1961. Oman was actually something

---

[26] 'The Gulf Cooperation Council: Prospects for the 1990s', Muscat, Ministry of Foreign Affairs Archive.

of an exception in this regard, at least once the Dhofar War was over, as it was larger than all the other states apart from Saudi Arabia and far less vulnerable than any of them to hostile territorial claims based on past possession (with the possible exception of Qatar). One consequence of this difference of situation was that Oman's perspective on Gulf security in the later part of the 1970s tended to prioritise the construction of multilateral frameworks designed to protect the Strait of Hormuz, whereas the perspectives of at least some of its neighbours increasingly seemed to prioritise questions of internal security. This second perspective would come to dominate the thinking of the rulers of the Arab Gulf states after the Iranian Revolution of 1978–1979.

The Iranian Revolution saw the overthrow of the pro-Western regime of Shah Reza Pahlavi by wave after wave of popular protest, and its replacement, after a brief period of uncertainty, by the Islamic Republic, under the leadership of Ayatollah Khomeini. Under Khomeini's leadership, the Islamic Republic of Iran repudiated the country's previous foreign policy orientation altogether, and the United States, previously the Shah's key ally and source of arms, was denounced as 'the Great Satan'. At the same time, the Soviet Union was characterised as 'the lesser Satan': Iran adopted a position of 'neither East nor West'. All the same, the Iranian Revolution completely transformed the Cold War dimensions of regional politics, and with them the dynamics of regional discussions about collective security. The most powerful pro-Western state in the region was suddenly implacably hostile to the United States. There could therefore be no prospect whatsoever of achieving the kind of collective security arrangement which Oman had been advocating earlier in the decade, which would have involved both Iranian and American participation. At the same time the Iranian Revolution massively exacerbated fears among Arab Gulf states that Iran posed a direct and immediate threat to their own security. The idea that Iran might 'export' its revolution, with the Shia populations of Bahrain and Saudi Arabia as its bridgehead, into the Arabian Peninsula took a powerful hold on the imagination of the region, encouraged by persistent rhetoric from within the new Iranian political structure explicitly calling for such pan-Islamic expansionism. Where before Iran might have been viewed with suspicion, and efforts made to exclude it from collective security arrangements, Iran was now seen, in some quarters, as the primary threat to the stability of the Arab Gulf states. Oman, however, took a rather different view and moved effectively to confirm that relations with the Islamic Republic of Iran would continue as relations with the Shah's Iran had done before.

In June 1979, Oman's Undersecretary in the Ministry of Foreign Affairs, Yusuf bin Alawi, visited Tehran to confirm with the new government that all existing agreements between Oman and Iran remained intact. An official Omani statement following this visit emphasised Oman's 'close historical, religious and geographical links with Iran' and looked 'forward keenly to the expansion of our relations and to making the region in which we live together a safer place to live in'.[27]

It was in this new regional context, created by the Iranian Revolution, that Oman made a further attempt to persuade its immediate Arab neighbours to develop a collective security arrangement. Oman's 1979 proposal reflected both the impossibility of including Iran and the ongoing development of Oman's relationship with the United States (which we will discuss later in the chapter). The new idea was that the six Arab Gulf states would raise $100 million for a system of minesweepers and radar to fund a collective naval force, with contributions from the United States, Britain and Germany, to protect the Strait of Hormuz. This proposal was tabled at a meeting of Foreign Ministers in Taif in October 1979, which had been convened to discuss how to respond to the call issued by the new Iranian government to 'export' its revolution throughout the Gulf. Iraq, which continued to offer its own proposals, widely regarded as schemes for acquiring a dominant role in the Gulf, was not invited to this meeting, and nor, of course, were the Iranians. Perhaps unsurprisingly, given the anxieties aroused by the new regime in Iran – felt most acutely in Saudi Arabia and Bahrain with their significant Shia populations – the emphasis of the discussions at Taif shifted from a focus on the Strait of Hormuz (on which the Omani proposal was centred) towards considerations of internal security.

If the Revolution of 1979 put an end to any prospect of Iranian involvement in collective regional security arrangements, the events of 1980 simultaneously ruled out Iraq and propelled the six Arab Gulf states into an agreement among themselves. The Iranian Revolution had created new tensions between Iraq and Iran, not least because Iraq, under Saddam Hussein, came to view the turmoil created in Iran by the revolution as an opportunity to seize a decisive advantage over its neighbour in a struggle for political and military dominance in the northern Gulf. On September 17, 1980, Saddam appeared on Iraqi television with a copy

---

[27] Abd al-Aziz Al-Rowas, Minister of Information, quoted in *Al-Watan*, July 25, 1980, cited in Kechichian, *Oman and the World*, p. 101. For a more extended analysis of Arab Gulf perceptions of the Iranian Revolution and Oman's distinctive position in this regard, see Jones and Ridout, *Oman, Culture and Diplomacy*, pp. 159–168.

of the 1975 Algiers Agreement, which he tore up. Five days later Iraqi forces invaded Iran, opening the first phase of an Iran–Iraq war which was to last until 1988. From the outset this conflict threatened massive destruction and instability in the Gulf: both regimes were unpredictable and their conflict would soon escalate into the waters of the Gulf itself, posing a substantial threat to commercial shipping. While the Iranian Revolution may have appeared to the rulers of the Arab Gulf states as posing the most direct threat to their internal security, the outbreak of a war between the two largest Gulf powers seems finally to have galvanised into decisive action leaders who had previously either found it difficult or placed too low a priority on regional security to reach the necessary political compromises. Three main proposals were discussed at meetings between the six Arab Gulf rulers in Taif in January 1981 and then again at a meeting of their Foreign Ministers in Kuwait in February. Oman's proposal envisaged the most thoroughly integrated approach: it was a development of the scheme put forward back in 1979, and it entailed the formation of a joint military force by all six of the Arab Gulf states. Kuwait's proposal was minimalist by comparison, seeking to establish security cooperation on the basis of information sharing alone. A third proposal from Saudi Arabia, clearly influenced by its government's anxieties following the seizure by militant Islamists of the Grand Mosque in Mecca and the Shia uprising in its Eastern Province (both in 1979), focussed primarily on cooperation on internal security matters. Oman clearly suspected that the cooperation envisaged would fall far short of its own hopes for security cooperation backed by joint military force. Indeed, Oman's insistence on security cooperation apparently led to discussion among other parties of excluding Oman from the organisation under consideration.[28] But Oman, despite its reservations about the limited scope of what was proposed, which was essentially the Saudi internal security plan with summit meetings and aspirations for economic cooperation attached, accepted that this limited organisation was the best option available at the time, and in May 1981, along with Bahrain, Kuwait, Qatar, Saudi Arabia and the United Arab Emirates, it joined in founding the Cooperation Council of the Arab States of the Gulf, more commonly known as the Gulf Cooperation Council (GCC). Article Four of the new organisation's charter, in which its basic objectives are set down, made

---

[28] Matteo Legrenzi, *The GCC and the International Relations of the Gulf: Diplomacy, Security and Economic Coordination in a Changing Middle East* (London: I. B. Tauris, 2011), p. 32.

no specific reference to either security or military matters, but did specify that cooperation would be pursued in the economic sphere, in commerce, in culture, in education and in science and technology research. Of course, the absence of such references by no means meant that security issues were absent from the work and the remit of the GCC. In fact, as the first decade of its history will show, it was issues of internal and regional security that probably exercised its leaders most. Oman continued to press its agenda for regional security within the framework of the new organisation, while also, as we shall see, looking elsewhere to make sure that its own security priorities were properly addressed.

Oman had in fact been looking elsewhere for some time, very aware that attempts to establish a viable regional security structure with its immediate neighbours, however desirable, might not succeed, as indeed was the case. The Dhofar War meant that Oman was probably more acutely aware of its potential vulnerability and more immediately concerned with its position in the Cold War than any of its neighbours. This would certainly have shaped Sultan Qaboos's assessment of the situation in the early 1970s, in such a way as to encourage the exploration of security and military cooperation with the United States, even though this would almost inevitably give rise to concern and even criticism from other allies and neighbours. Relations with the United States were enhanced in 1972 and 1973 by the opening of reciprocal embassies in Muscat and Washington. Discussions about some form of military cooperation began at least as early as 1973. There would be no question of any American involvement in Dhofar: the British were seeking to limit reporting of their role and, with American troops still in Vietnam and anti-American views still dominant in the Arab world, neither Oman nor the United States would wish for anything so visible. But the United States was interested in making use of the RAF base on Masirah in the wake of the British withdrawal from the Gulf, during which this facility would be vacated. Oman granted U.S. military personnel access to Masirah for the first time in 1975, in the wake of Sultan Qaboos's visit to Washington in January of that year, in the context of an agreement which also marked the first Omani acquisition of American arms, in the form of wire-guided missiles which were deployed against PFLO holdouts in the area adjoining the border with PDRY. Both aspects of this deal – the missiles and the access to Masirah – emphasise the extent to which both Oman and the United States understood their relationship in terms of a shared perception of a Soviet threat: for the United States, access to Masirah would help support its air surveillance of the Soviet Indian Ocean fleet and more generally increase its capacity to operate in the Gulf, where the United States clearly believed the Soviet presence was becoming more and more threatening.[29] Perhaps the most powerful sign of that threat (even if, in the long term, it turned out to damage the Soviet Union far more than it threatened the Gulf) was the Soviet invasion of Afghanistan in December 1979, which Cold War analysts were quick to read as the fulfilment of the alleged Soviet dream of the Red Army dipping its boots in the Indian Ocean.

In the mid-1970s the U.S. government had developed its 'Twin Pillars' policy for securing its interests in the Gulf, in which its relations with Saudi Arabia and Iran were the key elements. But by 1979, this policy was completely obsolete as a result of the Iranian Revolution, and Masirah momentarily, and to some Omani chagrin, became part of an American operation against Iran, when it was used on April 24, 1980, as a staging post for the U.S. Air Force during its failed attempt to rescue American hostages being held by revolutionary students and other militants at the occupied U.S. Embassy in Tehran. Omani officials had already been obliged to deny persistent reports of American troops on Omani territory (Qais Zawawi in January 1980 and Abd al-Aziz al-Rowas the following month)[30] or that the United States was to establish military bases in Oman. The use of Masirah in the failed hostage rescue mission was not helpful in this regard. Nonetheless, only about six weeks later the State Department was able to announce that a ten-year renewable agreement had been reached with Oman regarding access to Masirah on an ongoing basis (as well as the possible use of facilities at Khasab in Musandam, Seeb and Thamrayt).[31] The State Department

---

[29] An illuminating presentation of how the Soviet threat in the Gulf was perceived in the United States can be found in Dennis Ross, 'Considering Soviet Threats to the Persian Gulf', *International Security* 6.2 (1981), pp. 159–180. Ross points to the Soviet capacity to undermine the 'northern tier' of pro-Western states between itself and the Gulf, particularly through its role in Iraq; the possibility that it might gain enough influence in the region to use oil supplies as a way of coercing European and East Asian allies into weakening their alliance with the United States; and its capacity to support and sustain a range of opposition movements in the region, from the PFLO in Oman, to that of Palestinians in Kuwait or various ethnicity-based movements among, for example, the Kurds of Iran. Although this article does not officially represent the views of the U.S. government, it is worth noting that at the time of its publication Ross was a member of the policy planning staff at the State Department and when he wrote it he was working in the office of the Secretary of Defense. His government career would later entail extensive involvement in the post-1991 Middle East peace process during the Clinton administration. Ross revisited the question of the Soviet threat three years later in 'The Soviet Union and the Persian Gulf', *Political Science Quarterly* 99.4 (1984), pp. 615–636.

[30] 'Rowas Denies Troops Stationed on Its Territory', *Washington Post*, February 15, 1980.

[31] 'US Announces Pact with Oman on Access to Airbases and Port', *New York Times*, June 6, 1980.

announcement indicated that the U.S. government would be seeking congressional approval for a package of economic and military support for Oman in return. For Oman it was crucial that this agreement not involve a permanent U.S. presence, but permitted instead the use of the facilities in question at Oman's request or in the event of a direct threat to Oman. The political effect of the facilities agreement was almost certainly as intended by both parties. It enhanced U.S. power projection in the Gulf and the Indian Ocean at a crucial time when U.S. plans for regional security had to be reassessed in light of the loss of one of its 'Twin Pillars', Iran. It secured for Oman the promise of American military assistance, close at hand, in the event of a major threat to its security. For both parties it was a concrete realisation of a shared political objective: holding the line against the possibility of Soviet expansion into or within the region. Some of Oman's neighbours and other Arab states, however, viewed this as a step too far in its accommodation of American interests, especially by those who saw themselves as leading the 'rejectionist' group, which opposed the United States on the basis of its support for Israel and which therefore criticised Oman for not agreeing to join in ostracising Egypt following President Sadat's signature of the Camp David Accords of 1978 and the subsequent peace treaty with Egypt in 1979.

By the middle of 1981 Oman had moved substantially beyond the moment in its modern history during which its status as a secure nation-state was under serious internal threat. Oil revenues had permitted the consolidating nation-state to make substantial investments in infrastructure, health, education and welfare. Oil revenues had also enabled significant military expenditure, first as part of the effort to defeat the PFLO in Dhofar and subsequently in building up Oman's capacity to withstand external threats. This military expenditure reflected the government's conviction that a modern military force was an essential asset in a volatile regional environment where external threats, paramount among them, from Oman's perspective, those from the Soviet Union, demanded close attention. Oman's efforts to persuade its immediate neighbours that external threats could best be met through collective organisation had only limited success. There would be no prospect of a regional security agreement involving Iran, especially after 1979. The GCC offered some potential for mutual protection, but not until 1984, when Oman's proposal for a modest joint force (Peninsula Shield) was adopted, did this take any material form. In 1990, as we shall see, the limitations of the initial GCC approach to regional security were vividly exposed when Iraq invaded Kuwait and the states of the Arab Gulf realised they had no alternative but to rely upon U.S. support to defend themselves.

Between 1981 and 1990 the wider world would experience a dramatic change which would have extensive repercussions for the region in general and for Oman in particular. In 1981 the United States was seeking to establish effective defences against a Soviet threat that seemed more powerful than ever. By 1990, the Soviet Union was on the verge of dissolution. In the early 1980s, the United States (and most of Oman's Arab allies) would actively or tacitly back Iraq in its war against the Islamic Republic of Iran (Iran was seen as a new menace in the region, and the war as an opportunity to have it removed or at least substantially contained). By 1990 Iran and Iraq had fought one another to a standstill, and although Saddam Hussein clearly did not recognise the fact, a Pax Americana was now being established in the Gulf. In 1981 Oman was trying to balance its Cold War alliance with the United States against its desire to maintain its good relations with Iran. By 1990 its alliance with the United States was firmly established, but there was no longer a Cold War to be fought. The story of how Oman's diplomacy responded to this new situation, and of how new domestic political institutions – including its elected Majlis ash-Shura – came into being to deal with the increasing complexity of the nation-state, will be told in the chapter that follows, which covers the period from 1981 to the end of the twentieth century.

7

Shura, Diplomacy and Economic Liberalisation, 1980–2000

Historical overviews of Oman since the 1970s almost invariably remark upon the speed of social and economic change. Many Omanis, particularly those older than about forty who have clear memories of what life was like in their own childhoods, also comment on how rapid and comprehensive the transformation of their country has been. A familiar trope is to contrast an Oman of the past, in which there were only three schools, few roads and a supposedly isolated tribal society, with the modern metropolis of Muscat in the late twentieth and early twenty-first century, with its shopping malls and ubiquitous mobile phones. Such accounts tend to lend credence to versions of Omani history that make 1970 a unique turning point and designate the recent past as a 'renaissance'. They also repeat the problematic logic of the 'modernisation thesis', which holds that all 'developing nations' are making their way towards a predestined state of modern development. As we have already seen, however, more discriminating histories tend to identify much stronger continuities between past and present, even as they recognise the extent of the social and economic transformation wrought with oil in recent decades. It is also noted, from time to time, that Oman has a more old-fashioned air than its other oil-rich neighbours. Muscat is not a high-rise city: municipal planning regulations have been used to shape a very different urban landscape from that of Abu Dhabi, Dubai or Doha. A sort of modern Omani vernacular has been developed in both public and private buildings, featuring predominantly white or pale walls, arched windows and crenellations apparently taken from the architecture of the country's forts. Most Omani citizens still observe the convention established during Sultan Qaboos's reign that national dress should be worn in public: this is particularly noticeable in government offices, but the white *dishdasha* with coloured cap or turban is still the outfit most frequently seen in the streets, malls, cafés and other public spaces in Muscat. Women, too, wear distinctive Omani combinations of *dishdasha*, *sarwal* (trousers) and *waqaya* (headscarf), even if the use of the *abaya* (a full cloak, not part of Omani clothing tradition) became increasingly prevalent in Oman, as elsewhere in the Gulf, from the 1980s, apparently in response to the pressures to express piety in public following the Iranian Revolution of 1979 and other regional developments.[1]

Comparisons between Oman and its neighbours made on this basis tend to settle for the conclusion that Oman has somehow managed to retain 'tradition' in the context of 'modernity' in ways which some of its neighbours may not have done. While this is undoubtedly convenient for developing Oman's niche in regional tourism (in which Oman can be advertised to visitors seeking an experience of 'authenticity' alongside their encounter with the rather brasher attractions of Dubai), it doesn't fully capture the dynamic of the historical experience, in which both dress and architecture represent not so much the persistence of the past in the present as the imaginative reconstruction of an idea of the past, for the purposes of establishing a shared culture for the contemporary nation. The Web site of the Centre for Omani Dress makes this very clear:

Since 1970, His Majesty Sultan Qaboos has initiated a number of changes in Oman in order to unify the people and modernize the country. One of his earliest directives was on the subject of Omani dress where a new national dress for men and women was declared. This initiative was not intended to replace the existing regional styles but to choose just one style that would become the nation's dress identity for the first time ever in the Sultanate of Oman.[2]

Continuity is not simply the fortuitous persistence of traditional values, practices and materials in the contemporary world. It is the

---

[1] The adoption of the *abaya* may also been seen in the broader context of Islamic revival (which will be discussed briefly later in the chapter), in which the performance of piety, including the wearing of the *hijab*, became much more prevalent in a wide range of majority-Muslim countries from the 1970s. Among key texts for understanding this movement and the role of dress within it are Saba Mahmood, *The Politics of Piety: The Islamic Revival and the Feminist Subject* (Princeton, NJ: Princeton University Press, 2005), and Leila Ahmed, *A Quiet Revolution: The Veil's Resurgence from the Middle East to America* (New Haven, CT: Yale University Press, 2011). An anthropology of Omani women, including their clothing practices, is to be found in Unni Wikan, *Behind the Veil in Arabia: Women in Oman* (Chicago: University of Chicago Press, 1991).

[2] http://www.centreforomanidress.com/#!omani-dress/c1ukr (accessed August 10, 2014).

consequence of a deliberate policy of productive conservation, and it has helped to constitute a conservative environment in which elements of past social and political practice secure substantial consensus around the legitimacy of the Sultan's rule and the general direction of government policy.

We have elsewhere sought to show some of the ways in which aspects of this conservative environment have contributed to the conduct of Omani diplomacy. In *Oman, Culture and Diplomacy* we suggested that Omanis today understand themselves to be inheritors of a set of social practices, dominated by an ethics or 'culture' of politeness, in which interpersonal graciousness combines with a pragmatic emphasis on keeping all possible channels of communication open.[3] One consequence of this culture is that public expressions of disagreement tend to be viewed as failures of tact. We proposed that one way of understanding the dominance of such an approach was to think of multiple dimensions of Omani life as being influenced by a very particular emphasis on *shura* – the practice of consultation as a way of arriving at important decisions. Like national dress and public architecture, *shura* in modern Oman can be understood as a deliberate contemporary production, not simply as an idea revived from the past. In the account that follows of the construction of political institutions in modern Oman, we consider both the practical and ideological effects of the emphasis placed on *shura*. As we shall see, *shura* as practice and as ideology has been taken up and used in new situations and for the development of political institutions which neither conform to conventional Western norms of 'democratic' government nor represent a simple replication of 'traditional' Omani administration of social and political life.[4]

---

[3] See Jones and Ridout, *Oman, Culture and Diplomacy*, pp. 39–67. Our account is indebted to the earlier work of Fredrik Barth, *Sohar: Culture and Society in an Omani Town* (Baltimore: Johns Hopkins University Press, 1983). We have also treated this feature of Omani life in relation to contemporary political organisation in Jeremy Jones and Nicholas Ridout, 'Democratic Development in Oman', *Middle East Journal* 59.3 (2005), pp. 376–392, and in Jeremy Jones, *Negotiating Change: The New Politics of the Middle East* (London: I. B. Tauris, 2007).

[4] See Hussein Ghubash, *Oman: The Islamic Democratic Tradition* (London: Routledge, 2006), for an extended treatment of *shura* in Omani life and politics. Ghubash's study does not extend its coverage beyond 1964, and although the author claims that *shura* is a 'democratic' practice and that modern Oman inherits this tradition, he makes no claims that Oman's contemporary political institutions are democratic. Nor, indeed, does he articulate the extent to which they may be building upon the inheritance of *shura*.

THE POLITICS OF *SHURA*

In its most general sense *shura* refers to the practice whereby the ruler, leader or *shaikh* consults with others before taking decisions of importance to the society, tribe or family which he heads. It is recommended in the Quran, where Allah encourages the Prophet Mohammed to seek the advice of his companions. In Oman it has a particular historical dimension in that the selection of the ruler or leader is to be achieved through *shura*. This is part of the contribution of the Ibadi religious heritage to successive generations of Omani rulers: because the Ibadis emerged from among those who opposed the dynastic succession in the Caliphate, Ibadis have traditionally insisted that their leader – in Oman, the Imam – be chosen through a consultation, typically among leading social and religious men of the community. These men, known as *ahl al-hall wal-'aqd*, do not constitute a standing institution, but derive from their social position the understanding that they are held to possess the qualifications to act on behalf of their community in taking such decisions. It would have been a variant of this process that led to the election of Imam Ghalib al-Hinai in 1952, and, as we shall see, aspects of this tradition have subsequently been adapted by Sultan Qaboos (and, presumably, those with whom he consulted on the matter) to guide the process of succession after his death. Both the general Islamic context for understanding *shura* and the specific Omani emphasis on the practice are key elements in its ideological value. Contemporary processes and institutions undertaken and established with reference to *shura* acquire legitimacy inasmuch as they are accepted as instantiations of a long-standing religious and social practice. The ideological dimension of *shura* in contemporary Oman can be seen as part of the process of 'nationalisation' described in the preceding chapter. As we shall see, the contemporary invocation of *shura* in relation to institutions like Majlis ash-Shura, Oman's elected parliament, helps situate it positively by association with an Omani national history. The emphasis on *shura* also contributes to a sense of national identity by incorporating elements of Imamate political practice with the dynastic rule of the Al Bu Said in the construction of a polity that can lay claim to a full and legitimate accommodation with Oman's most well-established political traditions and those who might otherwise demand their revival in more confrontational forms.

In practical terms, *shura* is simply a way of widening the range of experience and expertise available to a ruler in the decision-making process. This has more than a merely technical dimension, of course; it is also political. The process of consultation in *shura* seeks consensus, and decisions are supposed to be made only when unanimity is achieved rather than when a matter is put to a vote and a majority view prevails. This means that everyone involved in a *shura* process is understood to be in full agreement with the decision taken: there can in theory be no dissenting minority that might subsequently seek to undo the decision or advocate alternative points of view. In some ways this resembles the convention of collective responsibility that obtains in a number of parliamentary democracies (in the UK and Australia, for example), where government ministers are generally bound to support government policy whatever their individual reservations or disagreements may be. It differs from this convention, however, in at least two respects: governments in such democracies will sometimes resolve contentious issues amongst themselves by means of a vote designed to secure a majority view; members of such governments will sometimes resign their positions if they feel unable to continue to share responsibility for policies with which they disagree. The conventions associated with *shura* do not seem to encourage resignation from the decision-making group in the event of disagreement. Resignation would be a very clear act of public disagreement and would be regarded very negatively, indicating that the individual concerned placed his own views and interests above those of the group. This is precisely what Oman's culture of politeness very strongly discourages.

In order to understand the history of Oman's modern political institutions, it is helpful to keep the significant social and cultural influence of *shura* and its history firmly in mind, and thus to retain a sense of the specificity of institutions which, in many respects, resemble government institutions in other countries and cultures (cabinets, parliaments, national assemblies, Congress and so forth). This emphasis is particularly important when it comes to the more recent developments, from the early 1990s, where institutions in some cultures – including Western democracies – are understood in terms of their representative function. In Oman, as we shall see, members of such institutions as Majlis ash-Shura are considered advisers to the government rather than representatives of interest groups or constituents, let alone political parties. Of course, this understanding is complicated by the extent to which participation in Majlis ash-Shura continues to overlap with members' participation in tribal associations. In this respect the centrality of the principle of *shura* may function as a check on the kind of client–patron representation which tribal affiliations tend to encourage. There is a widely held view in Oman that *shura* provides safeguards against the kind of lobbying and influence-peddling that disfigure some of the West's most celebrated democratic political systems. This view often coincides with a suspicion that the formation of political parties is incompatible with the effective operation of *shura*, in that parties would become vehicles for fixed positions and social interests. In this view, political parties would force members to make their primary allegiance to the party rather than to the nation-state and deprive them of the capacity to consult with one another in the pursuit of consensus. We shall return to these questions of consultation, participation and representation in more detail in our account of the formation and development of the Majlis ash-Shura and related institutions.

Although the formation of Majlis ash-Shura, and especially the gradual introduction of an electoral process, is the aspect of modern Omani politics in which the principle of *shura* (and questions of its relationship to democracy) is most frequently discussed, it is clear that *shura* has had a significant role in the development of other and earlier Omani political institutions. One of these, which offers a further revealing example of the way in which Sultan Qaboos has created new practices and institutions which seek legitimacy through their appeal to popular understandings of Omani tradition, is the Meet the People Tour, in which the Sultan, accompanied by selected ministers and advisers, drives out into Oman, making camp at a series of locations, at which he receives and hears requests, listens to complaints and takes advice from local citizens. This practice was inaugurated in 1977, building on the Sultan's earlier practice of making short visits to locations across the country to meet individual Omanis near their homes. It seemed to function as an alternative way of achieving what in other Arab Gulf states was usually accomplished by the ruler's personal *majlis*, in which citizens were received at an official residence on a weekly basis. In other Arab Gulf states, such as Kuwait, for example, the ruler's *majlis* helps underscore a continuity of tribal leadership which the ruler wishes to maintain. In the case of Oman, the Meet the People Tour in place of the *majlis* might therefore be seen as an attempt to distance the Sultan from the interplay of tribal politics: in coming among the people he also marks out his social and political distinction from them.[5] In the late 1970s and 1980s this tour was often a month long, and sometimes more. These days the scale of the tour convoy and the apparatus of security and protocol around the event have transformed the nature of

---

[5] We have discussed such aspects of monarchical rule in the Arab World in Jones, *Negotiating Change*, ch. 5: 'Jordan and Morocco: The Authority of the Legitimate King', pp. 124–156.

the event: it has a far more ceremonial than practical function and has become part of what Dawn Chatty has characterised as the invention of tradition in Oman, which includes the annual National Day events (military parades, camel races), the construction of palaces, the development of military uniforms and medals and the design of a national flag and other emblems.[6] In its earlier form, the Meet the People Tour appears to have performed an important function in the process we have earlier called 'nationalisation', contributing to a sense that citizens belonged to a national entity whose leader they could see and with whom they could even, theoretically, speak one-to-one. This contrasted strongly with the near invisibility of Sultan Said after 1958. While it probably had almost no direct or measurable effect on government policy, it may be understood as part of a more general mobilization of the discourse and practice of *shura* as participation of a limited but tangible kind.

Perhaps most significantly, the Council of Ministers should be considered a *shura* institution, whose primary purpose is still to provide advice to the ruler. This differs, in principle and in practice, from other relationships between ministers and heads of state and government, such as those in which the head of government is a prime minister who is 'first among equals' or those in which ministers are the executive branch in a government structure where the head of state represents the sovereign people. In Oman the Sultan is sovereign in his own right and laws are issued, as decrees, in his name. As far as can be determined, meetings of Oman's Council of Ministers are primarily occasions at which the Sultan, or whoever chairs a session in his stead, listens to reports, proposals and ideas submitted by ministers. They are not conceived as occasions for the formulation of general government policy: ministers advise on their own areas of responsibility and it is the Sultan, rather than the Council of Ministers, who sets the overall direction of policy and who decides whether any particular proposal for action or legislation should be approved. The Council of Ministers is not a forum for ongoing policy-making so much

---

[6] Dawn Chatty, 'Rituals of Royalty and the Elaboration of Ceremony in Oman: View from the Edge', *International Journal of Middle East Studies* 41 (2009), 39–58 (40–41). Chatty notes that all traditions are in some sense 'invented', with the implication that they are no less authentic as a result. This view contrasts with Marc Valeri's in *Oman: Politics and Society in the Qaboos State*, which, although it draws on similar critical resources, such as Eric Hobsbawm and Terence Ranger's *The Invention of Tradition*, at times gives the impression that such inventions are to be deplored as inauthentic, as though there were some prior and preferable authentic tradition which had never had to be invented. See E. Hobsbawm and T. Ranger, *The Invention of Tradition* (Cambridge: Cambridge University Press, 2012).

as a meeting for the presentation of advice. The purpose of its consultation – *shura* – is to assist the Sultan rather than to advance its own autonomous agenda. That is not to say that ministers do not possess a high degree of autonomy in the management of their own ministries; the point is rather that when they meet as the Council of Ministers, they are not formally seeking one another's support, and nor do they generally seek to present a collective view to the Sultan. Consensus is established, therefore, around the Sultan's decision, following his receipt of his ministers' advice. Subsequent institutions, as we shall see, have begun with this structure largely as a kind of socio-cultural default: the extent to which Omanis have begun to experiment with alternative relations and modes of operation will be the measure of the novelty of institutions such as Majlis ash-Shura.

EXPANDING POLITICAL PARTICIPATION

In this section we discuss the process of gradual institution-building, in which the consultative bodies established in the 1970s have evolved into the current combination of one elected and one appointed assembly, or *Majlis* (majlis means assembly). Sultan Qaboos started to build a modern structure of government from the beginning of his reign in 1970. Initially this involved small consultative bodies composed of very senior ministers and advisers, but over time the scope of consultative mechanisms was extended to include, first, the State Consultative Council (1981) and then Majlis ash-Shura (1991), initially as an appointed body after a limited electoral process, which was then extended to allow women to vote and stand for election in 1994 and subsequently opened to universal adult suffrage from 2003. Alongside Majlis ash-Shura, Majlis a-Dowla, first appointed in 1997, came to form a bicameral legislative council known as Majlis Oman. In 2011 (as we shall see in Chapter 8), Majlis ash-Shura acquired the formal power to propose and enact legislation. This is the evolutionary sequence we trace here. Again, it is important not to see this process of institution-building in teleological terms. There was not a predetermined 'modern' state of affairs to be achieved through the gradual transformation of a 'traditional' practice – *shura* – into 'modern' institutions. Instead we might think of this process as one in which *shura* itself, as a process of discussion without predetermined outcomes, was encouraged as a way of building institutions capable of involving people in the economic and social development of the country.

Most analyses of Oman's political institutions trace the modern development of *shura* institutions to the establishment in 1979 of the Agriculture, Fisheries and Industries Council.[7] This body was appointed by the Sultan, with twelve members, and, according to the decree which established it, was intended to discuss economic policy and to encourage citizen participation in government decision-making. It represented the first formal expansion of forums through which the Sultan and his government might receive advice, beyond the Council of Ministers and the various interim and planning councils convened in the early 1970s (discussed in Chapter 5). The explicit reference in the decree to the extension of citizen participation makes its foundation significant in marking a shift in conceptions of state institutions to include the idea that citizen participation might be an end in itself, as well as a way of maximising the expertise in government service. This council functioned for slightly more than two years, during much of which time, it transpired, the Sultan was leading a process of consultation that would result in its replacement by a much larger body, the State Consultative Council (Majlis al-Istishari lil-Dawla), in 1981. For about a year a group of senior figures worked to prepare both the structure and the appointed membership of a new forty-five-member council; among these senior officials were Sayyid Fahd, the Deputy Prime Minister for Legal Affairs; Sayyid Hamad bin Hamood, the Minister for Diwan Affairs; Sayyid Badr bin Saud, the Minister of the Interior; Sayyid Mohammed bin Ahmad, formerly Minister of the Interior; Hamood bin Adballah al-Harthi; Yusuf bin Alawi; Salem al-Ghazali; and Mohammed Zubair. It is worth noting that these preparatory discussions were undertaken by men with political authority deriving from a range of sources: the Al Bu Said family, the tribes of the interior, the business community and Dhofar.

---

[7] Accounts which focus on the development of these institutions include Dale Eickelman, 'Kings and People: Oman's State Consultative Council', *Middle East Journal* 38.1 (1984), pp. 51–71; J. E. Peterson, *The Arab Gulf States: Steps Toward Political Participation* (Westport, CT: Praeger, 1988), pp. 102–108; Abdullah Juma Al-Haj, 'The Politics of Participation in the Gulf Cooperation Council States: The Omani Consultative Council', *Middle East Journal* 50.4 (1996), pp. 559–571 and 'The Political Elite and the Introduction of Political Participation in Oman', *Middle East Policy* 7.3 (2000), pp. 97–110; Uzi Rabi, 'Majlis al-Shura and Majlis al-Dawla: Weaving Old Practices and New Realities in the Process of State Formation in Oman', *Middle Eastern Studies* 38.4 (2002), pp. 41–50; and Marc Valeri, 'Liberalization from Above: Political Reforms and Sultanism in Oman', in Abdulhadi Khalaf and Giacomo Luciani (eds.), *Constitutional Reform and Political Participation in the Gulf* (Dubai: Gulf Research Center, 2006), pp. 187–210.

The new council (hereafter SCC) drew its members from three sectors of Omani public life: the government, the shaikhly families and tribes and the business community. Seventeen of the forty-five members were from the government; ten places were specifically reserved for undersecretaries, appointed ex officio, and seven were allocated by name to specific people. Seventeen members were drawn from the various regions of the Sultanate and were nominated by their *wali*, while the eleven members drawn from the business community were nominated by the Oman Chamber of Commerce (established in 1978). In 1983 the membership of the SCC was increased to fifty-five, mainly by increasing the number of members nominated from the *wilayat* or governorates from seventeen to twenty-five. Eickelman – whose analysis of the SCC is the most detailed – notes that there was some confusion regarding the responsibilities of those members drawn from the regions, with some understanding their appointment to derive from their position in their specific regional, ethnic or tribal groups, and their task to 'represent' the views and interests of these groups. The Sultan subsequently supported the view, also articulated by the Executive Bureau of the SCC, that each of them had a responsibility to 'represent' all of Oman. One reason, we suggest, for this confusion is that it was not entirely clear to what extent members were expected to 'represent' anyone. The creation of a state institution in which government policy could be discussed by people not involved in its formulation or implementation may in fact have been designed, at least in part, to counterbalance existing 'traditional' mechanisms of representation in which communities and individuals would seek to advance their interests by having their tribal *shaikhs* make representations on their behalf. The creation of such institutions is frequently considered to be part of an attempt either to erode the authority of such local sources of political power or to draw them into the state bureaucracy in order to supervise their activities more effectively and to align them with government policy, in a manner consistent with the nationalisation of legal and religious practices discussed in Chapter 5. Eickelman also points to a substantial overlap between the national government employees and the SCC members appointed from the regions, noting that nearly half of the regional members were in fact government employees. Since the government was the largest employer of Omani citizens at this time, and government employment was so strongly favoured as a source of both income and prestige among educated Omanis, this was perhaps inevitable, but it clearly raised enough concern about the likely tendency of government employees to take a government 'line' on all issues that the Sultan and the

SCC President, Khalfan bin Nasser al-Wahaybi, discussed the matter and declared that all members, including those appointed in the government category, were required to 'deliberate on all matters as Omani citizens, not as advocates of government policy'.[8] One conclusion to be drawn from this experience, and to be taken into consideration in analysing the subsequent establishment and development of Majlis ash-Shura, is that there is a sense in which Omani politics permits a far less clear distinction between government and governed than that which obtains in electoral democracies. Institutions such as those discussed here are not conceived as vehicles through which citizens can articulate or advance their *opposition* to the government, nor, indeed, pursue any inclination to change it (by removing one set of people from office and replacing them with another). They are understood rather as occasions in which citizens can contribute to and participate in the process of government, on terms which owe much to conventional understandings of social and political hierarchy and the culture of politeness. Critics have variously described this polity as authoritarian or paternalistic, and the institutions it has produced as politically powerless: to some extent these views measure the efficacy of these institutions in terms of their capacity to *oppose* government. Within a framework shaped by the discourse of *shura*, opposition is not seen as part of their role, however. Opposition as such was, in the early 1980s at least, still seen as something to be avoided, a concept usually imagined to entail attempts to overthrow the current order altogether, particularly bearing in mind that organisations with precisely that aim had seriously threatened the integrity of the state within most people's living memory.

Ten years after its foundation, the SCC was itself replaced by a new body, Majlis ash-Shura, in 1991, which has continued to develop for more than twenty years until the time of writing. The name of the new institution is, interestingly, more traditional than that of its predecessor and makes explicit the intention that it be considered a development of Omani *shura* practices. It also clearly represents a gradual extension of citizen participation in government beyond that offered by the SCC, since, even in its first incarnation, Majlis ash-Shura revised, in what can be called an inclusive direction, the terms upon which members were appointed and the nature of their relationship with government. Although far from creating a forum for the organisation of an opposition to the government or encouraging a more adversarial politics, Majlis ash-Shura was

---

[8] Eickelman, 'Kings and People', 59.

specifically conceived as an institution in which the government itself did not participate. It therefore emerged, in distinction to its predecessor, as a body comprising members of only two of the three groups specifically accommodated in the SCC – the people of the regions and the business community. Its identity as a national institution in which no particular interests were supposed to be represented was emphasised by the removal of any specific allocation of seats to defined groups or categories, such as the business community or private sector, as in the SCC.

Our account of the development of these political institutions has so far focussed on their endogenous nature, presenting them as the products of a specific and domestic intersection of policy and circumstance. This is an important emphasis, because it resists the temptation, to which some analysts have yielded, to understand the development of Oman's political institutions in comparative terms and to measure them and their efficacy by criteria drawn from institutions in other, mainly Western societies, which are unquestioningly established as norms from which any deviation is to be seen as a deficiency. But, all the same, Oman's political institutions have not emerged or been designed in a vacuum. So before proceeding to an account of the establishment of Majlis ash-Shura and Oman's gradual adoption of citizen elections to select its members, we turn briefly to consider the broader context in which these developments took place.

Two major events or processes were of particular significance: the first was the collapse of the one-party state regimes of Eastern Europe, which erupted into visibility during 1989 and accelerated in the following two years; the second was the Islamic revival, which had begun to gather strength in the 1970s and which had manifested itself in numerous ways, both social and political, throughout the region through the late 1970s and 1980s (from the revolution in Iran and the seizure of the Grand Mosque in Mecca in 1979, to the Mujahedin resistance to the Soviet invasion of Afghanistan and the rise of Islamist movements in north Africa, including the aborted electoral victory of the Islamic Salvation Front in Algeria in 1988). While Oman in the late 1980s did not resemble the one-party states of Eastern Europe, and nor did its government face the kind of direct mass challenge from political movements riding the Islamic revival, the conjunction of these two global developments clearly invited reflection within the Omani government and from Sultan Qaboos. An Omani government review of political institutions carried out in 1990 not only considered the potential for the gradual transformation of existing Omani institutions in relation to the ideas and practices of democracy (which had become such a prominent buzzword in mainstream global political discourse at that time) but also included analyses of the revolutions in Eastern Europe and the consequences for the region of the end of the Cold War.[9]

The social, political and intellectual origins of the Islamic revival are often located by historians and other scholars in Egypt, and some of the most significant studies of the phenomenon are based on field work conducted in Egypt.[10] The formation there, in 1928, of the Muslim Brotherhood and the influence of the thought and writings of its founder, Hassan al-Banna, of Sayyid Qutb and of numerous other Muslim intellectuals (many of them Egyptian or educated in Egypt) are frequently cited as crucial to the development of a widespread turn towards Islam as a source of solutions to both political and social problems. Some accounts tend to focus on the more extraordinary headline events associated with this, such as the assassination of President Sadat in 1981 and other activities by militants who took up arms against regional regimes in the name of *jihad*, or the violent suppression of Muslim Brotherhood activity, such as the military assault by government troops on the Syrian city of Homs in 1982. While such events certainly contributed to the wider regional and global context in which Sultan Qaboos contemplated the gradual extension of political participation in Oman, it seems likely that the more pervasive but less spectacular growth of a new everyday piety in numerous Muslim societies was a more immediate spur to reflection in Oman. This has been a complex and multifaceted process, manifesting itself in different ways in diverse Muslim societies. Its key characteristics, however, are perhaps best explained as a widespread conviction, shared by millions of people, that the just and dignified life is to be found through everyday religious practice in which individuals regulate their behaviour, their social interactions, their physical comportment, consumption and dress in such a way as to orient themselves and those around them towards the ethical conduct to which they are called by the Quran and the Hadith. A key aspect of this everyday public piety has been *da'wa* – the

---

[9] One substantial outcome of this review was a report by the Ministry of Foreign Affairs in 1990, which was subsequently augmented in 1994 with analyses of a wide range of democratic practices in non-Western and developing nations, with particular emphasis on Arab and Muslim countries.

[10] Two significant works, Gilles Kepel's *Muslim Extremism in Egypt: The Prophet and the Pharaoh* (Berkeley: University of California Press, 1985) and Saba Mahmood's *The Politics of Piety: The Islamic Revival and the Feminist Subject* (Princeton, NJ: Princeton University Press, 2005), are exemplary of this focus.

calling for others to join such practices, in individual and family life and in wider social organisation. This led to the proliferation of neighbourhood mosques, to the development of charities and social welfare organisations, including, of course, many educational initiatives by means of which this Islamic revival could be communicated through an entire society, as well as sermons on audio and video cassettes, numerous widely distributed texts and, from the later 1990s, Web sites.

In some Muslim societies this social organisation also extended into the political domain. In Egypt it saw the Muslim Brotherhood, technically illegal but practically tolerated by the Mubarak government, develop an extensive national political network (which would be the basis for its rise to power following the revolution of 2011). In Algeria it led to the rise of the Islamic Salvation Front, formed as a political party in 1989, which emerged as the largest party in the first round of parliamentary elections in 1991, only for the elections to be cancelled by a military coup in January 1992. It had also led to the less controversial emergence of Brotherhood-associated political parties in Jordan, where the Islamic Action Party is a substantial presence in parliament, and in Kuwait, where its representatives have held seats in the National Assembly since 1992. In the UAE, where Muslim Brotherhood members in exile from Nasser's attacks on their movement in the 1950s and 1960s had helped found a local organisation, Islah, in 1974, members and supporters of the movement gained considerable social and political influence, especially in education, winning the allegiance of a large number of young and educated Emiratis. In Qatar, Yusuf al-Qaradawi, an Egyptian religious scholar who had studied with the Brotherhood's founder, Hassan al-Banna, established and led a faculty for Islamic studies at Doha University in 1977 and subsequently gained a large international following for his writings and pronouncements on Islam and everyday life.

The Muslim Brotherhood was a Sunni organisation, and the Islamic revival more generally was strongly Sunni in character. It was accompanied by the rise of a politicised Islam among Shia Muslims, most significantly in the Iranian Revolution of 1979. In Oman this meant that the direct appeal of both movements was somewhat reduced: the non-sectarian emphasis shaped by Oman's Ibadi tradition limited the effects of the Islamic revival to a more general increase in public piety. The only significant Oman-based organisation associated with this phenomenon was a group called al-Da'wah wa al-Tabligh, which was active from the 1970s to the 1990s and numbered among its adherents a mixture of citizens, including some relatively affluent businesspeople. One additional and highly visible consequence, in Oman, of this regional resurgence in Islamism, has been the increased religiosity of everyday life. Conservative sentiments and views on issues such as women's dress and the consumption of alcohol and tobacco became much more widespread and confidently expressed in Oman from the early 1980s.

Even without much formal political organisation in Oman associated with the Islamic revival, it was significant that the younger generation, including students in higher education and recent graduates, comprised many citizens for whom this new religiosity had a strong appeal. Opportunities for this generation to participate in shaping the society they lived in were limited by government institutions and by the tribal structures in which power and authority lay with their fathers and grandfathers. The social and religious activity associated with the new religiosity gave some younger Omanis a sense that they could make a contribution. The impact of the Islamic revival on considerations of Omani political institutions was to bring to the forefront the question of participation. Did the new religiosity offer a challenge to the existing social and political order or was it an opportunity? Did the new composition and character of Omani society require that *shura* be extended to a much broader constituency? Finally, bearing in mind the succession of successful revolutions in Eastern Europe in the name of democracy, how might an extension of *shura*-based political participation be informed by an understanding of the development of democratic politics in Europe?

This was the context, then, in which Sultan Qaboos announced the establishment of Majlis ash-Shura in November 1990, on the occasion of Oman's twentieth National Day. In the speech in which he made the announcement, Sultan Qaboos hinted that he saw the replacement of the SCC by Majlis ash-Shura as part of an endogenous process shaped by previous Omani practice, as well as by reflection on political practices elsewhere in the world, stating that this latest development in Oman's political institutions was 'in accordance with our established tradition to work conscientiously and gradually at a pace which suits the life of our country. We should be open to the experiments of others to enrich the Omani experiment without imitation for the sake of imitation.'[11] The new body met formally for the first time, after a limited election process, in December 1991. The election process involved the nomination of candidates in each of Oman's 59 *wilayat* and the submission of a list

---

[11] Sultan Qaboos, National Day Speech, 1990. http://www.omaninfo.om/english/option .php?Action=PagePrint&CatID=154&PageID=515

of preferred candidates to the Deputy Prime Minister for Legal Affairs, who then, subject to the approval of the Sultan, chose one candidate from each *wilaya* to sit in Majlis ash-Shura. The selection of candidates for inclusion on the lists was entrusted to caucuses of leading citizens in each *wilaya*, who, according to Oman's Ministry of Information, participated on the basis of their 'valued opinion and experience': they were, in effect, instances of *ahl al-hal w'al aqd* at work. Along with this limited extension of the appointment process, perhaps the most significant change expressed by the formation of Majls ash-Shura was that government officials could not be members of the new body. As part of the same logic, in which the Majlis ash-Shura was understood less as part of the government than as a complement to government functions, it acquired the power not just to review legislation and make recommendations, but to question ministers in person and in public over their ministries' activities and performance. Majlis ash-Shura thus had the potential to provide new levels of accountability and transparency for Omani government. Another way of understanding how Majlis ash-Shura differed from its predecessor, the SCC, is to consider the distinction indicated by their names: Majlis al-Istishari lil-Dawla suggests a state council in which consultation is a more one-way process than the full reciprocal process implied by the term *shura*. As Sadek Sulaiman, a former senior Omani official and intellectual has explained:

It is important to make two observations here. The first is that the etymological form of *shura*, derived from the root *shawr*, or advice, means mutual consultation in its widest scope – a collective deliberation in which all parties are *exchanging* counsel. The term *shura*, as such, is to be distinguished from the term *istisharah*, which means one side seeking counsel from another, and from the term *tashawur*, which means mutual consultation but on a lesser scale than that envisioned in *shura* as a nationwide participatory political exercise. For instance, in my country, Oman, the present assembly was first named *al majlis al istishari*, and only several years later renamed as *majlis al shura*, thereby claiming a more democratic posture.[12]

The first Majlis ash-Shura sat, as specified in the decree that had established it, for a three-year term, at the end of which a new election of members took place. This time each *wilaya* with a population of more than thirty thousand citizens sent two members to sit in Majlis ash-Shura, which increased membership from fifty-nine to seventy-nine. It was

---

[12] Sadek Sulaiman, 'The Shura Principle in Islam', http://www.alhewar.com/SadekShura .htm (accessed August 16, 2014).

through the 1994 process that the first two female members of Majlis ash-Shura were appointed – Shukoor al-Ghammari in Muscat and Taiba al-Maawali in Seeb – both of whom served for what was at that time the maximum of two three-year terms. At the time of their first election, they were the only female members of a comparable body within the GCC states. Elections for the third session, held in October 1998, returned members to an expanded eighty-two-member Majlis ash-Shura. Around fifty thousand citizens, both men and women, participated in this process. Majlis ash-Shura did not have the power to propose legislation: its role was to scrutinise and advise on proposals submitted to it by ministers. It formed specialist committees to permit members to consider legislation in detail. Aspects of government policy deemed to be sensitive in terms of national security were excluded from consideration by Majlis ash-Shura: thus issues pertaining to the work of the Ministries of Oil, Defence and Foreign Affairs were not discussed there. Thus, while *shura* was understood to involve reciprocal council, the Sultan and his government continued to set the terms on which this reciprocity would work by limiting the acceptable topics for consultation as well as circumscribing eligibility to consult and be consulted. The early years of Majlis ash-Shura conformed to a familiar pattern in modern Omani political life, in which a gradual expansion of participation was directed from above. Membership of Majlis ash-Shura seems to have broadly reflected this emphasis, with members largely drawn from similar social groups to those who selected them – traditional shaikhly families and leading tribes, as well as merchant families – alongside some representation from more emergent elite groups, including those whose social status derived from having achieved an advanced education. Both the selection process and the constitution of Majlis ash-Shura itself could be considered a gradual redefinition of who counted as *ahl al-hal w'al aqd*. The next significant development in the history of Majlis ash-Shura would come in 2003, with the introduction of universal suffrage. We shall return to this development in due course, after resuming our more or less chronological account of significant political events in Oman in the 1990s and beyond.

DIPLOMACY: THE FIRST GULF WAR
AND THE MIDDLE EAST PEACE PROCESS

As the Omani government sought to understand the political implications of the collapse of the one-party states of Eastern Europe in relation to the extension of political participation, the global consequences of these events – the end of the Cold War, in short – were beginning to have significant consequences for the balance of power in the Gulf. Oman's foreign policy had been very strongly influenced, as we have seen, by Oman's particular experience of Cold War confrontation (in Dhofar). The end of the Cold War would therefore be an occasion for the invigoration of a more autonomous foreign policy during the 1990s. The first major consequences, however, for Oman would arise as a result of Iraq's ill-judged invasion of Kuwait in August 1990 and Oman's participation in the international coalition assembled under U.S. leadership to reverse it.

Iraq invaded Kuwait after a period of issuing increasingly threatening statements and demands that Kuwait reduce its oil production, the effects of which were suppressing the global price with negative consequences for Iraq, whose government claimed that Kuwaiti overproduction constituted an act of aggression. What lay behind these claims was Iraq's desire to strengthen its regional position by acquiring territory with good access to Gulf waters (which had also been an issue in its attack on Iran in 1980) and to use its military power to claim leadership of the Arab world and, more particularly, of the anti-American and generally less wealthy nations within it. Iraq therefore claimed Kuwait as its thirteenth province, taking less than two days to overwhelm the country and force its ruling al-Sabah family into exile. As part of this bid for political ascendancy in the Arab world, the Iraqi President, Saddam Hussein, linked his action to the Israeli occupation of Palestine, effectively insisting that he would accept no resolution of his country's 'dispute' with Kuwait until Israel had withdrawn from Palestine. For seven months Iraq occupied Kuwait, in the face of nearly unanimous international condemnation and a sequence of Security Council Resolutions, first imposing sanctions and eventually authorising the use of military force against Iraq. The United States assembled and led a military coalition, stationing substantial ground forces in Saudi Arabia, from which a ground assault was launched on February 24, 1991, following an air bombardment that had begun in mid-January. Iraqi forces withdrew entirely from Kuwait by the end of February and a ceasefire was declared, prior to an Iraqi surrender on March 3.

One of the misjudgements Saddam Hussein made in invading Kuwait was the assumption that the Soviet Union would play its traditional Cold War role and block any attempt by the United States to intervene directly in support of Kuwait. But the interests of the Soviet Union no longer lay with contesting American interests in the Gulf. Instead diplomatic cooperation with the United States had become an emergent objective in

Soviet diplomacy, and although President Gorbachev made last-minute attempts to avert the United States-led coalition's military assault on Iraq in January and February 1991, the Soviet Union had condemned the initial Iraqi invasion and had backed the UN resolutions upon which the military coalition had been assembled. Saddam Hussein's Iraq would get no Soviet protection. This misjudgement was related to and compounded by Iraq's failure to win any substantial support from within the Arab world which he aspired to lead. Iraq had presumably relied upon the continued solidarity of the so-called rejectionist camp within the Arab League, a group which overlapped substantially with those states that enjoyed Soviet backing of some kind. In the event a number of very different political allegiances superseded obsolete Cold War and declining pan-Arabist affiliations, and with the exception of abstentionist positions from Yemen and the PLO, Arab states largely rejected Iraq's position and many cooperated actively in the military coalition assembled by the United States to remove Iraqi forces from Kuwait. Oman was among them, contributing ground troops, making facilities available to U.S. forces (at Masirah and elsewhere, in keeping with the 1980 agreement) and providing locations for signals intelligence activity.[13] The American military presence in Oman during the build-up and the invasion itself was modest in comparison with the presence in Saudi Arabia. The American presence in Saudi Arabia was also a great deal more controversial, because Saudi Arabia had previously made its refusal to host such a presence on its soil a matter of religious and ideological principle, which Oman had not, and because it was new, whereas the American presence in Oman was simply making use of an existing arrangement.

The international and regional responses to Iraq's invasion of Kuwait made it very clear that both regional and international relations had undergone a major transformation. The region was no longer governed by a Cold War framework in which the Soviet Union and the United States would seek to prevent or negate any significant exertion of explicit power by the other in the Gulf. Existing regional structures, including the Arab

---

[13] Some sources suggest that Oman contributed as many as 25,500 ground troops, 75 tanks, 12 patrol ships and 50 combat aircraft to the coalition effort. The original source for these numbers is probably Joseph P. Englehardt, 'Desert Shield and Desert Storm: A Chronology and Troop List for the 1990–91 Persian Gulf Crisis', a Strategic Studies Institute Special Report, produced at the U.S. Army War College in March 1991. The author of this report was the Director of Middle East Studies in the Department of National Security and Strategy at the U.S. Army War College at the time, and his analysis may be assumed to reflect the U.S. government position on the Omani contribution. No Omani sources either confirm or contest this assessment.

League as the supposed guarantor of Arab unity through diplomacy and the GCC as a collective security body, had completely failed to protect Kuwait. The Arab states of the Gulf confronted the reality that their security would depend, given the present configuration of global and regional forces, on the presence of the United States in the region – a reality which several of them had in the past tried to deny. Oman's earlier arguments in favour of an American role in Gulf collective security now looked much more convincing to its GCC partners. Therefore, in the aftermath of war, with Kuwaiti independence restored but Iraq still hostile, if contained, the GCC was forced to rethink its previous reluctance to enter into a full and effective collective security arrangement. Indeed, the GCC attempt to develop such a structure had resumed even before the end of the war. At its 1990 summit, held in Doha on December 22–25, leaders established a committee, to be chaired by Sultan Qaboos, to consider options for a postwar security framework. This committee presented its findings at the 1991 summit in Kuwait, with a proposal for a 100,000-strong unified GCC military force its principal recommendation.

This proposal was consistent with the approach Oman had taken to regional security since the 1970s. It was also envisaged as a project compatible with wider cooperation, particularly with Iran. Oman had initially sought an arrangement for regional security that would incorporate not just the six GCC states, but also both Iraq and Iran. Although this was discussed at the Muscat Summit of November 1976, as we have seen (Chapter 6) it did not command much support. In 1990 and 1991, noting the restraint with which the Iranian government had conducted itself during the build-up to the First Gulf War, Omani diplomats continued to advocate including Iran, even though Iraqi participation was clearly not possible at this juncture. By the time the war was at an end, however, a new proposal emerged, in the form of the Damascus Declaration of March 6, 1991, in which the six GCC states, Egypt and Syria proposed the formation of an eight-nation defensive alliance, effectively combining Egyptian and Syrian military resources and manpower with the financial capacities of the GCC states. In practical terms this proposal relied upon the fact that Egyptian and Syrian troops were already stationed in the Gulf, as part of their contribution to the military coalition assembled to expel Iraq from Kuwait. Egypt and Syria would expect substantial financial benefits in return for their contribution. There was some doubt, however, about the Egyptian and Syrian military capacity, especially when compared with the scale and effectiveness so recently demonstrated by the United States. In political terms its appeal, in some quarters at least, was that Egyptian and Syrian forces would be less controversial than the Americans (whose presence in Saudi Arabia had already begun to arouse the opposition of Islamist groups and would later be a mobilising factor in the formation of Al-Qaeda). There was also some political interest in the prospect of an alliance which might consolidate a larger and broadly pro-Western Arab consensus, by including the previously 'rejectionist' Syrian government of President Hafez al-Assad alongside the already pro-Western Egyptian and Arab Gulf governments.

Omani diplomats viewed the proposal with reservations and, in consultations with the Iranian Foreign Minister in Muscat in mid-March, continued to explore the potential for including some form of Iranian participation (which, given the poor relations between Egypt and Iran at that time, would have to be as an alternative rather than an addition to the Damascus Declaration). GCC Foreign Ministers met in Kuwait in May 1991 to review arrangements for the GCC+2 security system. But Kuwait was already contemplating a separate arrangement, based on a bilateral pact with the United States, and with other GCC states also indicating that they might prefer to make separate arrangements both the Damascus Declaration and the Omani proposal for a joint GCC military force effectively dropped off the agenda. Just days after the Kuwait meeting of GCC Foreign Ministers, President Mubarak of Egypt announced that Egyptian forces stationed in Saudi Arabia would be withdrawn within three months. In September 1991 Kuwait signed a bilateral security pact with the United States, and Bahrain followed suit with a Defence Cooperation Agreement the same year. Oman has since opted to keep its own military cooperation with the United States within the framework of the original 1980 agreement, renewed in 1985, 1990, 2000 and 2010.

A second far-reaching consequence of the First Gulf War was that the U.S. government subsequently facilitated a series of negotiations which would jointly become known as a new Middle East peace process. As part of this process the 'core parties' – Israel and those Arab states whose territory Israel had occupied after the 1967 war (Palestine, Jordan, Syria) – were encouraged to develop bilateral negotiations with the aim of achieving individual peace treaties on a 'land for peace' basis. The negotiations involving the core parties, which began with an international conference in Madrid in October 1991, were augmented by a 'multilateral phase' in which other regional states would meet to discuss issues of mutual concern with a view to reaching accords that would create a positive context for any bilateral treaties achieved. Oman joined this phase of the peace process, which began in Moscow in January 1992, and established five multilateral working groups on, respectively, water, refugees, the environment, arms control and regional security, and regional economic development. By this point progress on the bilateral track still seemed unlikely, as the Likud-led Israeli government of Prime Minister Yitzhak Shamir was reluctant to engage in substantive discussions, but following the success of the Labor Party in parliamentary elections in Israel in June 1992, a new government, led by Yitzhak Rabin, seemed to offer hope that real progress could be made. Following the announcement of the Oslo Accords of 1993, in which Israel and Palestine reached a preliminary agreement designed to lead to a final 'land for peace' settlement, Oman started to take a much more active role in the unfolding peace process. The Omani government began to explore the possibility of simultaneously pursuing its interests in the Water Resources Working Group and contributing more generally to the peace process by developing a bilateral relationship with Israel. The multilateral process provided an appropriate space in which this potentially more contentious policy could be implemented; discreet meetings between Omani and Israeli diplomats could be held in the context of such meetings. Oman was one of five Arab states taking modest steps towards some kind of new accommodation with Israel at this time (the others were Bahrain, Morocco, Qatar and Tunisia), but having attracted criticism in the past from other Arab states for not joining the general Arab repudiation of Egypt's Camp David agreement with Israel ten years earlier, Oman's diplomats appeared to want to avoid such exposure on this occasion.[14]

Oman focussed on the Water Resources Working Group, for which it commissioned a scientific survey to assess the feasibility of establishing a regional research centre. The Working Group adopted the recommendations of this survey, which included a proposal that the research centre, to be established in Muscat, focus on desalination. In April 1994 Oman hosted a meeting of the Working Group in Muscat, which was attended by representatives of the Israeli government, including Deputy Foreign Minister Yossi Beilin. The latter had earlier participated in

---

[14] We offer a more extended analysis of Oman's diplomacy in this regard in Jones and Ridout, *Oman, Culture and Diplomacy*, pp. 231–249. There are also useful accounts in Uzi Rabi, 'Oman and the Arab-Israeli Conflict: The Reflection of a Pragmatic Foreign Policy', *Israel Affairs* 11.3 (2005), pp. 535–551, and Elisheva Rosman-Stollman, 'Balancing Acts: The Gulf States and Israel', *Middle Eastern Studies* 40. 4 (2007), pp. 185–208. Our own analysis of this period of Omani diplomacy also draws on documents made available to us during the course of our research by the Ministry of Foreign Affairs and the Middle East Desalination Research Center.

establishing discreet contacts with senior Omani officials and would visit Muscat again in November 1994, at the invitation of the Omani government, to help prepare for the visit of Yitzhak Rabin to Muscat, which took place at the very end of December 1994. The April meeting of the Water Resources Working Group had approved the Omani proposal for a desalination research centre, which was formally established as an institution of the peace process in December 1996, as the Middle East Desalination Research Center, with Oman, Israel, the United States, South Korea, and Japan as founder members. By this time Oman and Israel had also been able to make progress towards agreement on how they might establish some form of formal state-to-state relations, choosing, at Oman's suggestion, to do so via the establishment of reciprocal Trade Representative Offices in Muscat and Tel Aviv. This progress – like the peace process as a whole – was to some extent endangered by the assassination of Yitzhak Rabin in November 1995, but both sides succeeded in maintaining progress towards an agreement. Oman was one of a number of Arab states to send a delegation to Rabin's funeral, led by the Minister Responsible for Foreign Affairs, Yusuf bin Alawi. In January 1996 the agreement establishing the Trade Representative Offices was signed, and the Israeli office in Muscat was opened in May of that year. Oman delayed the opening of its own Trade Representative Office in Tel Aviv for some months, uncertain how to view the intentions of the new Likud Prime Minister, Binyamin Netanyahu, elected at the head of a new government in May 1996, but the office eventually opened in August 1996. The Omani government gradually recognised that the new Israeli government was unlikely to contribute to further progress in the wider peace process, and any plans for the development of Oman–Israel ties were soon put on hold. In September 2000, the Likud leader Ariel Sharon led a visit by party members with armed guards to the Haram al-Sharif in Jerusalem, provocatively affirming a commitment to permanent Israeli sovereignty of the city of Jerusalem. The Second Intifada broke out as Palestinians protested not just against this episode, but against the occupation, whose long-term goals it seemed to confirm. Oman closed its Trade Representative Office in Tel Aviv and relations with Israel were suspended. There have been occasional contacts since 2000, including a meeting between Yusuf bin Alawi and the Israeli Foreign Minister Tzipi Livni in Doha in 2008. The Middle East Desalination Research Center in Muscat has continued to function, commissioning research projects and expanding its membership (to include Jordan, the Palestinian Water Authority, Qatar, the Netherlands and Spain). This means that Israeli

FIGURE 17. Sultan Qaboos with Israeli Prime Minister Yitzhak Rabin, 1994.
Source: Israel Govt Press Office/AFP/Getty Images

experts and officials have visited Oman on occasions since 2000: channels
for communication remain open even as the Omani government continues
to insist that the reopening of the Trade Representative Offices is now con-
tingent upon progress towards a Palestinian state.

PARTICIPATION: ECONOMIC AND POLITICAL

The development of Oman's relations with Israel was not a universally popular policy, and the government was conscious that many of its citizens,
particularly those who had only encountered largely hostile popular Arab
media representations of Israel, would find this policy hard to square with
the way they understood Arab and Muslim solidarity. The coverage given
to the Palestinian struggle by Al-Jazeera (the Qatar-based satellite channel
established in 1996) clearly contributed to a stronger popular sense of solidarity with the Palestinians during the Second Intifada (after 2000).[15] So,

---

[15] Omani public opinion became more assertive in its expression of support for the
Palestinians and opposition to Israeli policy (and U.S. support for Israel). There were public protests in 2000, 2001 and 2002. These included a very public display of disapproval

while Omani foreign policy on such issues had, in the past, attracted criticism from other Arab countries and political organisations, its dialogue with the Israeli government in the mid-1990s had also been controversial on the domestic front. Not only were anti-Israel attitudes widely held among the Omani population, there were also those who claimed that the government's policy of dialogue and accommodation was evidence of its subservience to American interests. For some critics of the policy, Oman's dialogue with Israel was viewed as an indication that the 'modernisation' of the Sultanate was heading in the wrong direction: it was undermining Omani autonomy and corroding both Arab and Islamic solidarity. Especially for those whose views of the world had been shaped by the Islamic revival and for whom support for the Palestinian cause readily translated into calls for either complete rejection or even the destruction of Israel, their government's position on this question could be presented polemically as a litmus test for its political and religious legitimacy. There may have been no direct connection between the participation of an Israeli delegation in the meeting of the Water Resources Working Group in Muscat in April 1994 (see the second section of this chapter) and the arrests, the following month, of 430 people suspected by the government of conspiring to organise the overthrow of the Omani government. All the same, the episode of the 1994 arrests represents the emergence into public visibility of a serious social and political division within the Omani population to which issues of religion, foreign policy and political participation contributed.[16]

at the National Day celebrations in November 2000, at which a brass band from the U.S. Marines was booed in the stadium.

[16] Published analyses of these events draw substantially on information presented in Salem Abdullah, *Omani Islamism: An Unexpected Confrontation with the Government* (Annandale: United Association for Studies and Research, 1995), which is sympathetic to those arrested and argues, not unpersuasively, that organisations associated with the Islamic revival in the Gulf at this time focussed primarily on cultural and education matters and did not seek a direct confrontation with the state. He claims that the only action taken by those arrested was the circulation of a 'political statement' criticising the government's policy on Israel. Referring to a publication issued in 1995 in the name of the Voice of the Islamic Movement in Oman and entitled *Diwan al-Mathalem*, the author claims that 'the Islamic movement reiterated its firm belief in Omani national unity, its dedication to the achievements of the country, its antipathy towards insecurity and instability in Oman. It is obvious by reading the correspondence that confronting the authorities is the last thing on its mind. In general, the Omani Islamists may be considered moderates whose concern is reconciliation and temperance' (8). The United Association for Studies and Research (UASR) was founded in 1989 and closed in 2005. It was closely linked with the Muslim Brotherhood and was believed by U.S. government agencies to have been an office for Hamas. The UASR's assessment of the aims of the Omani Islamists may be accurate. Its involvement in publicising them seems to support Omani government claims that at least some of those arrested were associated with the Muslim Brotherhood.

The arrests were not immediately made public and were not officially acknowledged by the government until the end of August 1994. The accusation that those arrested had been building a network, with foreign support and illegal arms, which was designed to overthrown the Omani government would have brought back memories for many Omanis of the fairly recent past in which such networks (PFLOAG, NDFLOAG) certainly did pose a serious challenge to the stability of the state. When 160 of the 430 arrested were eventually tried, the proceedings were held in secret, there were no defence witnesses and the defendants did not enjoy legal representation. As a result it is hard to evaluate the gravity of the threat posed, other than to note that the government response suggests that it was taken very seriously indeed. Some independent reports of the arrests claim that no arms were found and that, while an organisation based on Islamist ideas was in existence, its main activity had been the distribution of leaflets criticising the government for hosting Israeli officials in April. There has been a widespread habit from the 1990s to the present day, shared by many security services in the region and beyond it, to assume that any form of coordinated association between people deemed to be 'Islamists' is evidence of the existence of a highly developed organisation and the likelihood of conspiracy. The presence of Egyptians and Jordanians among those arrested lent further credibility to suggestions that an international network, however modest, might be playing an active but clandestine role in Omani political life. The issue of interference by hostile foreign agents (governments or others) is particularly sensitive in light of the history of Oman between 1955 and 1975 (see Chapters 4 and 5). The State Security Court found the accused guilty and issued sentences ranging from the death penalty (in three cases, all of which were commuted to life imprisonment) to prison terms of between three and twenty years.

While the intentions of those arrested and the extent to which their activities did indeed constitute the nucleus of an armed threat to the Omani government remain unclear, analysis of the social composition of the group (if, indeed, it was a group) sheds some light on the nature of the problem their activities presented to the government. By far the largest number of those detained (based on data relating to 125 of them) were men aged between twenty-six and thirty-five, who made up 77 percent of those analysed. No fewer than 84 percent of those analysed were university graduates. Nearly 70 percent were Sunni and more than half came from Salalah. This begins to suggest the existence of a broad social category of people who had not yet been included in Oman's recent but limited expansion of political participation. These were people who were not part of the old elite, those from whom *ahl al-hall wal aqd* had traditionally been drawn, and who might therefore have participated in electoral colleges for the selection of Majlis ash-Shura members. But they possessed modern qualifications (in the form of degrees, many of them in science and engineering) which they felt ought to give them not simply access to better employment opportunities but the right to have their views heard as part of the *shura* process. Although many were 'wealthy by Omani standards' and some held government and civil service positions, they clearly did not perceive themselves as part of the contemporary elite.[17] Their dissatisfaction seems to have come from a combination of four factors: their feeling of economic and political exclusion; their global commitments based on Arab and Islamic solidarities; their sense that Oman's modern government had undermined, by means of its 'nationalisation' policies, distinctive aspects of Omani social and religious life; and, finally, their conviction that with their advanced education and religious piety, they were the people to whom the task of reform and cultural renewal should rightly fall. The question of how to contest or accommodate this emerging social group would continue to be one of the key issues for Omani government from the 1990s to the present day. The initial government response in 1994, in which an emphasis on secrecy and security-based solutions prevailed, seems to have given way to, or at the very least to have been subsequently complemented by, other measures, including, as briefly mentioned in Chapter 6, the closure of religious schools in which the teaching of Islam may not have conformed to the citizenship-focussed curriculum favoured in mainstream education. It is also very significant that in November the following year, on the occasion of the twenty-fifth National Day, Sultan Qaboos pardoned all those who had been convicted the previous year, an act which suggested a return to the approach taken to leading Dhofari rebels in the 1970s, emphasising a politics of inclusion and accommodation (from a position of greater strength on this occasion, of course) rather than seeking conflict or outright suppression.

The security-driven response to whatever challenge those arrested in 1994 were understood to represent was an example of Omani government agencies in a largely reactive mode, exhibiting a nervousness which was not otherwise apparent in government circles. It was during the mid-1990s, in fact, that developments on both economic and

---

[17] See al-Haj, 'Politics of Participation', p. 567.

political fronts gave clear evidence of significant, albeit gradual, change having been under consideration for some time. Perhaps most significantly, bearing in mind evidence of some public dissatisfaction with limited opportunities for economic and political participation, government policy showed signs of an attempt to see these problems as interrelated and an effort to find interrelated solutions. This is how we understand the two key events of 1995 and 1996: the launch of a new economic policy through the Vision 2020 conference in June 1995 and Sultan Qaboos's announcement, in November 1996, of the Basic Statute of the State, Oman's first written constitution, which among other provisions established Majlis a-Dawla as second chamber of an Omani parliament, Majlis Oman.

The Vision 2020 conference was held in Muscat in June 1995, with Deputy Prime Minister Qais Zawawi and Minister of State for Development Affairs Mohammed bin Musa al-Yusef presiding and with other speakers, including a Vice President of the World Bank and a number of other economic experts from international organisations and a range of Arab, Asian and Latin American countries. Both public and closed sessions were attended by members of Majlis ash-Shura and the Oman Chamber of Commerce and Industry (representing the local business community). It was clearly intended to mark a shift in Oman's economic policy in favour of 'liberalisation'.[18] It articulated a new development and planning strategy which would shape subsequent development plans through an emphasis on economic diversification, human resource development and privatisation, all supported by policies designed to secure macroeconomic balance. It offers a good way of understanding how the Omani government has sought to address the two most acute economic, and this ultimately political, problems it faces. The first is the simplest: that the oil upon which its economy depends is a non-renewable resource. The second is more complex, but no less intractable: that the labour force is composed predominantly of expatriate workers, while many Omani citizens are substantially underemployed. The broad aim

---

[18] We use the term 'liberalisation' here to indicate a set of economic policies which aim at encouraging the market rather than the state to drive economic activity (including privatisation, deregulation, free-trade regimes and incentives for private investment). We prefer this term to alternatives such as 'reform', because they carry with them a value judgement ('reform' implies that the former state of affairs is being improved upon) and because 'liberalisation' indicates a specific policy orientation (a liberal one). It emphasises the connection between such policies and the phenomenon of 'neoliberalism', which describes the broader global political consensus that such policies are preferable to others.

of Vision 2020, then, was to set in motion a transformation of the economy in which the role of oil would be substantially reduced and the role of Omani citizens in wealth generation would be substantially increased. Because the government also calculated that the success of this policy would depend upon the support of international financial institutions and foreign investment, the Vision 2020 conference also served to make this policy shift as visible as possible, and Mohammed bin Musa al-Yusef gave two press conferences during the event which were attended by a significant number of foreign journalists. In this way the Omani government could signal to important external audiences that it was 'open for business'.[19]

The Vision 2020 conference followed shortly after the publication of a report commissioned in 1991 by the Omani government from the World Bank. Noting that Oman's oil reserves would run out at present rates of extraction after eighteen years (by 2011–2012)[20] and that its gas reserves had a life span of forty-eight years, the report set down recommendations for how Oman might manage a transition towards a post-oil economy while holding onto the standard of living which its citizens had come to enjoy as a result of the country's oil-financed development. In particular, and in keeping with the general tenor of World Bank policy at the time, the report argued that the Omani government was currently spending 'an excessive proportion of the proceeds of [oil] extraction on current consumption' and recommended substantial reductions in the economic role of government in favour of an expanded private sector.[21] While there is some evidence that Omani policy-makers did not entirely agree with the World Bank assessment, the general direction of policy articulated at the Vision 2020 conference and in subsequent development plans was broadly in line with these recommendations.[22] The report argued that 'the dominance of public spending has been the major factor inhibiting the development of an independent and

[19] An indication of the success of the conference as a way of communicating to a global audience can be found in Richard Curtiss's article for the Washington Report on Middle East Affairs, which described Oman as 'an Arab model for developing nations everywhere.' http://www.wrmea.org/component/content/article/7936-oman-a-model-for-all-developing-nations.html (accessed June 3, 2014).

[20] Viable reserves have increased since then.

[21] World Bank, *Document on Sultanate of Oman: Sustainable Growth and Economic Development*, Report no. 12199-OM (Washington, DC, 1994), p. iii.

[22] The Omani Minister for Development at that time, Mohammed bin Musa al-Yusef, who played a key role in Vision 2020, notes in his 1997 PhD dissertation that Oman's development had until this point differed from processes in other developing nations, because it had not adopted the kind of structural adjustment programmes recommended by the

dynamic private sector ... Other factors include: a legal and regulatory framework that establishes serious barriers to investment and the entry of new firms as well as sanctioning monopolistic practices; discrimination against, and failure to promote or provide adequate protection to, foreign investment; and the preemptive role of the public sector in utilities, transport, communications, development banking, hotels and some areas of manufacturing.'[23] It is clear that subsequent efforts by the Omani government to encourage foreign investment, support the creation of new businesses and divest itself of state-owned enterprises have been consistent with this analysis.

The government had in fact begun to make and implement policies compatible with Vision 2020 as early as 1988, which is when concerted efforts to 'Omanise' the workforce had begun to be implemented within the framework of the fourth Five-Year Plan (1991–1995). This established regulations which required certain employment categories to be reserved for Omani citizens (these included lawyers, civil engineers, accountants, primary school teachers, nurses, accounts clerks, general car mechanics, general salespeople, leather workers, typists and newspaper vendors). In 1989 Oman's stock exchange, the Muscat Securities Market (MSM), had been established, and in 1994 the rules governing participation in MSM had been changed to allow non-Omanis to place money in investment accounts. In 1993 a new investment law had been announced permitting foreign nationals to hold up to 49 percent of any commercial company in Oman, with higher levels of up to 65 percent available with the approval of the Minister for Commerce and Industry or, above that, only with the approval of the Council of Ministers. The new law also contained protection against nationalisation. In 1994 foundations were also laid for a major aspect of diversification away from oil and into natural gas through the foundation of Oman LNG, a joint venture company in which the government took a 51 percent shareholding, with Shell Gas taking a further 30 percent, Korea LNG 5 percent, Mistubishi and Mitsui 2.77 percent each, Partex (Oman) 2 percent and Itochu Corporation 0.92 percent. In 1994 the

World Bank and the International Monetary Fund since the 1970s and that Vision 2020 represented a continuation of an existing Omani mix of state and market rather than a wholesale adoption of the 'neoliberal' agenda of the World Bank. See Mohammed bin Musa al-Yusef, 'The State and Market in Oman's Development: Conflict or Cooperation' (PhD diss, University College London, Development Planning Unit, 1997).

[23] World Bank, *Sultanate of Oman*, p. vii.

government also announced the establishment of the first independent power project in the country (in fact, the first in the Arab world)
which would involve the construction of a power station at Manah, on
a build-own-operate-transfer basis, by the United Power Company, a
joint-stock company formed for this purpose in 1995. In March 1995
Oman was one of seven governments to send representatives to a meeting of Indian Ocean littoral states convened by the government of
Mauritius (the other five were Australia, India, Kenya, South Africa and
Singapore) in order to discuss trade liberalisation and economic cooperation. This would lead to the formation in 1997 of the Indian Ocean
Rim Association for Regional Cooperation (IOR-ARC). These various
initiatives indicate a consistent policy in which Oman's long-standing
attachment to free trade was matched with a programme of domestic
liberalisation and a new level of engagement with a changing external
economic environment. Both the IOR-ARC initiative and the inclusion
of Korean and Japanese partners in the LNG project (South Korea and
Japan were to be the first major customers once the project was up and
running) were representative of Oman's conviction that its economic
prosperity would increasingly depend upon its relations with Asian
nations, even if its security was still inextricably bound up with the
United States.

The main structural changes envisaged in Vision 2020 were a reduction in crude oil's share of GDP from 37.2 percent in 1994 to 9 percent in 2020 and an increase in the share of GDP contributed by gas
from 0.9 percent in 1995 to 10 percent in 2020. Taken together these
changes would result in a non-oil GDP of 81 percent, as opposed to the
62.4 percent it constituted in 1995. The transformation of the labour
market involved targets in which the public sector should be 95 percent
'Omanised' by 2020, and the private sector 75 percent, compared with
rates of 68 and 15 percent in 1995. By 2005, the Omanisation of the
public sector had reached 80 percent, while Omanis in the private sector still comprised only 15 percent of the total workforce. These targets remain a reminder of the extent of the task the government set
itself in 1995. Human resources development remains, as we shall see
in the concluding chapter, a major social, economic and political problem for Oman. Encouraging Omani citizens to take employment in the
private sector has been a theme of a number of government initiatives
in recent years, including appeals to the population by Sultan Qaboos
himself.

Two months after the Vision 2020 conference, on September 11, 1995, Qais Zawawi was killed in a car accident near Salalah, in which a car driven by Sultan Qaboos was struck by another vehicle. Since his participation in Sultan Qaboos's small post-accession council in 1970, Qais Zawawi had played a central role in Omani government, serving as Minister of State for Foreign Affairs and subsequently as Deputy Prime Minister and Minister for Financial and Economic Affairs, the position he held at the time of his death. He had been particularly influential in recent years in leading the government's shift, exemplified by Vision 2020 and related economic planning, towards an economic policy of privatisation and engagement with the structures of globalisation such as Oman's application for membership of the World Trade Organization (WTO). The circumstances of his death, coming a little more than a year after the detention and conviction of Islamist activists, inevitably gave rise to fears that the car accident had in fact been an attempt on the life of the Sultan (who was injured in the crash). There is no evidence to suggest that such fears were justified, although some accounts continue to refer to the incident as 'unexplained'.[24] After his death the Ministry of Finance and Economy was effectively broken up into two ministries, Finance and National Economy. Ahmed bin Abdul Nabi Macki, another long-standing minister who had served the Omani government since 1970, was appointed Minister for National Economy, in which role he appeared also to enjoy supervision of the activities of the Ministry of Finance. In addition to Macki's, key economic portfolios in the Council of Ministers were those of Commerce and Industry, held by Maqbool bin Sultan, and Development, headed by Mohammed Musa al-Yusef, Minister of State for Development Affairs and the public face of the Vision 2020 project.[25] The reorientation of Oman's economic policy led by Qais Zawawi until his death and carried forward by the government in subsequent years was accompanied, as we have already noted, by political developments which were clearly intended to be complementary: the Basic Statute of the State

---

[24] See, e.g., Marc Valeri, 'Liberalization from Above', p. 189. Valeri also suggests here, but not in later publications, that the shift in economic policy, in which Qais Zawawi participated, followed his death. The Vision 2020 conference, at which this shift was presented, was held, as Valeri notes, in June 1995.

[25] Mohammed bin Musa al-Yusef was dismissed and subsequently jailed for corruption in 2001. Macki and Maqbool remained in office until 2011, when both were removed from the Council of Ministers in response to public protests.

would, among many other things, affirm Oman's constitutional commitment to the free market.

The Basic Statute of the State is Oman's written constitution. It was announced and promulgated by Sultan Qaboos on November 6, 1996, in the context of his Meet the People Tour and apparently after holding consultations with senior religious and legal scholars at his camp in the desert. The Basic Statute now provides the framework for all legislation in Oman. It also sets out a number of fundamental principles according to which the country is to be governed, specifying the scope of existing institutions and laying the foundations for the creation of new ones. In terms of fundamental principles, most attention has generally been paid to the definition of the government of the Sultanate as 'royal' and 'hereditary' (Article 5) and to the arrangements for royal succession that it establishes (and to which we shall turn shortly). Equally important is the provision in Article 9 that 'rule in the Sultanate shall be based on justice, *shura* and equality' and that 'citizens have the right ... to participate in public affairs.' If there was a residual sense in Oman that royal or 'Sultani' rule, with its hereditary characters, might be incompatible with the tradition of election by *shura* associated with the Imamate, the establishment of both of these principles alongside one another seems to have been intended to affirm that, in the modern Omani state, there is no contradiction between the two. While it might be argued that the hereditary principle set out in the Basic Statute involves far fewer people in the choice of the ruler than the process by which Imams had been chosen in the past (which involved, in any case, only a very limited number of participants), it could also be demonstrated that the Basic Statue, by enshrining citizen participation and providing scope for its ongoing extension, in effect redirected the *shura* principle away from the limited question of succession towards a potentially far wider conception of citizen participation in Omani government. This would be consistent with movement towards a constitutional monarchy, a direction in which it has occasionally been suggested Sultan Qaboos intends to lead Oman. The articles of the Basic Statute on the succession stipulate that the Sultan shall be chosen from among the male descendants of Sayyid Turki bin Said bin Sultan (provided he is a Muslim, born of Omani Muslim parents and is 'judicious and of sound mind'; Article 5). Responsibility for choosing a new Sultan falls on the 'Ruling Family Council', which is to meet within three days of the office being vacant to agree on a successor. In the event of their being unable to designate a successor, the Defence

Council will announce the appointment as Sultan of the person named in a letter previously prepared by the last Sultan. This provision (which was slightly revised in an amendment issued in October 2011 to add the Presidents of Majlis ash-Shura and Majlis a-Dowla, the President of the Supreme Court and his two oldest deputies) has understandably attracted much attention. It is, in itself, an unusual process that seems to retain at least some aspects of the electoral process associated with the Imamate. It also makes Oman unusual in relation to its Arab Gulf neighbours, where there is almost always a designated successor or Crown Prince in place. Interest is perhaps all the more acute because the Sultan has no children and the familiar process by which a son often succeeds his father will not take place. It is widely believed that there are at least two envelopes containing Sultan Qaboos's choice of successor (in the event of an inconclusive consultation), one held in Muscat and one in Salalah. Most analysts of the contemporary political scene in Oman tend to agree that the succession is most likely to pass to one of Sayyid Tariq's sons, of whom three are considered possible successors: Sayyid Assad, currently the Sultan's Representative, Sayyid Shihab, the retired Commander of the Navy, now an adviser without portfolio to the Sultan, and Sayyid Haitham, who is currently the Minister of Heritage and Culture.

The other innovation in the original Basic Statute to which attention has been widely and understandably paid is its provision for a new institution, Majlis Oman, which, as specified in the brief Article 58, is to be composed of the existing Majlis ash-Shura and a new body called Majlis a-Dawla (State Council). Article 58 simply states that 'the Law shall specify the jurisdiction of each, its term, sessions and rules of procedure ... the number of its members, the conditions they should satisfy, the way they are selected and appointed, the reasons for their dismissal and other regulatory provisions.' Majlis Oman was inaugurated in December 1997, following the election of the third session of Majlis ash-Shura, with Majlis a-Dawla convening for the first time with forty-two members, all appointed by the Sultan. Members have typically been appointed from among former senior government officials, including former ministers and ambassadors, as well as from members of the judiciary and the business community. It does not function as an upper house in the manner of many bicameral legislatures, but appears to have been envisaged as a complementary source of advice on legislation. Because it is not elected, its membership tends not to be influenced by tribal affiliation: it might be viewed as a more 'technocratic' body than Majlis ash-Shura. Because appointments are typically made after each Majlis ash-Shura election

FIGURE 18. Elections in Muscat, 1997.
Source: Mohammed Mahjoub/AFP/Getty Images

(their terms of office have been synchronised), it also gives the Sultan an opportunity to make marginal adjustments to the composition of Majlis Oman: for example, he has consistently appointed more women to Majlis a-Dawla than have ever been elected to Majlis ash-Shura. In 1997, when Shakur al-Ghammari and Taiba al-Maawali were still the only two women elected to Majlis ash-Shura, Sultan Qaboos appointed five women to the new Majlis a-Dawla. In subsequent years he has appointed nine, fourteen and fifteen women, for sessions during which Majlis ash-Shura either had only two or (for the 2000–2003 session) no female members.

Although these were the aspects of the Basic Statute that attracted most attention from observers at the time, three others deserve consideration. The first is that it contained, in Article 11, the provision that the economy of the Sultanate be based on free-market principles. Not only is this unusually prescriptive for a constitutional document, but it is also notable in that it indicates that the Omani leadership – and presumably Sultan Qaboos himself, since he is widely believed to have played a very substantial role in drafting the Basic Statute – saw a connection between political participation and the idea of a free market. In other words, as Oman began to contemplate pressing economic questions of the kind foregrounded in Vision 2020 and embarking on a programme of gradual privatisation of the economy, a specifically capitalist mode of organisation was explicitly proposed for the first time. As we have noted in Chapter 6, Oman's economy had until this time preserved significant non-capitalist elements. Although this provision of the Basic Statute has clearly helped create the conditions for subsequent legislation and international commitments, such as the Privatisation Law of 2004 and Oman's accession to the WTO, it has not yet been used (but could in the future) as a way to unravel any of the substantial and quasi-protectionist mercantile interests that dominate much of Oman's non-oil economy. The second is that Article 42 lists among the responsibilities of the Sultan 'issuing and endorsing legislation'. The point of interest here is the implication that the Sultan might at some point not be the only source of legislation and would therefore be in a position to endorse legislation issued by some other body, such as either chamber of Majlis Oman.[26] Here what we might call a carefully crafted 'gap' in the Basic Statute points, as does the orientation of *shura* towards political participation discussed earlier, in the direction of a constitutional monarchy. Or, at the very least, it makes such an arrangement possible within the terms of the existing constitution. The third aspect is that Article 33 guarantees 'the freedom to form associations on national bases, for lawful causes and with peaceful means in compliance with the Basic Statute', a clause which could readily be used to legitimise the formation of political parties (often supposed to be illegal in Oman), but, crucially, not those whose objectives conflict with the Basic Statute on issues such as the form of government (royal and hereditary) or the nature of the economy (free market). Interestingly, then, the terms in which the Basic Statute makes political parties possible also has the effect of prohibiting parties committed to either the revival of the Imamate or the promotion of a socialist or communist agenda. In seeking to keep options open for the future, the Basic Statute also shows signs of conscious efforts to rule out of any future politics those aspects of Oman's recent past which have been the source of the most acute political conflict.

The Basic Statute of the State created new institutions, formalised a number of political conventions and created a fairly open framework to permit future developments. In this respect it may be seen, historically,

---

[26] One of the political demands of protesters in Oman in early 2011 was that Majlis ash-Shura be granted the power to initiate legislation. In March 2011 Sultan Qaboos announced that this would take place, and in October 2011 the Basic Statute was in fact amended to include this provision in a much-extended revision of Article 58. See Chapter 8 for more on the protests of 2011 and the government responses.

as being of a piece with the politics of Oman Vision 2020. The two processes effectively yoked together the extension of political participation (on the basis of *shura*) and the liberalisation of the economy, a process which would also depend for its success upon a much higher level of citizen participation. While new challenges would emerge on the international front in the first decade of the twenty-first century, the question of the relationship between economic and political participation on the part of Oman's citizens would continue to be the most pressing concern for Oman's government and, increasingly, for its citizens, too.

8

Oman in the Twenty-First Century

The task of concluding a history with a consideration of the immediate past carries certain risks. Among them are the temptation to offer predictions that will later prove to have been wrong and the danger that in offering an account of the past ten years or so the writers will miss what later turns out to have been significant and focus instead on events that were not. In the case of Oman in the twenty-first century, however, it is reasonable to imagine that Oman's participation in events associated with the 'war on terror', the 'Arab Spring' (both of them terms that we will wish to question and perhaps replace) and the crisis over Iran and the threat of regional nuclear proliferation will still be of interest to readers for some time to come. We therefore turn to these events as the principal topics for discussion in this final chapter, before concluding it with a retrospective consideration of how the history we have set out across the book as a whole might help us understand the situation of Oman in the second decade of the twenty-first century.

One additional and crucial issue facing Oman at this juncture is, of course, the future direction of political leadership. The Basic Statute of the State outlines a process for the appointment of a new Sultan on the death of the incumbent. The Ruling Council meets to agree on a successor, and if they cannot reach agreement, the Defence Council then consults instructions prepared by the present Sultan. This arrangement does not address, however, any questions as to the scope and nature of future political leadership. Most Omanis have known no ruler other than Sultan Qaboos. His retention of formal responsibility for multiple aspects of government has almost certainly been possible only because of an exceptional degree of popular and political consensus over his legitimacy. It is unlikely that any successor will automatically inherit such strong support. Some significant changes in the roles and responsibilities of the Sultan and other leading political figures may therefore take place following the death of Sultan Qaboos. The history traced in this book suggests that any future arrangements for political leadership will be shaped by multiple considerations: the Ibadi character of Omani political culture; the nature of Oman's incorporation into global economic networks; Oman's need to balance its international and regional relations with great care; and, perhaps above all, the enduring question of how to respond appropriately to the economic and political demands for further development that will only grow louder and more pressing as the oil era draws to a close. These, however, are questions for the contemporary political analyst, informed, it is to be hoped, by a consideration of Oman's modern history. We close this book, therefore, not with speculation about that future, but with an attempt to identify the most significant aspects of the most recent phase in that history.

OMAN AND THE 'WAR ON TERROR'

When nineteen men, acting in the name of Al-Qaida, flew hijacked passenger planes into the World Trade Center in New York and the Pentagon in Washington, DC, on September 11, 2001 (with a fourth plane crashing in Pennsylvania), killing more than three thousand people, terrorism became the single most pressing issue facing many of the world's governments. The unprecedented scale of this attack on U.S. citizens on U.S. soil is now widely regarded as having led to a global transformation in which the security interests of the United States were to justify the inauguration of a 'war on terror'. A wide range of new military, intelligence, juridical and economic measures were taken as part of a worldwide effort, led by the U.S. government, to organise a new division of the world, between the 'terrorists' on the one hand and the 'international community' on the other. The stark terms of this supposed division were articulated by U.S. President George W. Bush in his address to a joint session of Congress on September 20, 2011: 'You are either with us, or you are with the terrorists.'[1] This was also the speech in which President Bush used the term 'war on terror' to describe the scope of the response to Al-Qaida's action.

---

[1] President G. W. Bush, 'Address to a Joint Session of Congress and the American People', http://georgewbush-whitehouse.archives.gov/news/releases/2001/09/20010920-8.html (accessed July 7, 2014).

This demand that everyone take sides in a new global conflict was sometimes and regrettably accompanied by descriptions of the actions to be taken as a 'crusade', pitting 'the West' against 'Islam'. For the people and governments of countries with significant or majority Muslim populations this presented some acute difficulties. Very few people endorsed the actions of Al-Qaida. Substantial sections of such populations, however, understood some of the grievances that had led to the development of Al-Qaida, and still others held strong views about the conduct of U.S. policy in the region, particularly as regards U.S. support for Israel. Many feared, however, that, simply by virtue of their religion, they risked being identified as enemies of a global superpower, clearly determined to take massive retaliatory action. One consequence of the American response to the Al-Qaida attacks was therefore that it suddenly became very difficult, and potentially very dangerous, for Muslims (either citizens or their governments) to express their opposition to any aspects of U.S. policy. At the same time it remained all the more imperative that such criticism and opposition be expressed, as aspects of U.S. policy and action in the years following the attacks were themselves fraught with danger, not simply for Muslims, but for the world. The series of wars that have followed, particularly in Afghanistan and Iraq, both of which continue to exact a huge toll in terms of human lives and freedoms, have so far failed in their initial objective of defeating Al-Qaida and its various offshoots. Although the Al-Qaida leader, Osama bin Laden, was assassinated in Pakistan by U.S. forces in May 2011, armed conflict involving Al-Qaida-related militants continues, not only in areas where the organisation had been active before 2001 (Afghanistan, Pakistan, Somalia, Yemen), but also in others where such movements had previously enjoyed little penetration (most notably Syria and Iraq). For Oman, then, the twenty-first century presented new international challenges, inextricably related to its strategic location, its cultural identity and its existing political alliances.

First of all, Oman was a long-standing ally of the United States, with which, as we have seen, it had a renewable facilities agreement under which the United States could make use of military bases in Oman. As a political ally and friend, Oman's government expressed unequivocally its condemnation of the Al-Qaida attacks and its solidarity with the United States. According to the U.S. Secretary of Defense at the time, Donald Rumsfeld, who met Sultan Qaboos in Oman on October 4, 2001, the Omani ruler's expressions of support were exceptionally clear. They met just as the United States was about to take military action against Afghanistan – the first airstrikes were only days away – and Rumsfeld writes that Sultan Qaboos had been 'emotional' in assuring him of Oman's support and that when he confirmed to him that the facilities at Masirah could indeed be used by U.S. Air Force C-130 military transporters as part of the operation against the Taliban, he had simply told him, 'We trust you. We're allies. I have nothing else to add.'[2] Oman's strategic location, both in relation to the Strait of Hormuz and in its relative proximity to Afghanistan, made Omani cooperation of particular value to the United States at this time and would do so for some years, as regards Afghanistan and also, although to a lesser extent, when the United States launched its campaign to overthrow the regime of Saddam Hussein in Iraq in 2003. Although Oman had made its objections to the action against Iraq known both publicly and privately, once the operation was under way it did permit the use of Masirah, Seeb and Thamrayt by the 320th, 321st and 405th Expeditionary Wings of the U.S. Air Force flying missions over Iraq.

Second, Oman had a border with Saudi Arabia. Saudi Arabia was both the origin and the ultimate target of Al-Qaida, at least at this stage in the development of its network of struggle. Its leader, Osama bin Laden, had been a Saudi citizen of Yemeni origin, and the origins of his antipathy to the Saudi ruling family lay in their acceptance, in the aftermath of the Iraqi invasion of Kuwait in 1990, of American troops stationed on what Osama bin Laden regarded as the soil of a sacred Muslim land. Although Al-Qaida's hostility to the United States would eventually come to dominate mainstream perceptions of its ideology, its decision to act against U.S. interests from the mid-1990s onwards arose from its aim of securing the withdrawal of U.S. troops from Saudi Arabia and the subsequent re-establishment there of an Islamic state based on the principles and practices it associated with the initial rule of the Prophet Mohammed. The Saudi origins of fifteen of the nineteen hijackers involved in the attacks of September 11 emphasised the extent to which the Saudi state harboured within it opponents with powerful ideological attachments to this Salafist vision and the willingness, too, to organise and execute violence in its pursuit. The Saudi government was therefore among the strongest supporters of the United States in its response to Al-Qaida and, as the dominant power on the Arabian Peninsula, would expect similar support for its own position from its immediate neighbours and GCC allies, including, of course, Oman. In

---

[2] Donald Rumsfeld, *Known and Unknown: A Memoir* (New York: Penguin Books, 2001), p. 381.

the longer term, as we shall see, this would lead to attempts by Saudi Arabia to mould the GCC into a political union with its own internal security as a primary collective objective. Thus, while Oman was quite ready to cooperate with its Saudi neighbours in preventing and containing the threat from Al-Qaida, it would be far less willing, eventually, to acquiesce in the Saudi political project for the GCC. Cooperation with Saudi Arabia would involve intelligence-sharing, border controls and action to stem the flow of money from the region to Al-Qaida, much of which was assisted by laundering operations and wealthy sympathisers in the UAE, Oman's other immediate neighbour in the GCC.

Third, Oman shared a border with Yemen, a state which, since its rapid unification in 1990 and a civil war in 1994, had been teetering on the brink of collapse. In the absence of effective government control of much of its territory, Yemen had become, as had Afghanistan before it, a preferred location for the establishment of training camps by organisations such as Al-Qaida. It had also been the site of one of the most significant Al-Qaida operations against an American target before September 11, 2001: the suicide attack on the naval destroyer the USS *Cole* in October 2000, while it was in harbour at the Port of Aden. Seventeen U.S. sailors were killed in this attack. This meant that Yemen was the focus of sustained U.S. efforts to hunt down and eliminate alleged terrorists, and had it not been for President Saleh's decision in 2001 to support the United States in these efforts, the country more generally could have become the target, as had Afghanistan, of U.S. military attacks. As it was, over the years following 2001, U.S. drones succeeded in killing a significant number of suspected terrorists on the ground in Yemen. These attacks persisted into 2014. At the same time, the consolidation of militants based in Yemen into the organisation Al-Qaida in the Arabian Peninsula (AQAP) during this period indicates the limits of this approach. The presence of AQAP and of other such militants in Yemen clearly made the control of the Oman–Yemen border a pressing security issue after 2001. Oman's relatively recent history of conflict with PDRY (see Chapter 5) means that this was, to some extent, a return to earlier preoccupations. In the context of the 'war on terror', it meant that Oman's allies and other neighbours would come to rely upon Oman's capacity to manage this situation for their own security. Part of Oman's response to the heightened threat posed from within Yemen has been to support the Yemeni government in its aspirations to build a stronger relationship with and perhaps even secure eventual membership of the GCC. But it has also sought to strengthen border security as a way of protecting the country from the consequences of the kind of state collapse that occurred in Somalia and that is now regarded as a real possibility in Yemen. The consequences of instability in the Horn of Africa (which include armed Islamist movements and maritime piracy) are already a security challenge for Oman and would be very significantly amplified if Yemen were to follow a similar path.

Finally, and more generally, as a Muslim nation, Oman shared a strong interest in working to correct widely held misperceptions in the West about the ethics and politics of Muslim people and their religion. This was particularly pressing in the light of a damaging polarisation encouraged by influential commentators and popular media outlets, especially in the United States. The task of Omani diplomats was to maintain a dialogue with U.S. policy-makers in which they could hope to counter some of the most damaging consequences of popular anti-Muslim sentiment. One important aspect of this dialogue involved, as we shall see in the next section, trying to persuade the U.S. government of the merits of engagement with Iran. The long-standing American hostility towards Iran, arising from the revolutionary events of 1979 and, in particular, the holding of American hostages by radical students in Tehran, had been heightened in the years immediately following the terrorist attacks of 2001. Even though Iran played no part in these attacks, President Bush was nonetheless (as we shall see) to create a public perception that it might as well have done so, by including it in the 'Axis of Evil', whose existence he proclaimed in the 2002 State of the Union address. Oman therefore sought to combine its participation in measures to combat real terrorism with efforts to combat the fantasy versions produced in the American imagination.

In addition to the assistance offered to military operations in Afghanistan, Oman made practical contributions to counterterrorist efforts by joining the United States' Container Security Initiative in November 2005; securing an agreement with Saudi Arabia on cross-border transit in December 2006; taking financial transparency measures to limit money laundering, including actions in the context of the Oman–U.S. Free Trade Agreement signed in 2006; establishing a National Committee for Combating Terrorism in January 2007; securing the conviction, in an Omani court in 2009, of a businessman for helping to plan and fund attacks in Oman and activities for a terrorist organisation in Pakistan; and ongoing measures to enhance security on its border with Yemen.

Alongside these activities Oman also increased its own military capacity through extensive arms purchases and general military and security expenditure in the first decade of the twenty-first century. In October 2001, in a deal that had clearly been in the works for some time and therefore cannot be seen as a direct response to the increased international and regional tension after the terrorist attacks of September, Oman concluded the purchase of 12 F-16 aircraft as part of a $825 million package. In 2006 Oman spent $48 million on a Javelin anti-tank system, and it was reported to have contracted for C-130J Hercules transporters in 2009 and eighteen further F-16s in 2010. These purchases were part of what Fred Lawson has described as 'a veritable arms race' in the Gulf that accelerated after 2007.[3] Oman's annual military expenditure from 2008 to 2011 is estimated by Anthony Cordesman to have ranged between $4.1 and $4.8 billion representing between 6.4 and 8.5 percent of GDP, the second-highest percentage in the GCC, and in 2008 a higher percentage than that allocated by Saudi Arabia.[4] That Oman's expenditure represented such a high proportion of GDP, larger in percentage terms than its much wealthier neighbours, was of course due to Oman's lower GDP; it also tended to confirm the suggestion that this expenditure was not always motivated purely by identifiable needs in relation to specific threats, but was sometimes driven by a sense of regional competition almost entirely detached from strategic or tactical considerations of security.[5] Such purchases may also be understood as a response to heightened international and regional tension, much of which does arise from the security challenge posed by terrorism, even if the actual purchases of, say, anti-tank systems do not seem to correspond directly, if at all, to the kind of threat posed by terrorists. As we shall see, this kind of expenditure, which for the UAE, Bahrain and Saudi Arabia may be motivated by threat perceptions that Oman does not share (in which Iran is seen as hostile, as discussed later), is not entirely consistent with Oman's more general approach to regional security and represents an aspect of its security policy that may come under increasing pressure as the resources to sustain it become more difficult to find and justify.

---

[3] Fred H. Lawson, 'Security Dilemmas in the Contemporary Persian Gulf', in Mehran Kamrava, *International Politics of the Persian Gulf* (Syracuse, NY: Syracuse University Press, 2011), p. 53.

[4] Anthony Cordesman, *The Gulf Military Balance in 2012* (Washington, DC: Center for Strategic and International Studies, 2013), pp. 54–55.

[5] See, e.g., Kenneth Katzman, who writes that Oman's 2011 purchases were 'in part to keep pace with its Gulf neighbors, including UAE and Bahrain'. Kenneth Katzman, *Oman: Reform, Security and US Policy* (Washington, DC: Congressional Research Service, 2011), p. 9.

In addition to its participation in regional and international anti-terrorist actions, Oman has also, at least once during the same period, contemplated the possibility of terrorist activity on its own territory. Although the main instance of such activity (a series of arrests and convictions in 2005) turned out to have nothing to do with the Sunni-Salafist networks associated with Al-Qaida, the wider political context – the heightened tension we have alluded to – meant that the 2005 events gave rise to more extensive concern than did the arrests of 1994 discussed in Chapter 7.

In January 2005 rumours reported in the media and circulating in Omani Internet forums suggested that the Omani authorities had arrested as many as three hundred people suspected of involvement in a terrorist conspiracy, specifically to attack the Muscat Festival, due to begin on January 21. The Muscat Festival, offering concerts, other entertainment and social activities, had for some time been a target of criticism by religious conservatives. The BBC, citing reports from Associated Press and *Al-Hayat*, spoke of 'at least 100 suspected extremists' and of the capture of 'a cargo of arms,' apparently intercepted on the Yemeni border.[6] The Omani government did not respond until an official statement from the Minister of Information, Hamad bin Muhammad al-Rashdi, in which he told the Oman News Agency on January 30 that 'there have been some arrests but there is no need to exaggerate them and accord them a greater magnitude than in reality'.[7] Because the Minister did not explicitly deny the reports of the number arrested, nor comment on the question of whether a 'cargo of arms' had been seized or on whether an attack on the Muscat Festival had been planned, his statement was widely taken by the regional and international media as a de facto confirmation of the earlier reports[8] and produced media summaries such as 'Oman has acknowledged the detention of hundreds of nationals amid a crackdown on Al Qaida'.[9] In fact, the number of arrests was far lower, probably around twenty, with a further ten men detained in February. Most important, it appeared that those arrested were all Ibadis and that they had no involvement whatsoever with external organisations. The

---

[6] BBC News, 'Oman "Arrests Hundreds over Plot"', Wednesday, January 26, 2005, 16.39 GMT, http://news.bbc.co.uk/1/hi/world/middle_east/4209645.stm (accessed July 11, 2014).

[7] http://www.middle-east-online.com/english/?id=16582 (accessed July 19, 2014).

[8] See, e.g., 'Oman Confirms Security Arrests', *Al Jazeera*, Sunday, January 30, 2005, http://english.aljazeera.net/NR/exeres/5CED2F72-4E11-4D31-84E5-39685875B0FA.htm (accessed July 19, 2014).

[9] See, e.g., http://www.menewsline.com/stories/2005/february/02_02_2.html (accessed July 19, 2014).

Al-Qaida connection had turned out, as John E. Peterson noted, to be 'undoubtedly unfounded'.[10]

In April and May thirty-one detainees were tried by the State Security Court, accused of being members of an illegal secret organisation, which, it was claimed, had a public political dimension as well as an underground armed wing that sought to overthrow the present government and replace it with an Ibadi Imamate. The defendants were predominantly well educated, and several of them held positions in educational and religious organisations. They were all Ibadis. Unlike the situation in 1994, the trials were public and the defendants had legal counsel. Six were convicted of being leaders of the conspiracy and received sentences of twenty years, twelve others received ten-year terms, a further twelve received seven years and one a one-year sentence. There were demonstrations in support of the defendants in Muscat on the day before the verdicts were announced and after their announcement. A former member of Majlis ash-Shura, Taiba al-Maawali, who had attended the trial and had published critical remarks on Oman Sablah (an online forum) about government officials, was arrested in June and sentenced to eighteen months in prison, subsequently reduced on appeal to six. She was eventually released in January 2006. Like those convicted in May, she continued publicly to affirm her loyalty to Sultan Qaboos, blaming his advisers for misleading him.[11] A poet and journalist who revealed her arrest, and who had earlier been active in revealing details of the January arrests, was also briefly detained but released without charge.[12] On June 9 all of the thirty-one convicted in May received royal pardons and were released. In June there was also a trial – conducted in a military court – of around eighteen members of the armed forces, who were accused and convicted of participation in a conspiracy to overthrow the government, receiving prison sentences of between three and twenty-five years. All of those convicted were pardoned in July and released.

While these events were primarily local in both their inspiration and their implications, and represented a threat to the stability of the Omani government very different in character to that presented by transnational networks such as Al-Qaida or other regional organisations like AQAP and the Islamic State of Iraq and al-Sham (ISIS), the broader context

[10] J. E. Peterson, 'Oman: Omanis, Ibadis and Islamism'; first published on the Web Site of the Tharwa Project (tharwaproject.com), February, 28, 2005, now available at http://www.jepeterson.net/comment.html (accessed July 19, 2014).

[11] http://www.middle-east-online.com/english/?id=16582 (accessed July 19, 2014).

[12] http://www.theguardian.com/books/2006/mar/16/voicesofprotest (accessed June 23, 2014).

of the 'war on terror' ensured that they received more extensive international media attention and that, as a result, questions about Oman's national security have continued to be seen by many analysts, and perhaps also by the Omani government, as inextricably linked to the terrorist threat posed by Al-Qaida and the rise of Salafist movements in Iraq and Syria.

OMAN, IRAN AND THE GCC

As we have already seen, Oman has for a long time placed considerable importance on the maintenance of good relations with Iran. This means Oman has been in the unusual position of enjoying such relations with both Iran and the United States, a position that from time to time has enabled its diplomats to act as discreet facilitators of contacts between two countries that do not have regular channels of communication with one another. The election of Mohammed Khatami as President of Iran in May 1997 created conditions in which prospects for a substantive Iran–U.S. rapprochement seemed greater than at any time since the 1979 Iranian Revolution. Khatami's election was widely seen as a repudiation of a conservative Iranian politics in which hostility to the United States was a key ideological component, and was accordingly welcomed by a number of American analysts who urged their government to take advantage of the opportunity it provided to seek better relations. President Khatami himself emphasised his desire to take part in a 'dialogue of civilisations': a term apparently designed to offer an alternative to a widely circulated idea that the world now faced a 'clash of civilisations' in which the 'Christian' West was destined to face an almost existential conflict with an Islamic world.[13] In 1998 President Khatami made a very well received appearance on the U.S. cable news channel CNN, in which he spoke of his admiration for American civilisation, reiterated his call for dialogue and described the absence of Iranian relations with the United States as 'a tragedy'.[14] The following year the U.S. government made its first attempt to open up a diplomatic channel with Iran by means of a letter, written by President Clinton to President Khatami, indicating that although the U.S. government possessed intelligence linking the Iranian Revolutionary Guard to a bombing in Saudi Arabia three years earlier in which nineteen American citizens had been

---

[13] An influential (and widely criticised) text affirming this idea was Samuel Huntington's 'The Clash of Civilizations', *Foreign Affairs* 72.3 (1993), pp. 22–49.

[14] http://www.cnn.com/WORLD/9801/07/iran/interview.html (accessed June 30, 2014).

killed, it nonetheless harboured 'no hostile intentions towards the Islamic Republic of Iran'.[15] The letter was delivered, at the President's request, by the Omani Minister Responsible for Foreign Affairs, Yusuf bin Alawi, on July 20, 1999. A written response was received in Washington in September and was not viewed as sufficiently positive for the U.S. government to make further efforts to open a dialogue with Iran. This moment of apparent opportunity soon passed. Although Khatami was re-elected in 2001, his room for political manoeuvre had been significantly limited by the resurgence of conservative opposition to his policies and perspectives. But the real obstacles to progress were generated in the United States in January 2002 when President Bush, giving his first State of the Union address after the Al-Qaida attacks on New York and Washington of September 11, 2001, named Iran as one of three countries in an imagined 'Axis of Evil', against which the 'war on terror' must be waged. Bush alleged that, along with North Korea and Iraq, Iran was colluding in the production of weapons of mass destruction and that its policies directly threatened the security of the United States. By the time the conservative Mahmoud Ahmadinejad was elected President of Iran in 2005, U.S. attitudes towards Iran had hardened into a posture of almost implacable hostility.

Much of this hostility on the part of the U.S. government was fuelled by growing concerns that Iran might be actively seeking a nuclear weapons capability. Iran's ambitions to develop a nuclear industry and U.S. fears that Iran was also seeking a nuclear weapons capability made the issue of Iranian nuclear power one of the most contentious and difficult problems facing the region in the first decade of the twenty-first century. It was not just a question of regional nuclear proliferation – worrying enough in itself – but also the way this question would come to intersect with other points of contention and conflict: Iran's relationship with the beleaguered Syrian regime; Israel's desire (as the region's only possessor of nuclear weapons) to maintain what it perceived to be a vital strategic advantage over a state it increasingly viewed as its major regional antagonist; and Iran's role as a supporter of the Iraqi government of Nour al-Maliki and the implications of its growing influence, especially for its major economic and political rival for influence in the Gulf, Saudi Arabia. For Oman, therefore, any successful intervention to assist Iran and the United

---

[15] For details of this letter and related correspondence, see http://www2.gwu.edu/~nsarchiv/NSAEBB/NSAEBB318/#doc2 (accessed June 30, 2014). See also Jones and Ridout, *Oman, Culture and Diplomacy*, pp. 170–171.

States in improving their bilateral relations would almost certainly have to address this issue.

In 2002 an Iranian dissident disclosed the existence of secret nuclear facilities in Iran. Subsequent investigations by the International Atomic Energy Authority (IAEA) suggested that Iran was in violation of its obligations under the Nuclear Non-Proliferation Treaty (NPT) for failing to declare uranium enrichment activities. The IAEA eventually reported Iran to the United Nations Security Council (UNSC) in February 2006 for non-compliance with the safeguards agreement of the NPT, and in December 2006 the UNSC passed Resolution 1737, demanding that Iran suspend all enrichment activities and imposing sanctions until such time as Iran could demonstrate full compliance. Subsequent resolutions from 2007 to 2010 tightened these sanctions in the face of Iran's perceived failure to suspend uranium enrichment. Talks between Iranian negotiators and representatives of the five permanent members of the UNSC and Germany (the group known in this context as P5+1) were held from 2006, following earlier efforts by the three EU members of this group (France, Germany, UK). Attempts to resolve the issue were frequently accompanied by uncompromising and threatening rhetoric on both sides, ranging from President Ahmadinejad's public announcements about the success of the enrichment programme in April 2006 and Iran's capacity to be a regional leader in August 2007, to President Bush's more or less explicit calls for 'regime change' in Iran and his suggestions that Iran was risking the outbreak of world war by seeking nuclear weapons, both also in 2007.[16] The U.S. government's bellicose position was somewhat compromised by its own intelligence community, however, which published an analysis at the end of 2007 suggesting that Iran had suspended efforts to develop a nuclear weapons capability in 2003 and that it would be unable to acquire such a capability for at least eight years. This analysis was consistent with much earlier U.S. intelligence, in which Iran was consistently reported to be many years away from acquiring such a capability. After this disclosure and the change of administration in the United States, the threat that the United States might intervene militarily in Iran, which had begun to appear credible, receded, and although tensions remained, a slightly less febrile atmosphere prevailed.

In November 2013, the Associated Press reported that a provisional deal had been reached in Geneva between P5+1 and Iran regarding Iran's

---

[16] See F. Gregory Gause III, *The International Relations of the Persian Gulf* (Cambridge: Cambridge University Press, 2010), pp. 176–178.

development of a nuclear power capability and that the agreement had been facilitated by Omani diplomacy over five sessions of talks between Iranian and American officials held in Muscat starting in March of that year. The agreement established a Joint Action Plan and provided for ongoing consultations between technical experts and negotiators in order to reach a comprehensive agreement within six months.

Oman, as we have seen (Chapters 6 and 7), had for many years maintained good relations with Iran, both during the rule of the Shah and since the Revolution of 1979. Oman's government had consistently opposed and argued against both the United States and its own GCC partners, advocating engagement with Iran rather than its exclusion from regional politics. Consistent with this position, Omani diplomats tended to downplay anxieties about Iran's nuclear ambitions. They may privately have accepted that Iran may indeed have been seeking to develop a weaponisation capability, while recognising that, from an Iranian perspective, such an ambition was entirely understandable (fuelled as it was by fears of encirclement, sporadic outbursts of regime change rhetoric from Washington, the implacable hostility of a nuclear Israel, and so forth). In private conversations with Iranian counterparts Omani officials are believed – by the United States – to have adopted a more critical stance, urging Iran to 'accommodate the international community's concerns on the nuclear file'.[17] But the public position was that Oman accepted Iran's own claim that its nuclear programme was purely for legitimate civil energy purposes. While Oman's public position sought to lower the temperature wherever possible, its diplomats were also working behind the scenes to assist both Iran and the United States – which had no means of communicating directly with one another – in resolving a number of issues. These included negotiating the release from detention in Iran of three U.S. citizens detained on suspicion of espionage in 2009 while hiking in Kurdistan. First, in September 2010, Sara Shourd was released, on bail, following a payment of 5 billion Iranian rials (about U.S.$450,000), deposited in the Muscat branch of the Iranian Bank Melli. Then, after their trial and conviction in July and August 2011, Joshua Fattal and Shane Bauer were also released, on payment of similar sums. On each occasion the releases involved public appearances in Muscat, which allowed Omani officials to take credit for their involvement without explicitly claiming responsibility. It was suggested in various media that, in order for the terms of U.S. sanctions on Iran not be violated, the bail payments had been made by Sultan Qaboos himself.

[17] http://www.wikileaks.org/plusd/cables/06MUSCAT126_a.html (accessed June 30, 2014).

FIGURE 19. Protests outside Majlis ash Shura, 2011.
Source: Mohammed Mahjoub/AFP/Getty Images

Throughout the period in which the Iranian nuclear issue had been taking shape – largely under the presidency of Mahmoud Ahmadinejad (2005–2013), whose often inflammatory rhetoric had led many to abandon earlier hopes of Iran's return to the 'international community' of states acceptable to the United States – the Omani government continued to maintain contacts with Iran at the highest level. In August 2009, Sultan Qaboos went ahead with an official three-day visit to Tehran, in spite of local protests and international condemnation of President Ahmadinejad's re-election in June of that year, which was widely alleged to have been fraudulent. It is unlikely that the subsequent diplomatic breakthroughs could have been achieved had this visit – which had been scheduled for June 28 and then postponed – not taken place. For although the Geneva agreement between the United States and Iran was reached after Ahmadinejad had been replaced by Hossein Rouhani (regarded much more favourably by the United States), the groundwork, including, it seems, the first Muscat meeting between American and Iranian officials, had been laid while Ahmadinejad was still in office. Here it seems that Omani diplomacy's tendency to view particular governments and rulers as transient when compared with more enduring geo-strategic realities had been vindicated.

These Omani efforts to assist Iran in reaching agreement on the nuclear issue and improving its relations with the United States coincided, not surprisingly, with developments on the bilateral front. In March 2014, President Rouhani visited Muscat on his first official visit to an Arab country. During this visit agreements were signed for Oman to purchase 10 billion cubic metres of natural gas a year from Iran. As part of these agreements the two sides envisaged the construction of a gas export pipeline from Iran to Oman. Talks about a gas deal between Oman and Iran had been going on intermittently for more than eight years, and Oman had previously encountered some pressure from the United States (keen to isolate Iran in the context of the nuclear crisis), whose officials had sought to persuade Oman to seek alternative solutions to its future energy needs. The 2014 deal suggested that Oman was now confident it could proceed with this major economic project without U.S. objections.

Oman's conduct of its relationship with Iran differed significantly from the approaches taken by most of its GCC partners, particularly since the Revolution of 1979.[18] With the exception of Qatar, whose government, at least from the mid-1990s, had developed a less antagonistic relationship with the Islamic Republic, other GCC states have tended to view Iran with suspicion. In the case of Bahrain, there are long-standing fears the country's substantial Shia population might identify more with their Iranian co-religionists than with their Sunni rulers, fears intensified by the leading role taken by Shia citizens in the major protest movement of 2011. In the case of the UAE, there are outstanding territorial disputes over Abu Musa and the Tunbs, which is a continuing source of potential tension, while the presence of a significant number of Iranians living and working in the UAE simultaneously serves to encourage good relations. Perhaps most significantly, as far as the overall disposition of political forces in the Gulf is concerned, Saudi Arabia generally views Iran as a rival regional hegemon, as a source of potential subversion (especially of the Kingdom's Shia population) and as a threat to both regional and global security. Iran's nuclear ambitions, of course, heightened these Saudi anxieties in the first decade of the twenty-first century. These divergences of opinion and policy as regards Iran between Oman and other GCC states are indicative of a wider difference in perspective, which became increasingly visible at the end of the first decade of the twenty-first century. As Saudi Arabia sought simultaneously to promote the idea of a

---

[18] See Jones and Ridout, *Oman, Culture and Diplomacy*, pp. 153–182.

full-fledged political union and to assert itself more forcefully in foreign policy terms (supporting Sunni opposition to the Shia-led Iraqi government and leading Arab opposition to Bashar al-Assad in Syria), Oman began to make explicit its opposition to the direction in which the GCC was being taken. An early indication that Oman had reservations about moves towards greater union was its decision to abstain from plans for a monetary union in December 2006.

On December 7, 2013, during a plenary session of the Manama Dialogue (a summit organised annually by the International Institute for Strategic Studies) held just a few days before the annual GCC Summit itself, Oman's Minister Responsible for Foreign Affairs, Yusuf bin Alawi, made an impromptu intervention from the floor to respond to a presentation by the Saudi Foreign Minister, Nizar bin Obaid Madani. Madani had set out proposals for a GCC political union, arguing that GCC member states should 'loosen their grip on traditional concepts of sovereignty'.[19] Taking the microphone to reply, Yusuf bin Alawi stated unequivocally that Oman would not take part in any such unification project. He later confirmed Oman's position to Agence France-Presse: 'We will not prevent a union,' he said, 'but if it happens we will not be part of it.' The idea of such a union had been mooted back in 2011, and a special mid-year summit had been held in Riyadh in 2012 to discuss the issue. Neither Sultan Qaboos nor the President of the UAE attended this meeting. The issue was apparently due to be discussed again at the 2013 GCC Summit in Kuwait. In the event the summit agreed to the formation of a joint military command, and this was followed by an announcement (by the head of the Saudi National Guard) that a new 100,000-strong GCC military force would be set up.[20] But, although the former Saudi intelligence chief, Prince Turki, indicated after the GCC Summit in Kuwait that he believed Saudi Arabia, Kuwait, Bahrain and Qatar would pursue plans for the formation of a union,[21] there was little explicit support for the project and the summit's communiqué made no reference to it. By March 2014 further political divisions within the GCC emerged, when the governments of Saudi Arabia, Bahrain and the UAE withdrew their ambassadors from Qatar, in response to Qatar's supposed support for groups associated

---

[19] Proceedings of the Manama Dialogue, 2013: The 9th IISS Regional Security Summit, Kingdom of Bahrain, December 2013, p. 26. http://www.iiss.org/-/media/Silos/Conference%20Proceedings/The%20Manama%20Dialogue/Manama-Dialogue-2/Manama%20Dialogue%202.pdf

[20] *EIU Country Report Oman*, March 2014, Economist Intelligence Unit, p. 25.

[21] Ibid., December 2013, p. 18.

with the Muslim Brotherhood in the context of the protests and political upheavals in the region since 2011.

Although Oman has distanced itself from moves towards GCC political union and has continued to conduct its foreign policy, most notably as regards relations with Iran, in a way that differs from the dominant approach favoured by Saudi Arabia, Oman continues to benefit from its membership of the GCC and is not likely to wish to leave the organisation. Certain contradictions in Oman's relationship with the rest of the GCC, and with Saudi Arabia in particular, became visible, however, in the context of the political upheavals of 2011, in which, as we shall see, Oman experienced a period of political unrest unprecedented since the end of the Dhofar conflict in the 1970s. As political unrest challenged a number of GCC states – particularly Bahrain, which, like Oman, lacked the financial resources of the other four member states – the GCC agreed to an aid package in which both Oman and Bahrain would receive $10 billion over a period of ten years in order to finance social and economic measures that, it was hoped, would meet some of the demands articulated by protesters. For Oman, this was, of course, a welcome move by its allies, but it came just a few days before troops from Saudi Arabia and the UAE were dispatched to act against protesters in Bahrain. Oman did not participate in this action, and given its later and very public opposition to proposals for political union, it may be imagined that this move was much less welcome. For Oman, this move may have been especially unwelcome, as it might also have been understood to be part of a broader Saudi-led regional strategy to resist the supposed political advances of Shia movements (in Iraq, for example), a strategy in which Oman, standing as it does outside the Shia–Sunni division and valuing its relationship with Iran, was not keen to participate. So while the Omani government clearly believes that the country has continued to benefit from membership of the GCC in very tangible ways, it has also had to square such economic advantages with questions about collective participation in political projects that do not correspond with its perception of its own interests.

DOMESTIC POLITICAL DEVELOPMENTS: OMAN AND THE 'ARAB SPRING'

In the first half of 2011 a significant number of Omani citizens participated in sustained protests across the country, variously demanding a range of social, economic and political changes. These events have been interpreted in the wider context of regional political upheavals that global English-language media of the time called the 'Arab Spring'.[22] They involved mass popular mobilisations against authoritarian regimes in Tunisia, Egypt, Libya, Bahrain, Yemen and Syria. These revolutionary protests resulted in the overthrow, first, of Tunisia's Zine el Abedine Ben Ali in January 2011 and subsequently of Egypt's President Hosni Mubarak (February 2011), Yemen's President Saleh (June 2011) and, finally, Libya's Colonel Gaddafi, who was captured and killed by Libyan opposition forces in October 2011 after a NATO-supported military operation to topple his regime. In Bahrain the government of the ruling al-Khalifa family called on its GCC allies Saudi Arabia and the UAE for support in suppressing a protest movement calling for the overthrow of the monarchy, and several thousand troops from the Saudi and Emirati armed forces were deployed against protesters who had established a camp at the Pearl Roundabout in the capital city Manama. Protests in Bahrain have continued ever since, and at the time of writing no political solution has been achieved. Protests against the Syrian government also met strong resistance from the military and security forces. As had been the case with Libya and Colonel Gaddafi, the United States, echoed by its European allies and some regional governments, called publicly for President Bashar al-Assad to step down. But on this occasion the United States did not intervene directly. The conflict, however, was internationalised, largely by means of Islamist movements funded and armed by sympathisers (most notably in Saudi Arabia, the UAE and Qatar). In the summer of 2014 one of the Islamist groups most active in the struggle against the Assad government, known as the Islamic State of Iraq and al-Sham, declared an independent Caliphate in contiguous regions of Iraq and Syria, building on both the position it had secured within Syria over the preceding years and a renewed struggle against the Baghdad government. The conflict in Syria and its increasing coincidence with the highly militarised political struggles in Iraq is likely to be a major regional problem that Oman and others will need to address in the years to come.

All of these uprisings and conflicts shared characteristics that transcended their local circumstances and situations. In most cases, there was a sense of an Arab identity being asserted, and the simultaneity of the events clearly intensified this. There was also a strong element of subaltern resistance to the domination of global politics and economics by the

---

[22] For a discussion of the most appropriate term to use, see Tariq Ramadan, *Islam and the Arab Awakening* (Oxford: Oxford University Press), pp. 2–4.

United States and its postcolonial allies, exacerbated by the effects of the global financial crisis of 2008 and the following years. At the same time, there was also a strong current of pro-Western desire at play, often in one and the same movement, as some middle-class participants in the protest movements identified 'Western' democracy as an alternative to a failed one-party or police state. Also, to various degrees, in each situation there were questions of religious identity at stake. On occasion, this too was a way of crystallising, articulating and mobilising a general political hostility to the forces of globalisation and American hegemony, as well as an expression of local affiliations and practical solidarities. In Egypt the first major beneficiary of Mubarak's overthrow turned out to be the Muslim Brotherhood, while in Tunisia democratic elections led to the establishment of a government led by Ennahda, a political party with a clearly Islamist agenda. Neither Ennahda nor the Muslim Brotherhood had initiated the protests, however: in both cases the established Islamist political parties did not join forces with the protestors until weeks after they had begun mobilising. Activists in Egypt accused the Muslim Brotherhood of political opportunism. Eventually their established political organisation made them much more effective than the initial protest groups after Mubarak had been overthrown. In Syria (and the related conflict in Iraq), sectarian conflict and the ideology of *jihad* have come to the fore. In Bahrain, although class and poverty were also major factors (as indeed they were, to various degrees, in all of the individual cases), one of the main driving forces in the protest movement was a long-standing politics of Shia grievance against a regime perceived as representing only a minority Sunni elite.

Of course, each of these situations was also shaped by very particular historical and political circumstances and histories, and each sequence of events was played out in relation to specific local relationships and concerns. In Oman the local circumstances resembled many of those that gave rise to the movements in Tunisia and Egypt. On the one hand, there was widespread economic distress, much of it caused by unemployment, particularly among the younger generation, many of whom had seen their education as a pathway to successful careers and livelihoods but had been disappointed by the reality that the state itself could not provide them all with jobs. This disappointment was exacerbated by a perception shared by young Arab citizens in many countries, including Oman, that their social lives did not give them the range of freedoms – of self-expression, consumption and personal development – they had hoped for. The two disappointments went hand in hand: unemployment made it hard or impossible to establish an independent household; limited incomes put the pleasures of consumption out of reach. Where these frustrations were experienced in a social and political setting in which the conservative pull of family and tradition remained powerful, and either the state or religious authority continued to place tangible limits on many modes of personal self-expression, the disaffection of the younger generation could readily be directed at a structure that seemed to be the cause of both the economic and the social dimensions of the problem. In such circumstances the idea that other people – and particularly those of an older generation – might not just be responsible for and immune to such problems, but might even be profiting from the situation, became particularly hard to accept. It is perhaps for this reason that the economic and political dimensions of the protests in Oman came together around the corruption of political life by private economic interests.

Perhaps the most striking difference between the character of the protests in Oman and those elsewhere in the region, including those in Bahrain, where the economic and social situation may be said to have been most like Oman's, was that the various tensions and discontents do not appear to have taken the form of a demand for the overthrow of the regime. The popular chant of 'al-Sha'b Yurid Isqat al-Nizam' (the people demand the overthrow of the regime) was not heard in Oman, and at several protests, particularly those with explicitly political demands, participants publicly affirmed their loyalty to Sultan Qaboos. One common explanation given for this in Oman was that people did not generally hold Sultan Qaboos responsible for the shortcomings of the government. Instead it was his ministers, advisers and other men of wealth and influence who were believed to be at fault and who were frequently accused of corruption, incompetence and offering poor advice to the Sultan. James Worrall, reporting conversations with Omani citizens in August 2011 about the protests earlier in the year, notes that '[a] common theme in these conversations was that corrupt merchants and senior ministers had clearly pulled the wool over the sultan's eyes and were taking advantage of him for their own personal aims'.[23] It may also be observed, in this context, that none of the leaders forced out of power by the 'Arab Spring' protests were monarchs, a fact that might support a widely held belief that hereditary rulers enjoy a higher degree of political legitimacy in Arab societies than 'presidents for life', four of whom (Ben Ali, Mubarak, Salih,

---

[23] James Worrall, 'Oman: The "Forgotten" Corner of the Arab Spring', *Middle East Policy* 19.3 (2012), pp. 98–115 (99).

Gaddafi) were ousted in 2011.[24] However, it is also worth noting that other monarchs did face much more direct criticism than Sultan Qaboos, among them King Mohammed VI of Morocco, King Abdullah of Jordan and, above all, King Hamad of Bahrain, whose countries experienced events much more closely resembling political revolution than any of the other monarchs. The mere fact of monarchy was clearly no proof against protest.[25] Sultan Qaboos's position may have been stronger not simply because he is a monarch rather than a president, but also because he is not a 'successor'. Having ruled since 1970, he is the only ruler most Omanis have known. He is also widely seen as the 'first' ruler of the country in its current incarnation. By contrast, the kings of Jordan and Morocco are both the successors and sons of long-serving predecessors who live on in public memory. By the same token, Ben Ali, Mubarak and Assad, three of the presidents for life' who attracted the most widespread opposition, were all 'successors' who were always at risk of unflattering comparisons with illustrious predecessors: Bourguiba, Nasser and Hafiz al-Assad. Only Colonel Gaddafi, who seized power in Libya a year before Sultan Qaboos's accession in 1970 and who was, in effect, the founder as well as the leader of the Libyan Arab Jamahiriya, appears to be an exception to the rule that a certain primacy was a key element in a ruler's political legitimacy when facing protests such as those of 2011. Interestingly, the widespread belief that President Mubarak was preparing his son Gamal to succeed him in Egypt exacerbated popular perceptions that his rule had become illegitimate.

Although the protests in Oman in the first half of 2011 were clearly inspired by developments elsewhere, they were certainly not a copy-cat phenomenon. Many of the grievances expressed now had been expressed before, in muted and sporadic ways, and for some time. The emergence in Oman of social media and, in particular, blogs and discussion forums such as the Sablah had allowed for a level of public conversation about social and political problems not previously available in print and broadcast media. Critical views of government policy and performance on a range of topics, including gossip and speculation about the business interests of government ministers, therefore circulated far more widely than ever before. From time to time the government would intervene to control

---

[24] See Jeremy Jones, *Negotiating Change*, pp. 124–156, and Roger Owen, *The Rise and Fall of Arab Presidents for Life* (Cambridge, MA: Harvard University Press, 2014). pp. 125–138.

[25] See Sean L. Yom and F. Gregory Gause III, 'Resilient Royals: How Arab Monarchies Hang On', *Journal of Democracy* 23.4 (2012), pp. 74–88.

FIGURE 20. Sultan Qaboos with President Rouhani of Iran, 2014.
Source: Photo by Mohammed Al Rashdi

or prohibit certain kinds of speech online, with sites being blocked and the authors of particularly critical comments arrested and sometimes charged with various offences.[26] Among the participants in such forums were relatively young and well-educated adults and students, some of whom expressed frustration at the lack of personal freedom and a sense of political stasis. Others – often from similar backgrounds – expressed views more commonly associated elsewhere with Islamist movements. Objections to U.S. policies in the region, especially with respect to Israel, were widely shared, and underlying concerns about Oman's own relationships with both the United States and Israel were widespread and would occasionally manifest themselves in polite protest events, which the police and security services made no attempt to prevent. One rather striking example of such a protest – notably among a relatively elite and privileged sector of Omani society – took place during the National Day

[26] Omania.net, e.g., was shut down in November 2006. See 'Ali Al Zuwaidi, blogging as Bin Daris, convicted in April 2009', http://www.muscati.com/2006_11_01_archive.html (accessed July 7, 2014).

parade of 2000, when a brass band of the U.S. Marine Corps was booed during its performance in the stadium, in front of Sultan Qaboos and the visiting U.S. Secretary of Defense.

The protests of 2011 started on January 17, with around two hundred people gathering in Muscat to protest against government corruption and to call for wage increases and price cuts. They carried banners which claimed that 'rising prices have destroyed the dreams of ordinary people'. The police were present but did not intervene.[27] Teachers took strike action in February, contesting a government decision to increase employee pension fund contributions from 6 to 8 percent of their salaries and to reduce the government's contribution to teachers' housing, utilities and transport costs.[28] More substantial protests began later in February, and on February 18 the second so-called Green March, involving around five hundred people, called for wage rises, price cuts and the resignation of government ministers believed to be corrupt. The ministers most frequently named in this and subsequent protests were the Minister of National Economy, Ahmad bin Abdul Nabi Macki, and the Minister for Commerce and Industry, Maqbool bin Sultan.[29] The protesters' demands were presented in the form of a petition to the Diwan, which issued a statement via the Oman News Agency on February 23 confirming that the protesters' 'message' had been 'conveyed' to the Sultan.[30]

Towards the end of February, protests began to spread beyond Muscat, to Salalah and particularly to Sohar, where they took on a more confrontational character. Sohar is one of Oman's oldest cities, historically associated with its traditions of maritime trade and navigation (it is the mythical birthplace of Sindbad, for example). Today it is the site of a major port-industrial complex which was first developed from 1998 and which now includes a refinery, several petrochemical plants, a steel plant, two power plants and a water desalination plant. The port opened in 2002 and an associated free zone in 2010. The plans for its eventual development suggested that the complex should provide around forty thousand jobs either in the industrial zone itself or in the surrounding

---

[27] http://english.ahram.org.eg/NewsContent/2/8/4196/World/Region/Omanis-protest-high-cost-of-living,-corruption.aspx (accessed July 7, 2014).

[28] http://www.muscatdaily.com/Archive/Stories-Files/Oman-school-teachers-go-on-strike (accessed July 7, 2014).

[29] Others included the Ministers of Justice, Housing and Labour and the Attorney General.

[30] http://m.gulfnews.com/news/gulf/oman/message-of-green-march-protesters-delivered-to-sultan-qaboos-1.766655 (accessed July 22, 2014).

Batinah area. As Oman's largest industrial development, Sohar is perhaps the most likely location for the emergence of labour-related political unrest, and the intensity of the protests that occurred there from the end of February 2011 suggests that labour relations and issues of employment were among the most powerful motivating factors in Oman's protest movement. Protests began in Sohar on February 26, with attempts to blockade the port and the establishment of a permanent camp at Kurra Ardiyah – the 'Globe' roundabout. Protesters also targeted the Sohar branch of the Indian-owned hypermarket, LuLu, which was first blockaded and subsequently attacked and burned. These actions suggested that resentment of Indian participation in Oman's economy was among the feelings driving some of those involved. On February 27 police used tear gas and rubber bullets in an attempt to break up the camp at Kurra Ardiyah. Scores of protesters were arrested and one man – a thirty-six-year old businessman – was shot and killed. Protesters returned to the roundabout in Sohar, and protests in Salalah grew to involve several thousand people, with platforms erected to enable speakers to address the crowd. Meanwhile in Muscat a sit-in was inaugurated outside Majlis ash-Shura, with participants articulating economic demands similar to those already expressed elsewhere but with a more explicit focus on their desires for political change, including the allocation of legislative powers to Majlis ash-Shura. The death in Sohar clearly shocked Omani society, and the emphasis on an ultra-peaceful, almost non-demonstrative and silent mode of protest outside Majlis ash-Shura appears to have been, at least in part, a response to this wider public mood.

Sultan Qaboos had already begun to respond to the demands being made, presumably as a result of the petition presented via the Diwan the previous week. On February 27 a special session of Majlis ash-Shura was convened, charged with examining the demands submitted by the protesters, and a minor reshuffle of the cabinet involved Maqbool bin Sultan being moved from the Ministry of Commerce and Industry to the Ministry of Transport, the appointment of Madeeha al-Shibaniyah as Minister of Education, as well as some reshuffling of junior positions. A day later the Sultan announced that fifty thousand new jobs would be created, along with new unemployment benefits and higher allowances for students. On March 1 he announced the establishment of a consumer protection authority, removed the power to initiate prosecutions from the Royal Oman Police so that they rested entirely with the Office of the Public Prosecutor and set up a commission to look into the question of legislative powers for Majlis ash-Shura. During the following month, protests continued and, in addition to the sit-in in Muscat and various renewals of the Kurra Ardiyah camp in Sohar, involved a series of strikes in key sectors, including Omantel, PDO, WJ Towell, Oman Air and a number of Muscat hotels. During the same period, Sultan Qaboos made a series of further responses, including some quite significant political developments. Among these were, on March 5, the replacement of two very senior ministers, General Ali bin Majid al-Maamari (a key adviser to the Sultan on security issues since his appointment in 1989) as Minister in the Sultan's Office and Sayyid Ali bin Hamood al-Busaidi as Minister of the Royal Court. Two days later, in a further set of royal decrees, Sultan Qaboos abolished the Ministry for National Economy, thereby effectively dismissing Macki from the cabinet, and made a series of further cabinet changes, which included the definitive departure of Maqbool, too. He also established a National Audit Committee and set up a commission to look into the possibility of the establishment of cooperatives. In his account of the Omani protests, James Worrall speculates that this largely unnoticed development might be of particular significance in relation to the possibility of the formation of political parties, which, he notes, are currently 'banned'.[31] As we discussed in Chapter 7, the Basic Statute of the State can be understood as implicitly permitting their formation: the 'ban' is more a matter of perception than law.[32] The Basic Statute's absence of a formal prohibition might then be supplemented if there were positive moves to encourage the formation of new kinds of association. On March 13 the Sultan announced that the Majlis Oman would be given 'legislative and regulatory powers', through an amendment to the Basic Statute of the State. He also announced that the Inspector-General of Police and Customs would be retiring, a move that was widely interpreted as a recognition that the actions of the police in Sohar had been excessively heavy-handed.

However, as protests continued, primarily in Salalah and Sohar, further police action to clear the reoccupied camp at Kurra Ardiyah led to clashes between police and stone-throwing protesters and to a second violent death, on April 1. Protests in Sohar gradually wound down in early April, but it was not until mid-May that the larger protests in Salalah were eventually dispersed by force. Police made several hundred

[31] Worrall, 'Oman: The Forgotten "Corner"', p. 107.
[32] In an interview with the authors in 2008, Sultan Qaboos confirmed that Article 33 of the Basic Statute could be the basis for the formation of political parties in Oman.

arrests in Salalah, but once nearly all of those arrested had been released, within about a week, apparently as a result of representations made to the *wali* by tribal leaders, the demonstrators announced that their protest was at an end.

The effects of the protests have continued to reverberate in Omani politics ever since. The elections to Majlis ash-Shura in October 2011 saw at least three candidates publicly associated with the protest movement elected to an assembly that was now to have legislative powers (although precisely how these powers would be exercised remained unclear as the new Majlis convened). In a break with previous practice the post of Chairman of the Majlis ash-Shura was assigned on the basis of a vote of Majlis members rather than by appointment of the Sultan, and the speech given at the opening of the first Majlis session was given by the newly elected Chairman, Shaikh Khalid bin Hilal al-Maawali (also, interestingly, its youngest member) rather than, as had been the case before, by the Sultan. During 2012 a number of activists who had used social media to continue to criticise the government were arrested. Prominent among those arrested were a group of activists who had travelled to Fahud to express their solidarity with a strike of oilfield workers there. In 2013 a number of activists in Samail prison briefly went on a hunger strike in an attempt to get their appeals, which they claimed had been delayed, heard in court. After the hunger strike ended, their appeals were heard and about half of them were upheld. In any event all those detained were pardoned by the Sultan shortly thereafter and released. In August 2013 one of the three Majlis members associated with the 2011 protests, Talib al-Maamari, was arrested along with other protesters during an action staged to draw attention to dangerous emissions from the petrochemical plants at Sohar. His conviction for undermining the state and illegal gathering was overturned by the Supreme Court in December 2013. An additional and interesting complication in this case was that, as a member of Majlis ash-Shura, Talib al Maamari might have expected immunity from prosecution unless that was waived by a vote of two-thirds of the Majlis. The Majlis was not in session at the time of his arrest, in which case his immunity could be waived only by the Chairman, who indicated, via Twitter, that he had not done so.[33]

Government action against its critics was followed, from the end of 2013, with very significant moves against the corruption that many critics

---

[33] http://gulfnews.com/news/gulf/oman/oman-shura-council-member-s-verdict-overturned-1.1295606 (accessed July 28, 2014).

had identified as a major cause for complaint. In December, trials began
of a number of senior government officials and business leaders, mainly
for bribery associated with major infrastructure projects. On February
27, 2014, the Chief Executive Officer of the Oman Oil Company, Ahmad
al-Wahaibi, was found guilty of accepting bribes, abusing public office
and money laundering. A former adviser at the Ministry of National
Economy (abolished in 2011), Adel al-Raisi, was convicted of organising
the payment of an $8 million bribe to Ahmad al-Wahaibi by Myung Jao
Yoo of the Korean company LGI in connection with LGI's bid for a petrochemical plant at Sohar. On March 9, the Managing Director of Galfar
Contracting and Engineering, Mohammed Ali (an Indian national), was
convicted at the end of a series of trials of paying bribes to PDO, receiving a total of fifteen years in prison. On May 18, 2014, Mohammed
bin Nasir al-Khusaibi, formerly the Secretary General at the Ministry
of National Economy (and briefly appointed Minister of Commerce in
2011), pleaded guilty and was convicted for paying a $1 million bribe to
Mohammed al-Amri, Undersecretary at the Ministry of Transport and
Communication in connection with a contract as part of the first phase of
the Muscat International Airport development. He received a three-year
prison sentence and a fine of 800,000 Omani riyals. Mohammed al-Amri,
who pleaded not guilty, also received a three-year sentence and a fine of
RO 1.2 million.[34] Not only were these convictions of high-level officials
associated with high-profile projects, significant in their own right, the
fact that they received press coverage, beyond the Internet, in Omani
print publications suggests that the government was concerned that its
actions in this respect be widely recognised and politically effective.
Another development that may turn out to have some long-term political significance, and that seemed to be a further response to the political dimensions of the 2011 protests, was the introduction of elections
to provincial councils, which were held for the first time in December
2012. Government responses to the protests of 2011 did not show a consistent pattern and probably revealed the existence of various attitudes
among senior figures to the range of problems they represented. On the
one hand, restrictive moves against some of the more prominent and out-
spoken of the government's critics, coupled with generous promises of

---

[34] See http://www.reuters.com/article/2014/02/27/us-oman-corruption-sentences-idUSBREA
1Q1OW20140227; http://www.reuters.com/article/2014/03/09/us-oman-corruption-
sentences-idUSBREA28oIo20140309; http://uk.reuters.com/article/2014/05/18/uk-
oman-corruption-sentences-idUKKBNoDYoFC20140518 (all accessed August 4, 2014).

FIGURE 21. Sultan Qaboos, Muscat 2013.
Source: Mohammed Mahjoub/AFP/Getty Images

benefits and allocations of state resources to job creation, suggest a tendency to rely upon the resources of the state, in its present form, to maintain social peace. On the other, the anti-corruption campaign, which was much more vigorous than anywhere else in the Gulf at the time, and the incremental developments in terms of political representation, suggested a cautious experiment with alternative possibilities and some interest in securing the participation of a younger and more 'liberal'-minded generation of the elite in political decision-making.

FUTURE CHALLENGES

In these three situations – the protests of 2011 and responses to them; the regional tensions and differences over Iran and political union; and the challenge posed by Islamist movements, including those committed to violent opposition – can be found many of the key issues now making the most pressing demands upon Oman, its government and its citizens. In many respects these demands also confront other countries in the region, particularly Oman's partners in the GCC. Of course, in each case the issues present themselves in different ways, sometimes for economic reasons (there is a world of difference, for example, between the economy of Qatar, with its tiny population and vast gas reserves, and Oman's) and sometimes arising from specific social and cultural differences, including, in Oman's case, many of those that have arisen from the historical experiences of, for example, the Ibadi tradition; the relationship with East Africa; and the consequences of three centuries of rule by a merchant rather than a tribal elite. Therefore, while our analysis here shares some fundamental assumptions with other recent scholarship on the Arab Gulf states in general, in order to tease out the specific character of these situations in Oman, we need to draw upon the understanding of Oman's particular historical trajectory that we have developed here.[35] The key issues at stake in the three situations discussed in this chapter can be analysed, in turn, in three broad clusters of related questions, for which the shorthand terms might be politics, economics and security.

In the first, political, cluster of issues, Oman (like all its GCC neighbours) confronts a number of questions. What is the appropriate mode of political participation through which citizens can contribute to the making of key decisions? How can a set of institutions, some of which have roots in long-standing social and political practices (*shura*, the balancing of tribal and other interest groups), accommodate the expectations of a generation for whom the contemporary world offers significantly different models for political participation and representation, including, of course, democracy as promoted from time to time in the region by the United States? What is the relationship between political representation achieved through state institutions and representation across the diversity of media platforms that have become such a ubiquitous aspect of contemporary life in Oman?

---

[35] See, in particular, Kristian Coates Ulrichsen, *Insecure Gulf: The End of Certainty and the Transition to the Post-Oil Era* (London: Hurst, 2011), and Sean Foley, *The Arab Gulf States: Beyond Oil and Islam* (London: Lynne Riener, 2010). It is striking that in a book that is otherwise and rightly concerned to understand the present and future of the Arab Gulf states outside the frameworks usually imposed by assuming the centrality of oil and the model of the rentier state (including due attention to the political uses of traditional cultural practices), Foley's focus on the similarity of the situations facing each of the Arab Gulf states seemingly prevents him from attending to one of Oman's most specific differences: the role of Ibadism. In assessing responses to the Iranian Revolution, for example, Foley writes, 'For the Shia Muslims of Iran and elsewhere in the Gulf, the message was clear: only Sunni Arab Muslims would be permitted to participate in the economic and political life of the Gulf region' (54–55).

We have already detailed the various gradual and sometimes tentative moves to extend political participation in Oman. It is not at all clear whether these have a specific intended destination.[36] It is sometimes suggested that Sultan Qaboos may envisage Oman becoming a constitutional monarchy, in which, for example, a prime minister takes the role of head of government and in which the composition of the government itself might no longer be determined solely by the Sultan, but might also involve a formal relationship with one or both chambers of the Majlis Oman.[37] However these institutional structures develop, it is clear enough that the formal conditions are in place for the development of a much more representative political system. It is much less clear, however, to what extent the underlying social and economic situation makes such development possible or likely. There are long-standing aspects of Omani politics that might inhibit developments in an explicitly democratic-representative direction. These include the complex nature of pre-political family and social affiliations among citizens and a strong preference for consensus and non-antagonistic politics, at least among those who compose what we might call the governing elite (of leading families and business interests). The economic situation, even today – and this situation will become more acute in future years – is such that governments whose members are also involved in a competitive and representative political system will find it just as difficult as the present government (if not more so) to resist the temptation to address economic demands from their constituents by falling back on familiar tactics of subsidies and welfare provision. The cluster of issues we raise here under the heading of 'political' are therefore, as we have already seen, closely connected to those that we group under the heading of 'economic'.

The second cluster, economic issues, gives rise to a number of questions, which the policies developed in the Vision 2020 process discussed in Chapter 7 were an initial attempt to answer. But, as we have seen, the ambitious targets, for diversification and Omanisation, in particular, proved beyond reach. One of the biggest challenges at present is that really significant economic diversification will require Omani citizens

---

[36] Elsewhere we have questioned the logic that 'democratic development' in Oman should be understood in terms of a movement towards a known destination. See Jones and Ridout, 'Democratic Development in Oman', pp. 376–392.

[37] The idea that a constitutional monarchy might evolve is raised by, inter alia, Jeffrey Lefevre, in 'Oman's Foreign Policy in the Twenty-First Century', *Middle East Policy* 17.1 (2010), pp. 99–114, who attributes this suggestion to the former U.S. Ambassador to Oman, George Cranwell Montgomery.

themselves to participate to an unprecedented extent in wealth-producing work. We have already indicated, in Chapter 6, some of the ways in which the development of the Omani economy from the 1970s differed from the capitalist model against which it is sometimes, and often rather critically, evaluated. Beyond even those features of the economy – subsidies, state ownership, and so forth – which have led many analysts to describe Oman (along with other Arab Gulf States) as a rentier state,[38] it is also worth considering a rather more structural distinction between the Omani economy and capitalism as such.

Capitalism as a distinct historical economic formation has depended upon wage labour as the primary means of wealth production. This has typically meant majority adult participation in productive work (even if at some moments the system appears to benefit from a certain level of unemployment, too). This has never been a feature of Oman's economy. This is not to say that Omanis have no history of work, of course.[39] But for much of their history, Omanis have worked, not to produce the kind of wealth that can be put into circulation as capital, but simply to provide basic levels of subsistence for themselves and their families and other dependents (in fishing and agriculture). During the only period in which Omani wealth was derived substantially from productive labour – during the mid-nineteenth century in Zanzibar, a moment when the Omani economy perhaps most closely resembled the capitalist economies of its own time – most of the labour involved was slave labour. The amount of productive labour required in oil extraction, refining and distribution is very low, and oil's dominant role in the economy has given Omanis no reason to revise a shared and historically situated understanding of work: that work is necessary to secure an appropriate standard of living for oneself and one's dependents, and that it may also be a way of securing social position through the development of networks, but not that it is a means of contributing to economic growth in the way that a capitalist economy demands. Economic growth of this kind depends upon the production of substantial surplus value, which can be achieved only when significant sectors of the population work more than is necessary for their own subsistence, and do so in areas that produce exchangeable commodities. That so many Omanis work in the public sector and continue to treat their employment there in traditional terms rather than

---

[38] See, e.g., Beblawi, 'The Rentier State in the Arab World'.

[39] The widely disseminated idea that Gulf Arabs have no history of working or that they possess some kind of cultural predisposition to idleness is a racist misunderstanding.

according to the ideology of work that has developed under capitalist conditions (where citizens, broadly speaking, have learned to think of working as almost a moral good) reflects long-standing social attitudes to work. This results in continued dependence upon migrant labour at all levels in the directly productive sectors of the economy and presents substantial obstacles to the development of productive alternatives to oil as part of a policy of economic diversification.

These contradictions also have consequences for education in Oman, inasmuch as education has been widely identified – by international agencies, economic analysts and the government, too – as central to securing the kind of capitalist diversification sought.[40] What Oman faces, in common with other Arab Gulf States, is a serious mismatch between the education system and the skills needed to support economic development through diversification. There are several reasons for this. One is that education is still widely seen as involving the acquisition, not of skills that might be put to use in productive work, but of qualifications that will secure entry into the kind of employment that confers upon the holder an appropriate social position. Another is a lack of capacity in crucial technical and scientific fields and a tendency, among many Omani university entrants, to avoid studying the subjects that might prepare them most effectively for productive work. These problems are exacerbated by the fact that demand for people with scientific and technical expertise can still often be satisfied by recourse to non-Omani professionals, many of whom typically accept salaries lower than those which Omanis who are not as well qualified could expect to receive in government service. Elsewhere in the Arab Gulf, governments have sought to address aspects of this problem and to engage more generally with the idea that a 'knowledge economy' might be a viable non-industrial mode of production, by importing elite higher education, most notably from the United States. The New York University campus in Abu Dhabi is an example of this tendency, although even here the number of Emirati students as a proportion of an international cohort is relatively small. A former Omani Minister of Education, now Chairman of Majlis a-Dawla, Yahya bin Mahfoudh al-Mantheri, has written critically of such initiatives, expressing concern that they simply involve the consumption of educational commodities rather than the development of educational processes that might embed themselves in public and economic life and so make a substantive

[40] See various Arab Human Development Reports.

contribution.[41] Oman has taken a different route, encouraging the development of its own private higher education providers, generally with programmes validated by universities in the UK.

But it remains the case that the greatest social prestige still attaches to Sultan Qaboos University, where, in addition, a small majority of the students are women, who as graduates will continue to face considerable social obstacles to their full participation in the kind of work that produces wealth. There may be limits on the capacity of higher education to do more than reproduce existing social norms. It is also clear that the younger generation of Omani citizens experience considerable frustration at the interface between the expectations associated with a university education and the employment opportunities actually available to graduates. The problem appears to be with both supply and demand simultaneously. There are not enough Omanis with the right education for the kind of work that the economy might demand from them, while at the same time there is a shortage of employment opportunities for the expanding number of Omani graduates seeking work. The results of the mismatch can be seen in the protests of 2011, which clearly demonstrated the existence of aspirations frustrated, and in the government response, which was to create more public sector jobs (which are, of course, unlikely to be wealth-producing). Thus the initial response appears only to compound the problem it seeks to solve.

If the problem can be only partially addressed by improving the supply of appropriately skilled Omanis to the labour market, as seems to be the case, is there anything that can be done to address the problem from the demand side? Why has the private sector been slow to create jobs for Omani citizens? We have already mentioned the availability of skilled (and cheaper) alternatives to Omanis in key roles, but this does not fully account for the problem, which may also be attributable to the same historically determined approach to economic activity that has prevented the emergence in Oman of the kind of ideology of work required for a functioning capitalist economy. Here the problem lies not with workers who are unwilling to work so much as with business owners who prefer to invest in commerce rather than production, and again, for entirely comprehensible reasons: this is how merchants in Oman have typically built their businesses, and there has been very little in the economic transformations of the oil era to encourage them to do otherwise. If Oman

---

[41] Gari Donn and Yahya al-Mantheri, *Globalisation and Higher Education in the Arab Gulf States* (Oxford: Symposium Books, 2010).

and the other Arab Gulf states are indeed rentier states, they were so for long before oil: as we have seen (Chapter 2) the only substantial historical Omani example of an economy based on the investment of commercial surpluses in production is the development of clove plantations on Zanzibar from the 1830s.[42] The agency system that developed in the second half of the twentieth century, through which many major Omani businesses derived significant portions of their income from the access they gave foreign businesses to Oman's growing consumer markets, is far more typical of Omani business practice and requires only very limited, if any, investment in production.

The third cluster of issues concerns the security of the region. As we have seen in Chapter 7, Oman's view of regional security has tended to combine arguments in favour of a more inclusive system of regional cooperation, which might, for example, include Iran, with a continued willingness to rely upon and support the role of the United States, first as an 'over the horizon' power in the Gulf and, from the 1990s onwards, as an increasingly visible and assertive presence. We have seen how this policy is, on the one hand, consistent with a broader GCC approach in which the United States is welcomed, at least implicitly, as the ultimate security guarantee, while on the other, it diverges at times, as on Iran, from the approach favoured by other GCC states. In the past decade the differences between the Omani view and the policies adopted by the rest of the GCC have been accentuated, even as certain basic contradictions in GCC policy have become increasingly apparent. In addition to the differences over Iran, Oman harbours reservations about the direction taken by Saudi Arabia (and with it Qatar) in response, first, to the establishment of the post-Saddam government in Iraq and, more recently, to the civil war in Syria. Saudi Arabia, along with other significant Arab states, including Egypt and Jordan, viewed the postwar success of political parties and leaders in Iraq (the United Iraqi Alliance) who explicitly identified themselves as Shia with grave concern.

In December 2004 King Abdullah of Jordan spoke to the *Washington Post* about his fears of a 'Shiite crescent' reaching from Iran across to Lebanon. In September 2005 the Saudi Foreign Minister, Prince Saud bin Faisal, complained that, as a consequence of the war to overthrow Saddam Hussein, in which Saudi Arabia had supported the United States, Iraq was being handed over to Iran. For several years the fear – widely

---

[42] For an extended discussion of the proposition that the Arab Gulf states were rentier states before oil, see Foley, *Arab Gulf States*.

dismissed as a 'myth' by more thoughtful commentators – of a 'Shiite crescent' achieving a dangerous and pro-Iranian hegemony seemed to have become one of the underlying motivations for regional security in Saudi Arabia. At the same time, as early as 2004, Sunni-identifying Salafist jihadis, emerging from an organisation initially called Tawhid wal Jihad and subsequently Al-Qaida in Iraq, and led by the Jordanian Abu Musab al-Zarkawi, had embarked on a violent campaign of resistance against the United States–backed and Shia-led government in Baghdad and against the continued American presence in Iraq. Eventually the logic of Saudi political support for Sunni opposition to supposed Shia advances in the region extended into Saudi (and Qatari) financial support and, it is alleged, the supply of arms to Syrian opposition forces seeking the over-throw of the government of President Bashar al-Assad, among them the Salafist Jabhat al-Nusra, widely regarded as an Al-Qaida-related organi-sation and designated as a 'terrorist organisation' by the U.S. government in 2012.[43] It was from the convergence and sometimes the competition among such groups in Syria and Iraq that the Islamic State in Iraq and ash-Sham (ISIS) would emerge and, in mid-2014, achieve such striking military success in Syria and Iraq that its leader, Abu Bakr al-Baghdadi, would announce the creation of a new Caliphate in the territory under its control.

Oman's perspective on such issues, and, in particular, the anti-Shia anxieties that seem to have driven Saudi Arabia and Qatar into their calculatedly expedient (but miscalculated) support for armed Salafism in Iraq and Syria, was of course shaped by its own history of standing apart from Sunni–Shia rivalry. From an Ibadi perspective, not only is Sunni–Shia competition or hostility not a significant factor in Omani life, but sectarian division within Islam, as such, is to be avoided. Badr bin Hamad al bu Saidi, Secretary General in the Ministry of Foreign Affairs, tried to explain the Omani view in a talk at the Oxford Centre for Islamic Studies in 2007, arguing that there was in fact no real religious basis for

[43] http://www.nytimes.com/2012/10/15/world/middleeast/jihadists-receiving-most-arms-sent-to-syrian-rebels.html?pagewanted=all&module=Search&mabReward=relbias%3Ar%2C{%222%22%3A%22RI%3A12%22}&_r=0; http://www.nytimes.com/2012/12/09/world/middleeast/syrian-rebels-tied-to-al-qaeda-play-key-role-in-war.html?pagewanted=all; http://www.nytimes.com/2012/12/11/world/middleeast/us-designates-syrian-al-nusra-front-as-terrorist-group.html?module=Search&mabReward=relbias%3Ar%2C{%222%22%3A%22RI%3A12%22}; http://www.ft.com/cms/s/2/f2d9bbc8-bdbc-11e2-890a-00144feab7de.html#axzz2klonIM7Q (accessed August 29, 2014, for a detailed account of Qatar's role).

this division and that it existed only as the basis for the pursuit of political objectives: 'There is not a profound religious conflict at the heart of Islam. The idea that such a conflict exists is a myth, and those who propagate it do so either from a malicious desire to provoke conflict, or from a lack of understanding and familiarity with everyday life in the Islamic world.'[44]

From a more pragmatic perspective, the attempt to organise regional security in the interests of Saudi Arabia's national security by promoting the idea of a region divided along sectarian lines carries some very particular dangers for Oman. Two serious threats to regional security could follow. One is that tension between Iraq and Iran could be exacerbated to the point of confrontation, particularly in the event that virulently anti-Shia elements in Iraq achieve greater political power or that their actions lead to the effective dismemberment of Iraq as a unitary state. This could very readily lead to a wider war in the Gulf with potentially very damaging consequences for Oman. Another is that as Salafist movements gain ground in Iraq and Syria, they will also do so in Yemen. Since Yemen's growing instability seriously limits its capacity to counter the activities of armed non-state actors within its borders, this could lead to a new kind of 'blowback' in which Saudi Arabia finds itself under assault from the very Islamist movements it had previously and expediently funded in the first place, just as it did in the 1990s. Oman, as a neighbouring state, could find its own security seriously compromised in such an eventuality.

There is probably little more that Oman can do to correct this counterproductive approach to regional security other than to continue to argue the case that it is counterproductive and that better solutions lie in seeking to engage and cooperate with Iran. If the United States – whose government clearly views Saudi and Qatari support for Salafist movements with considerable alarm – can also be persuaded that the path away from this dangerous collision lies via Tehran, then Omani diplomacy may have a constructive role to play. Beyond this specific and pressing crisis, however, Oman's circumstances may also lead to an increasing emphasis on the interconnectedness between the issues we have here separated into three distinct clusters, between questions of regional security, economic stability and political participation. The recognition that these issues are profoundly interconnected is sharpened, for Oman in particular, by the

---

[44] Badr bin Hamad al bu Saidi, 'Untangling Religion and Politics in the Middle East' (Oxford: Oxford Centre for Islamic Studies, 2008).

likelihood, given existing reserves, that its oil will run out some time shortly after 2030.[45]

The horizon imposed upon policy-making in Oman by the likely exhaustion of its oil reserves functions as a deadline for key aspects of economic and social policy, and has serious ramifications for more exclusively political questions as well as for Oman's approach to regional security. It makes the project of diversification, which has proceeded far less rapidly than had been proposed in the Vision 2020 document, very urgent indeed. It means that, even if diversification is relatively successful, the time will soon come when the government will no longer be able to respond to the kind of unrest experienced in 2011, nor to the more general effects of economic distress, through increases in public expenditure, in subsidies, job creation schemes, benefit increases and price controls. It raises the question of income tax, which oil revenues have effectively postponed. With the question of income tax there comes, almost inevitably, the question of political representation. The loss of oil revenues will limit the present government's capacity to secure the continued allegiance of all elements of the traditional ruling alliance whose fortunes we have tracked throughout this history, raising the prospect that, as has happened on several occasions over the past two hundred years, alternative visions and political coalitions organised around them could gain ground. It is very likely that there will be an Islamist dimension to such political developments. This may give the present government a strong incentive to extend political representation, if only as a means to secure the basis, through taxation, for government revenues sufficient to maintain the ruling alliance. Significant reductions in government revenues as a result of declining and vanishing oil reserves will also limit defence expenditure. We have already indicated that Oman's expenditure in this area is out of proportion to its capacity and need to deploy the weapons it has purchased. As it becomes ever clearer that regional security depends upon successful engagement with political and economic issues, the case for military expenditure may, in any case, become less and less persuasive (although Oman's major suppliers will no doubt seek to counter any such effect).

---

[45] The U.S. Energy Information Agency Analysis of 2013 gave Oman's oil production ratio in 2010 as 16 (meaning 16 further years of reserves at current rates of production). See http://www.eia.gov/countries/cab.cfm?fips=MU (accessed August 9, 2014). Kristian Coates Ulrichsen suggests that '[b]oth Bahrain and Oman are projected to exhaust their existing oil reserves by 2025'; see Ulrichsen, *Insecure Gulf*, p. 77.

Life in Oman after oil will not be wholly unfamiliar. It is unlikely that the oft-cited and somewhat fatalistic Arab Gulf prediction that future generations will live a desert lifestyle similar to that of the Bedouin before the advent of oil will prove to be accurate. In some important respects, in Oman there will be a great deal of continuity between the pre- and post-oil periods. But this is not because things will return to how they were before, but rather because so many aspects of the way things are now are already a continuation of the way things were before rather than a radical departure from the past. That is why this book has dwelt quite so extensively on the relatively distant past. Modern Oman goes back a long way.

It may be the case that some important aspects of the past we have described earlier part in this book are no longer as important as once they were or that some of them have disappeared altogether. The perennial need to unify the country against fissiparous tendencies, including powerful alternative centres of power either within the Al Bu Said or among tribal rivals, has more or less disappeared. With it the centrifugal tendencies pulling the coast and interior apart from one another, or the risk of parts of the country being drawn into the sphere of influence of hostile neighbours (Wahhabis, PDRY), have also receded almost to nothing. Omani rulers in Muscat no longer have to contend with the day-to-day political involvement of a major external power in their conduct of government, as they did during the periods of the most intense British supervision of Omani politics. Nor is it necessary to engage in complex negotiations over the very basis of the Omani economy, as was the case through much of the mid-nineteenth century over the question of slavery. More generally, like the territorial unity of the country, its independence is no longer in question.

However, even in touching upon those aspects of Oman's past that no longer seem to be part of the contemporary experience, one might note some striking continuities. As we have argued, Oman's economy has never fully conformed to capitalist norms, in terms of either the predominance of wage labour or the centrality of production. We may note, in this context, that the presence of a large number of migrant labourers in Oman, while it does not involve the same legal or living conditions as those experienced by plantation slaves in Zanzibar, does indicate the persistence of dependency upon non-Omani, non-citizen labour. Other enduring aspects of Omani life, or contemporary incarnations of long-standing social and political issues, include questions about the role of religion in public life; the relationship between government and the business community (both

Omani and expatriate); sustained negotiation of a central and asymmetrical relationship with a major global power (the United States in place of Great Britain); and, perhaps most important, the primary importance of economic exchange in the Indian Ocean and the social, cultural and security implications that arise from it.

As Oman looks east into and across the Indian Ocean region, which is where its primary external commercial interests have been located for many years, its next major infrastructure development project is an indication of current priorities. In 2007 work began on the construction of a new port at the fishing village of Duqm. Duqm lies outside the Gulf and in an area of Oman some distance from present-day urban centres, more or less halfway between Muscat and Salalah. The port construction is part of a much larger project, Duqm Special Economic Zone, which is taking shape along 80 kilometres of the coast and will involve, in addition to the container port, a dry dock, an industrial zone with a refinery, a petrochemical plant and a gas pipeline fed from the Duqm field inland from the port, as well as tourism, education and training facilities, a whole new town and an international airport, with a capacity of 500,000 passengers a year, which opened for its first flights on July 23, 2014. The port is a joint venture between the Omani government and the Port of Antwerp. The significance of Duqm is that it lies outside the Gulf, offering a logistical alternative to Dubai and other ports from which traffic must pass through the Strait of Hormuz. This not only gives it considerable commercial potential, such that some commentators suggest it could even come to rival Dubai and Singapore, it also has potential security implications, as a port that could provide repair and resupply for navies operating in the Indian Ocean.[46] At the moment this might seem to appeal most obviously to the U.S. Navy, whose Central Command and Fifth Fleet are currently stationed in Bahrain. In the longer term, however, a new major global power might come to replace the United States in the Gulf, just as the United States gradually replaced the British. Duqm might become a key element in the development of both commercial and security relationships between Oman and China, and in China's gradual involvement in the regional security environment.

Meanwhile China is giving clear signs of its own interest in the Indian Ocean. Of particular relevance to Oman, particularly in consideration

---

[46] C. Raja Mohan, 'The Great Game Folio: Arabian Ports', *Indian Express*, May 2, 2014, http://indianexpress.com/article/opinion/columns/the-great-game-folio-arabian-ports/ (accessed August 9, 2014).

of continuities between the past we have explored here and the future into which we are peering, is the Chinese role in the development of Gwadar. This former Omani possession, sold by Sultan Said to Pakistan in 1958 (see Chapter 4), has been under development as a joint project by the governments of Pakistan and China for the expansion of the port and the construction of a major transport link with Kasha in Xinjiang. In 2013 management of the entire project was handed over to China Overseas Port Holdings. One immediate benefit for China might be a massive reduction in the time and risk involved in transporting oil from the Gulf to its main port at Shanghai. In the longer term, one might begin to imagine Gwadar and Duqm as key hubs in the emergence of a revitalised Indian Ocean and the return, with a difference, of the Indian Ocean commercial and cultural networks out of which modern Omani economic and political life first grew.

Bibliography

Abdullah, M. M., 'The First Saudi Dynasty and Oman, 1795–1818', *Proceedings of the Fourth Seminar for Arabian Studies* (1970), pp. 34–40.

Abdullah, S., *Omani Islamism: An Unexpected Confrontation with the Government* (Annandale: United Association for Studies and Research, 1995).

Ahmadi, K., *Islands and International Politics in the Persian Gulf: Abu Musa and the Tunbs in Strategic Perspective* (London: Routledge, 2008).

Ahmed, L., *A Quiet Revolution: The Veil's Resurgence from the Middle East to America* (New Haven, CT: Yale University Press, 2011).

Aitchison, Sir C. U., *A collection of treaties, engagements, and Sunnuds relating to India and Neighbouring Countries*, vol. VII: *Containing the treaties etc. relating to Sind, Baloochistan, Persia and Herat; Turkish Arabia and the Persian Gulf; and the Arabian and African Coasts* (Calcutta: O. T. Cutter, Military Orphan Press, 1865).

al-Azri, K., *Social and Gender Inequality in Oman: The Power of Religious and Political Tradition* (London: Routledge, 2012).

Albaharna, H. M., *The Legal Status of the Arabian Gulf States: A Study of Their Treaty Relations and Their International Problems* (Manchester: Manchester University Press, 1968).

Al Bu Saidi, B. H., *Untangling Religion and Politics in the Middle East* (Oxford: Oxford Centre for Islamic Studies, 2008).

al-Haj, A. J., 'The Political Elite and the Introduction of Political Participation in Oman', *Middle East Policy* 7.3 (2000), pp. 97–110.

'The Politics of Participation in the Gulf Cooperation Council States: The Omani Consultative Council, *Middle East Journal* 50.4 (1996), pp. 559–571.

al-Hashimy, M. S., *Imam Salim bin Rashid and the Imamate Revival in Oman, 1331/1913–1338/1920* (PhD diss., University of Leeds, 1994).

al-Khalili, M., *Oman's Foreign Policy: Foundation and Practice* (Westport, CT: Praeger, 2009).

Allen, C. H., Jr., 'The Indian Merchant Community of Masqat', *Bulletin of the School of Oriental and African Studies* 44.1 (1981), pp. 39–53.

al-Maamiry, A. H., *Oman and Ibadism* (New Delhi: Lancers, 1980).

al-Nami, A. K., *Studies in Ibadhism* (Open Mind, 2007).

al-Naqeeb, K. N., *Society and State in the Gulf and Arab Peninsula: A Different Perspective* (London: Routledge, 2012).

Alpers, E. A., 'The East African Slave Trade', in Z. A. Konczacki and J. M. Konczacki (eds.), *An Economic History of Tropical Africa*, vol. 1: *The Pre-Colonial Period* (London: Frank Cass, 1977), pp. 206–215.

al-Qasimi, M., *The Myth of Arab Piracy* (London: Routledge, 1988).

al-Salimi, A., 'The Transformation of Religious Learning in Oman: Tradition and Modernity', *Journal of the Royal Asiatic Society* 21.2 (2011), pp. 147–157.

al-Yousef, M. M., *Oil and the Transformation of Oman* (London: Stacey International, 1996).

The State and Market in Oman's Development: Conflict or Cooperation (PhD diss., Development Planning Unit, University College London, 1997).

Ansari, M. H., 'Security in the Persian Gulf: The Evolution of a Concept', *Strategic Analysis* 23.6 (1999), pp. 857–871.

Appadurai, A., 'Number in the Colonial Imagination', in Carol A. Breckenridge and Peter van der Veer (eds.), *Orientalism and the Postcolonial Predicament* (Philadelphia: University of Pennsylvania Press, 1993), pp. 114–135.

Bang, A., *Sufis and Scholars of the Sea: Family Networks in East Africa, 1860–1925* (New York: Routledge, 2003).

Barth, F., *Sohar: Culture and Society in an Omani Town* (Baltimore: Johns Hopkins University Press, 1983).

Beblawi, H., 'The Rentier State in the Arab World', in Giacomo Luciani (ed.), *The Arab State* (London: Routledge, 1990), pp. 85–98.

Bennett, N. R., *A History of the Arab State of Zanzibar* (London: Methuen, 1978).

Bhacker, M. R., *Trade and Empire in Muscat and Zanzibar: The Roots of British Domination* (London: Routledge, 1994).

Bierschenk, T., 'Oil Interests and the Formation Of Centralized Government In Oman, 1920–1970', *Orient* 30.2 (1989), pp. 205–219.

Birks, J. S., and C. A. Sinclair, *The Sultanate of Oman: Economic Development, the Domestic Labour Market and International Migration*, no. 179611 (Geneva: International Labour Organization, 1978).

'The International Migration Project: An Enquiry into the Middle East Labor Market', *International Migration Review* 13.1 (1979), pp. 122–135.

Bissell, W. C., *Urban Design, Chaos, and Colonial Power in Zanzibar* (Bloomington, IN: University of Indiana Press, 2011).

Campbell, G., *The Structure of Slavery in Indian Ocean Africa and Asia* (London: Frank Cass, 2004).

Chakrabarty, D., *Provincializing Europe: Postcolonial Thought and Historical Difference* (Princeton, NJ: Princeton University Press, 2000).

Chatterjee, P., *The Nation and Its Fragments: Colonial and Postcolonial Histories* (Princeton, NJ: Princeton University Press, 1993).

Chatty, D., *Mobile Pastoralists: Development Planning and Social Change in Oman* (New York: Columbia University Press, 1996).

'Rituals of Royalty and the Elaboration of Ceremony in Oman: View from the Edge', *International Journal of Middle East Studies* 41 (2009), pp. 39–58.

Chaudhuri, K. N., *Trade and Civilisation in the Indian Ocean: An Economic History from the Rise of Islam to 1750* (Cambridge: Cambridge University Press, 1985).

Chubin, S., and S. Zabih, *Foreign Relations of Iran: A Developing State in a Zone of Great Power Conflict* (Berkeley: University of California Press, 1974).

Cooper, F., *Plantation Slavery on the East Coast of Africa* (New Haven, CT: Yale University Press, 1977).

Cordesman, A., *The Gulf Military Balance in 2012* (Washington, DC: Center for Strategic and International Studies, 2013).

Cees Corsten, C., S. Mahrooqi, and P. Engbers, 'Good Vibrations in Fahud', *Leading Edge*, 24.8 (August 2005), pp. 827–830.

Davies, C. E., *The Blood-Red Arab Flag: An Investigation into Qasimi Piracy, 1797–1820* (Exeter: University of Exeter Press, 1997).

Dawisha, A., *Arab Nationalism in the Twentieth Century* (Princeton, NJ: Princeton University Press, 2003).

DeVore, M., 'The United Kingdom's Last Hot War of the Cold War: Oman, 1963–1975', *Cold War History* 11.3 (2011), pp. 441–471.

Donn, G., and Y. al-Mantheri, *Globalisation and Higher Education in the Arab Gulf States* (Oxford: Symposium Books, 2010).

Eickelman, D., 'From Theocracy to Monarchy: Authority and Legitimacy in Inner Oman, 1935–1957', *International Journal of Middle East Studies* 17.1 (1985), pp. 3–24.

'Kings and People: Oman's State Consultative Council', *Middle East Journal* 38.1 (1984), pp. 51–71.

Englehardt, J. P., *Desert Shield and Desert Storm: A Chronology and Troop List for the 1990–91 Persian Gulf Crisis*, Strategic Studies Institute Special Report (Carlisle, PA: U.S. Army War College, 1991).

Foley, S., *The Arab Gulf States: Beyond Oil and Islam* (London: Lynne Riener, 2010).

Gause, F. G., III, *Oil Monarchies: Domestic and Security Challenges in the Arab Gulf States* (New York: Council on Foreign Relations, 1994).

The International Relations of the Persian Gulf (Cambridge: Cambridge University Press, 2010).

Ghazal, A., *Islamic Reform and Arab Nationalism: Expanding the Crescent from the Mediterranean to the Indian Ocean (1880s–1930s)* (London: Routledge, 2010).

Ghubash, H., *Oman: The Islamic Democratic Tradition* (London: Routledge, 2006).

Guha, R., *Dominance Without Hegemony: History and Power in Colonial India* (Cambridge, MA: Harvard University Press, 1998).

Halliday, F., *Arabia Without Sultans* (Harmondsworth: Penguin, 1974).

Revolution and Foreign Policy: The Case of South Yemen (Cambridge: Cambridge University Press, 1990).

Hawley, D., *The Trucial States* (London: George Allen & Unwin, 1970).

Heard-Bey, F., *From Trucial States to United Arab Emirates: A Society in Transition* (London: Longman, 1982).

Hobsbawm, E., and T. Ranger, *The Invention of Tradition* (Cambridge: Cambridge University Press, 2012).

Hoffman, V., *The Essentials of Ibadism* (Syracuse, NY: Syracuse University Press, 2012).

Hourani, A., *Arabic Thought in the Liberal Age, 1798–1939* (Cambridge: Cambridge University Press, 1983).

Hourani, G., *Arab Seafaring in the Indian Ocean in Ancient and Early Medieval Times*, revised and expanded by John Carswell (Princeton, NJ: Princeton University Press, 1995).

Hughes, G., 'A "Model Campaign" Reappraised: The Counter-Insurgency War in Dhofar, Oman, 1965–1975', *Journal of Strategic Studies* 32.2 (2009), pp. 271–305.

Huntington, S., 'The Clash of Civilizations', *Foreign Affairs* 72.3 (1993), pp. 22–49.

Jafari-Valdani, A., 'The Geo-Politics of the Strait of Hormuz and the Iran–Oman Relations', *Iranian Review of Foreign Affairs* 2.4 (2012), pp. 7–40.

Jeapes, T., *SAS Secret War: Operation Storm in the Middle East* (London: Greenhill Books, 2005).

Janzen, J., *Nomads in the Sultanate of Oman*: Tradition and Development in Dhofar (Boulder, CO: Westview Press, 1986).

Jones, C., 'Military Intelligence, Tribes, and Britain's War in Dhofar, 1970–1976', *Middle East Journal* 65.4 (2011), pp. 557–574.

Jones, J., *Negotiating Change: The New Politics of the Middle East* (London: I. B. Tauris, 2007).

Jones, J., and N. Ridout, 'Democratic Development in Oman', *Middle East Journal* 59.3 (2005), pp. 376–392.

  Oman, Culture and Diplomacy (Edinburgh: Edinburgh University Press, 2012), pp. 155–160.

Katzman, K., *Oman: Reform, Security and US Policy* (Washington, DC: Congressional Research Service, 2011).

Kechichian, J. A., *Oman and the World: The Emergence of an Independent Foreign Policy* (Santa Monica, CA: Rand Corporation, 1995).

Kelly, J. B., 'A Prevalence of Furies: Tribes, Politics and Religion in Oman and Trucial Oman', in D. Hopwood (ed.), *The Arabian Peninsula* (London: George Allen & Unwin, 1972), pp. 107–141.

  Arabia, The Gulf and the West (London: Weidenfeld & Nicolson, 1980).

  Eastern Arabian Frontiers (Westport, CT: Praeger, 1964).

  'Hadramaut, Oman, Dhufar: The Experience of Revolution', *Middle East Studies* 12.2 (1976), pp. 213–230.

  Sultanate and Imamate in Oman, vol. 7. (London: Royal Institute of International Affairs, December 1959).

Kennet, D., 'The Decline of Eastern Arabia in the Sasanian Period', *Arabian Archaeology and Epigraphy* 18 (2007), pp. 86–122.

Kepel, G., *Muslim Extremism in Egypt: The Prophet and the Pharaoh* (Berkeley: University of California Press, 1985).

Landen, R. G., *Oman Since 1856* (Princeton, NJ: Princeton University Press, 1967).

Lawson, F. H., 'Security Dilemmas in the Contemporary Persian Gulf', in M. Kamrava (ed.), *International Politics of the Persian Gulf* (Syracuse, NY: Syracuse University Press, 2011), pp. 50–71.

Lefevre, J., 'Oman's Foreign Policy in the Twenty-First Century', *Middle East Policy* 17.1 (2010), pp. 99–114.

Legrenzi, M., *The GCC and the International Relations of the Gulf: Diplomacy, Security and Economic Coordination in a Changing Middle East* (London: I. B. Tauris, 2011).

Lightfoot, D. R., 'The Origin and Diffusion of Qanats in Arabia: New Evidence from the Northern and Southern Peninsula', *Geographical Journal* 166.3 (2000), pp. 215–226.

Limbert, M. E., *In the Time of Oil: Piety, Memory and Social Life in an Omani Town* (Stanford, CA: Stanford University Press, 2010).

    'Oman: Cultivating Good Citizens and Religious Virtue', in Eleanor Abdella Doumato and Gregory Starrett (eds.), *Teaching Islam: Textbooks and Religion in the Middle East* (Boulder, CO: Lynne Rienner, 2007), pp. 103–124.

Lorimer, J. G., *Gazetteer of the Persian Gulf, Oman, and Central Arabia,* (Calcutta: Superintendent Government Printing, 1915).

Mahmood, S., *The Politics of Piety: The Islamic Revival and the Feminist Subject* (Princeton, NJ: Princeton University Press, 2005).

Maurizi, V., *History of Seyd Said* (Cambridge, Oleander Press, 1984).

Menoret, P., *The Saudi Enigma: A History* (London: Zed Books, 2005).

Moaddel, M., *Islamic Modernism, Nationalism, and Fundamentalism: Episode and Discourse* (Chicago, University of Chicago Press, 2005).

Morris, J., *Sultan in Oman* (London: Faber & Faber, 1957).

Newsinger, J., *British Counterinsurgency: From Palestine to Northern Ireland* (Houndmills: Palgrave, 2002).

Nicolini, B., 'Historical and Political Links between Gwadar and Muscat from Nineteenth Century Testimonies', *Proceedings of the Seminar for Arabian Studies*, 32 (2001), pp. 281–286.

    Makran, Oman and Zanzibar: Three-Terminal Cultural Corridor in the Western Indian Ocean (1799–1856) (Leiden: Brill, 2004).

Onley, J., *Britain and the Gulf Shaikhdoms, 1820–1971: The Politics of Protection* (Doha: Georgetown University School of Foreign Service in Qatar, Center for International and Regional Studies: 2009).

    The Arabian Frontier of the British Raj: Merchants, Rulers, and the British in the Nineteenth-Century Gulf (Oxford: Oxford University Press, 2007).

    'The Politics of Protection in the Gulf: The Arab Rulers and the British Resident in the Nineteenth Century, *New Arabian Studies* 6 (2004), pp. 30–92.

Oonk, G., 'Gujarati Business Communities in East Africa: Success and Failure Stories', *Economic and Political Weekly*, 40.20 (May 14–20, 2005), pp. 2077–2081.

O'Reilly, M. J., 'Omanibalancing: Oman Confronts an Uncertain Future', *Middle East Journal* 52.1 (1998), pp. 70–84.

Owen, R., *The Rise and Fall of Arab Presidents for Life* (Cambridge, MA: Harvard University Press, 2014).

Pearson, M., *The Indian Ocean* (London: Routledge, 2003).

Peterson, J. E., 'Britain and "The Oman War": An Arabian Entanglement', *Asian Affairs* 7.3 (1976), pp. 285–298.

'Guerrilla Warfare and Ideological Confrontation in the Arabian Peninsula: The Rebellion in Dhufar', *World Affairs* 139.4 (1977), pp. 278–295.

'Oman: Omanis, Ibadis and Islamism', First published on the website of the Tharwa Project (tharwaproject.com), February 28, 2005, now available at http://www.jepeterson.net/comment.html.

Oman in the Twentieth Century: Political Foundations of an Emerging State (London: Croom Helm, 1978).

'Oman's Diverse Society: Southern Oman', *Middle East Journal* 58.2 (2004), pp. 254–269.

Oman's Insurgencies: The Sultanate's Struggle for Supremacy (London: Saqi Books, 2007).

The Arab Gulf States: Steps Toward Political Participation (Westport, CT: Praeger, 1988).

'The Revival of the Ibadi Imamate in Oman', in R. B. Serjeant and R. L. Bidwell (eds.), *Arabian Studies III* (London: Hurst, 1976), pp. 165–188.

Potts, D., *The Arabian Gulf in Antiquity*, vols. 1 and 2 (Oxford: Clarendon Press, 1990).

Pouwels, R. L., *Horn and Crescent: Cultural Change and Traditional Islam on the East African Coast, 800–1900* (Cambridge: Cambridge University Press, 1987).

Price, D. L., *Oman: Insurgency and Development* (London: Institute for the Study of Conflict, 1975).

Priestland, J. (ed.), *The Buraimi Dispute: Contemporary Documents, 1950–1961*, vol. 2 (Slough: Archive Editions, 1992).

Prestholdt, J., *Domesticating the World: African Consumerism and the Genealogies of Globalisation* (Berkeley: University of California Press, 2008).

Rabi, U., 'Majlis al-Shura and Majlis al-Dawla: Weaving Old Practices and New Realities in the Process of State Formation in Oman', *Middle Eastern Studies* 38.4 (2002), pp. 41–50.

'Oman and the Arab Israeli Conflict: The Reflection of a Pragmatic Foreign Policy', *Israel Affairs* 11.3 (2005), pp. 535–551.

The Emergence of States in a Tribal Society: Oman Under Said bin Taymur, 1932–1970, (Brighton: Sussex Academic Press, 2006).

Raja Mohan, C., 'The Great Game Folio: Arabian Ports', *Indian Express*, May 2, 2014.

Risso, P., 'Cross-Cultural Perceptions of Piracy: Maritime Violence in the Western Indian Ocean During a Long Eighteenth Century, *Journal of World History* 12.2 (2001), pp. 293–319.

Oman and Muscat: An Early Modern History (London: Croom Helm, 1986).

Rosman-Stollman, E., 'Balancing Acts: The Gulf States and Israel', *Middle Eastern Studies* 40.4 (2007), pp. 185–208.

Ross, D., 'Considering Soviet Threats to the Persian Gulf', *International Security* 6.2 (1981), pp. 159–180.

'The Soviet Union and the Persian Gulf', *Political Science Quarterly* 99.4 (1984), pp. 615–636.

Rumsfeld, D., *Known and Unknown: A Memoir* (New York: Penguin Books, 2001).

Ruzayq, H. M., *History of the Imams and Seyyids of Oman*, translated by George Percy Badger (London: Hakluyt Society, 1871).

Sheriff, A., 'Localisation and Social Composition of the East African Slave Trade, 1858–1873', in W. G. Clarence-Smith (ed.), *The Economics of the Indian Ocean Slave Trade in the Nineteenth Century* (London: Frank Cass, 1989), pp. 131–145.

Slaves, Spices & Ivory in Zanzibar (London: James Currey, 1987).

Skeet, I., *Muscat and Oman: The End of an Era* (London: Faber & Faber, 1974).

Smiley, D., with P. Kemp, *Arabian Assignment* (London: Leo Cooper 1975).

Subrahmanyam, S., *The Career and Legend of Vasco da Gama* (Cambridge: Cambridge University Press, 1999).

Sulaiman, S., 'The Shura Principle in Islam', http://www.alhewar.com/SadekShura .htm.

Takriti, A. R., *Monsoon Revolution: Republicans, Sultans and Empires in Oman, 1965–1976* (Oxford: Oxford University Press, 2013).

Taryam, A. O., *The Establishment of the United Arab Emirates, 1950–85* (London: Croom Helm, 1987).

Tibbets, G. R., *Arab Navigation in the Indian Ocean Before the Coming of the Portuguese, Being a Translation of 'Kitab al-Fawaid fi usul al-bahr wal-qawaid'* (London: Royal Asiatic Society of Britain and Ireland, 1971).

Townsend, T., *Oman: The Making of a Modern State* (London: Croom Helm, 1977).

Trabulsi, F., 'The Liberation of Dhuffar', *Pakistan Forum* 3.2 (1972), pp. 8–13.

Ulrich, B., *Constructing Al-Azd: Tribal Identity and Society in the Early Islamic Centuries* (PhD diss., University of Wisconsin-Madison, 2008.)

'Oman and Bahrain in Late Antiquity: The Sasanians' Arabian Periphery', *Proceedings of the Seminar for Arabian Studies* 41 (2011), pp. 377–385.

'The Azd Migrations Reconsidered: Narratives of Ab Muzayqiya and Malik b. Fahm in Historiographic Context', *Proceedings of the Seminar for Arabian Studies* 38 (2008), pp. 311–318.

Ulrichsen, K. C., *Insecure Gulf: The End of Certainty and the Transition to the Post–Oil Era* (London: Hurst, 2011).

Valeri, M., 'Liberalization from Above: Political Reforms and Sultanism in Oman', in Abdulhadi Khalaf and Giacomo Luciani (eds.), *Constitutional Reform and Political Participation in the Gulf* (Dubai: Gulf Research Center, 2006), pp. 187–210.

Oman: Politics and Society in the Qaboos State (London: Hurst, 2009).

Vink, M. P. M., 'Indian Ocean Studies and the "New Thalassology"', *Journal of Global History* 2.1 (2007), pp. 41–62.

Wallerstein, I., 'Incorporation of Indian Subcontinent into Capitalist World-Economy', *Economic and Political Weekly*, 21.4 (1986), pp. PE 28–PE 39.

The Modern World-System II: Mercantilism and the Consolidation of the European World-Economy (Berkeley: University of California Press, 2011).

Wikan, U., *Behind the Veil in Arabia: Women in Oman* (Chicago: University of Chicago Press, 1991).

Wilkinson, J. C., *Arabia's Frontiers: The Story of Britain's Boundary Drawing in the Desert* (London: I.B. Tauris, 1991).

'Arab–Persian Land Relationships in Late Sasanid Oman', *Proceedings of the Seminar for Arabian Studies* 3 (1973), pp. 40–51.

The Imamate Tradition of Oman (Cambridge: Cambridge University Press, 1987).

'The Oman Question: The Background to the Political Geography of South-East Arabia', *Geographical Journal* 137.3 (1971), pp. 361–371.

Water and Tribal Settlement in South-East Arabia: A Study of the Aflaj of Oman (Oxford: Clarendon Press, 1977).

Worrall, J., 'Oman: The "Forgotten" Corner of the Arab Spring', *Middle East Policy* 19.3 (2012), pp. 98–115.

Yom, S. L., and F. G. Gause III, 'Resilient Royals: How Arab Monarchies Hang On', *Journal of Democracy* 23.4 (2012), pp. 74–88.

Zahlan, R. S., *The Origins of the United Arab Emirates: A Political and Social History of the Trucial States* (London: Macmillan, 1978).

Index